**Research & Education Association**

The Best Teachers' Test Preparation for the

GACE®
Basic Skills

Judith F. Robbins, Ph.D.

Susan T. Franks, Ed.D.

Dana Sparkman, Ph.D.

Kymberly A. Harris, Ph.D.

Georgia Southern University
Statesboro, GA

Visit our Educator Support Center at:
www.REA.com/teacher

Planet Friendly Publishing
GREEN EDITION
✔ Made in the United States
✔ Printed on Recycled Paper
Text: 10%   Cover: 10%
Learn more: www.greenedition.org

At REA we're committed to producing books in an Earth-friendly manner and to helping our customers make greener choices.

Manufacturing books in the United States ensures compliance with strict environmental laws and eliminates the need for international freight shipping, a major contributor to global air pollution.

And printing on recycled paper helps minimize our consumption of trees, water and fossil fuels. This book was printed on paper made with **10% post-consumer waste**. According to Environmental Defense's Paper Calculator, by using this innovative paper instead of conventional papers, we achieved the following environmental benefits:

**Trees Saved: 8 • Air Emissions Eliminated: 1,604 pounds
Water Saved: 1,413 gallons • Solid Waste Eliminated: 474 pounds**

For more information on our environmental practices, please visit us online at **www.rea.com/green**

Research & Education Association

61 Ethel Road West
Piscataway, New Jersey 08854
E-mail: info@rea.com

**The Best Teachers' Test Preparation for the
Georgia GACE® Basic Skills Test**

Published 2010
Copyright © 2009 by Research & Education Association, Inc.
All rights reserved. No part of this book may be reproduced in any form without permission of the publisher.

Printed in the United States of America

Library of Congress Control Number 2008942501

ISBN-13: 978-0-7386-0397-1
ISBN-10: 0-7386-0397-X

The competencies presented in this book were created and implemented by the Georgia Professional Standards Commission and Pearson Education, Inc., or its affiliate(s).

REA® is a registered trademark of Research & Education Association, Inc.

About Research & Education Association

Founded in 1959, Research & Education Association is dedicated to publishing the finest and most effective educational materials—including software, study guides, and test preps—for students in middle school, high school, college, graduate school, and beyond.

REA's Test Preparation series includes books and software for all academic levels in almost all disciplines. Research & Education Association publishes test preps for students who have not yet entered high school, as well as for high school students preparing to enter college. Students from countries around the world seeking to attend college in the United States will find the assistance they need in REA's publications. For college students seeking advanced degrees, REA publishes test preps for many major graduate school admission examinations in a wide variety of disciplines, including engineering, law, and medicine. Students at every level, in every field, with every ambition can find what they are looking for among REA's publications.

REA's practice tests are always based upon the most recently administered exams and include every type of question that you can expect on the actual exams.

REA's publications and educational materials are highly regarded and continually receive an unprecedented amount of praise from professionals, instructors, librarians, parents, and students. Our authors are as diverse as the fields represented in the books we publish. They are well-known in their respective disciplines and serve on the faculties of prestigious high schools, colleges, and universities throughout the United States and Canada.

Today, REA's wide-ranging catalog is a leading resource for teachers, students, and professionals.

We invite you to visit us at *www.rea.com* to find out how REA is making the world smarter.

Acknowledgments

We would like to thank Larry Kling, Vice President, Editorial, for his editorial direction; Pam Weston, Vice President, Publishing, for setting the quality standards for production integrity and managing the publication to completion; Alice Leonard, Senior Editor, for project management and preflight editorial review; Diane Goldschmidt, Senior Editor, for post-production quality assurance; Christine Saul, Senior Graphic Artist, for cover design; Rachel DiMatteo, Graphic Artist, for test design; and Jeff LoBalbo, Senior Graphic Artist, for post-production file mapping.

We also gratefully acknowledge Christina Alex and Anne McGowan for copyediting, Kathy Caratozzolo of Caragraphics for typesetting, Ellen Gong for proofreading, and Brooke Graves for indexing the manuscript.

About the Authors

Dr. Susan Franks, the coauthor of the reading section of this test preparation book, has a distinguished career as an Associate Professor of Early Childhood Education in the Department of Teaching and Learning at Georgia Southern University, Statesboro, Georgia. Dr. Franks earned her Ed.D. from Virginia Polytechnic Institute and State University in Elementary Education with a specialty in Curriculum and Instruction. Dr. Franks is a frequent presenter at national and international conferences. She has an ongoing program of consultant work with classroom teachers.

In her early career, Dr. Franks played a major role in the development and implementation of a formal, written K–8 curriculum for the Choctaw Tribal School District, Choctaw, Mississippi.

Dr. Judith F. Robbins, coauthor of the GACE Basic Skills reading section, enjoys a long-term career as an Associate Professor of Early Childhood Education at the College of Education at Georgia Southern University where she conducts courses in Language Arts, with the additional focus on Lab School participation by student teachers. In addition, Dr. Robbins is a faculty member at the Center for Excellence in Teaching at Georgia Southern University. The center is a uniquely faculty-driven institution that is dedicated to the inspiration and advancement of outstanding and innovative teachers. Her Ph.D. was earned at Florida State University with a major in Reading and Language Arts. Dr. Robbins is frequently invited to be a presenter at national and international conferences.

Drs. Franks and Robbins collaborate often on programs and publications for teachers.

Dr. Dana Sparkman, author of the mathematics portion of this book, has devoted her career to the education of teachers. Dr. Sparkman earned her Ph.D., with a major in Elementary Education, from the University of Alabama. As an Assistant Professor in the Department of Teaching and Learning at Georgia Southern University, Dr. Sparkman teaches a full range of mathematics courses for future teachers. She is a current member of the Georgia Council of Teachers of Mathematics, and the Georgia Educational Research Association. Dr. Sparkman often presents papers at international and national conferences.

Dr. Kymberly A. Harris, author of the writing portion of this book, earned her Ph.D. with a special emphasis on Interdisciplinary Education, at the University of Alabama. She is also a member of the Teaching and Learning Department at Georgia Southern University where she teaches, among others, the Practicum and Field Study courses. Dr. Harris is a frequent presenter at national and international conferences.

Contents

CONTENTS

Introduction

About This Book

REA's *The Best Teachers' Test Preparation for the GACE Basic Skills Test* is a comprehensive guide designed to assist you in preparing to take the GACE Basic Skills Test, which is a requirement to teach in Georgia (unless an exemption is granted). To help you to succeed in this important step toward your teaching career in Georgia schools, this test guide features:

- An accurate and complete overview of the GACE Basic Skills Test

- The information you need to know about the exam

- A targeted review of each subarea

- Tips and strategies for successfully completing standardized tests

- Diagnostic tools to identify areas of strength and weakness

- Two full-length, true-to-format practice tests based on the most recently administered GACE Basic Skills Test

- Detailed explanations for each answer on the practice tests. These allow you to identify correct answers and understand not only why they are correct but also why the other answer choices are incorrect.

When creating this test prep, the authors and editors considered the most recent test administrations and professional standards. They also researched information from

GACE BASIC SKILLS

the Georgia Department of Education, professional journals, textbooks, and educators. The result is the best GACE test preparation materials based on the latest information available.

About Test Selection

The GACE are conducted during morning and afternoon test sessions. Test sessions are four hours in length. The morning session has a reporting time of 7:45 A.M. and ends at approximately 12:30 P.M. The afternoon session has a reporting time of 1:00 P.M. and ends at approximately 5:45 P.M. You may select tests for a single test session or for both the morning and afternoon test sessions.

The number of tests you may register to take in one test session is determined by the assessment(s) for which you are registering. Each assessment consists of one or more tests. Because you are registering for an assessment that includes multiple tests, you may take one, two, or all three Basic Skills Tests in the same test session.

About the GACE Basic Skills Test

The purpose of the GACE Basic Skills Test is to assess the knowledge and skills of prospective Georgia teachers in the areas of reading, mathematics, and writing. The GACE Basic Skills Test contains these three sections:

- Reading: Test code 200 (approximately 42 selected-response questions)

- Mathematics: Test code 201 (approximately 48 selected-response questions)

- Writing: Test code 202 (approximately 42 selected-response questions and a constructed-response assignment)

What Does the Test Cover?

The following table lists the objectives used as the basis for the GACE Basic Skills Test and the approximate number of questions in the Reading, Math, and Writing tests. A thorough review of all the specific skills is the focus of this book.

Test Framework

Basic Skills	Objectives	Skill	Approximate Number of Selected-Response Questions
Reading Test I (Test Code 200)	0001	Understand the main idea and supporting details in written material.	**42**
	0002	Identify a writer's purpose and point of view.	
	0003	Analyze the relationship among ideas in written material.	
	0004	Use critical reasoning skills to evaluate written material.	
	0005	Use reading strategies to comprehend written materials.	
	0006	Determine the meaning of words and phrases.	
Mathematics Test II (Test Code 201)	0007	Understand number properties and number operations.	**48**
	0008	Understand measurement concepts and principles of geometry.	
	0009	Understand statistical concepts and data analysis and interpretation.	
	0010	Understand problem-solving principles and techniques.	
Writing Test III (Test Code 202)	0011	Recognize unity, focus, and development in writing.	**42** (60% of Test Score) Constructed-Response Assignments: 1 (40% of Score)
	0012	Recognize effective organization in writing.	
	0013	Recognize effective sentences.	
	0014	Recognize Standard American English usage.	
	0015	Demonstrate the ability to prepare a developed composition on a given topic using language and style appropriate to a given audience, purpose, and occasion.	

How Is the GACE Basic Skills Test Scored?

Your total raw score is converted to a scaled score. A scaled score is a combination of the number of scorable questions you answer correctly on the selected-response section of the test and the scores you received on any constructed-response assignments and then converted to a scale from 100 to 300. The score of 220 is the passing score for any GACE test. The passing score for each test is established by the Georgia Professional Standards Commission and is based on the professional judgments and recommendations of Georgia educators. "Pass" or "Did Not Pass" status is based on your total score for each test. If you meet the passing score, your total test scaled score is not reported in order to preclude the use of GACE scores for purposes other than Georgia educator certification (e.g., employment, college admission screening).

What Is the Passing Score for the GACE Basic Skills Test?

The passing scaled score for each part is 220. There is no composite or combining all three tests. Each must be passed.

When Will I Receive My Score Report, and What Will It Look Like?

Your scores are reported directly to the Georgia Professional Standards Commission and are automatically added to your certification application file. Your scores are also reported to the Georgia institution of higher education or other agency that you indicated when you registered. Of course, as with any important document, you should keep a copy for your permanent records.

Unofficial test scores are posted on the Internet at 5:00 P.M. Eastern Time on the score report dates listed on *www.gace.nesinc.com/GA3_testdates.asp*. For each test date, the unofficial scores are kept on the Internet for approximately two weeks. You may only view these scores once during the posting period for security reasons.

Can I Retake the Test?

If you wish to retake a test, you may do so at any subsequent test administration. Please consult the GACE website at *www.gace.nesinc.com* for information about test registration. The GACE website also includes information regarding test retakes and score reports.

Who Administers the Test?

The Georgia Professional Standards Commission (PSC) has contracted with Evaluation Systems to assist in the development and administration of the Georgia Assessments for the Certification of Educators® (GACE®). The GACE tests are aligned with state and national standards for educator preparation and with state standards for the P–12 student curriculum (Georgia Performance Standards).

For additional information you can contact:

> **GACE Program**
> Evaluation Systems
> Pearson
> P.O. Box 660
> Amherst, MA 01004-9002
> **(800) 523-7064** or **(413) 256-2894**

For operator assistance, call between 9:00 A.M.–5:00 P.M., Eastern Time, Monday through Friday, excluding holidays.

The Automated Information System is available 24 hours daily.

> **Fax: (413) 256-7082** (Registration forms may not be transmitted by fax.)

When Should I Take the Test?

Georgia law requires that teachers demonstrate mastery of basic skills, professional knowledge, and the content area in which they are specializing.

To receive information on upcoming administrations of the GACE Basic Skills Test, consult the GACE website at *www.gace.nesinc.com*.

Do I Pay a Registration Fee?

To take the GACE, you must pay a registration fee. For information about the fees, log on to *http://www.gace.nesinc.com/GA3_testfees.asp*.

How to Use This Book

When Should I Start Studying?

It is never too early to start studying for the GACE Basic Skills Test. The earlier you begin, the more time you will have to sharpen your skills. Do not procrastinate! Cramming is not an effective way to study because it does not allow you the time you need to think about the content, review the subareas, and take the practice tests.

What Do the Review Sections Cover?

The targeted review in this book is designed to help you sharpen the basic skills you need to approach the GACE Basic Skills Test, as well as provide strategies for attacking the questions.

Each teaching area included in the GACE Basic Skills Test is examined in a separate chapter. The skills required for all three areas are extensively discussed to optimize your understanding of what the examination covers.

Your schooling has taught you most of the information you need to answer the questions on the test. The education classes you took should have provided you with the know-how to make important decisions about situations you will face as a teacher. The review sections in this book are designed to help you fit the information you have acquired into the competencies specified on the GACE. Going over your class notes and textbooks together with the reviews provided here will give you an excellent springboard for passing the examination.

Studying for the GACE Basic Skills Test

Choose the time and place for studying that works best for you. Some people set aside a certain number of hours every morning to study, while others prefer to study at night before going to sleep. Other people study off and on during the day—for instance, while waiting for a bus or during a lunch break. Only you can determine when and where your study time will be most effective. Be consistent and use your time efficiently. Work out a study routine and stick to it.

When you take the practice tests, simulate the conditions of the actual test as closely as possible. Turn off your television and radio, and sit down at a table in a quiet room, free from distraction. On completing a practice test, score it and thoroughly review the explanations to the questions you answered incorrectly; however, do not review too much at any one time. Concentrate on one problem area at a time by reviewing the question and explanation, and by studying the review in this guide until you are confident that you have mastered the material.

Keep track of your scores so you can gauge your progress and discover general weaknesses in particular sections. Give extra attention to the reviews that cover your areas of difficulty, so you can build your skills in those areas. Many have found the use of study or note cards very helpful for this review.

How Can I Use My Study Time Efficiently?

The following study schedule allows for thorough preparation for the GACE Basic Skills Test. The course of study presented here is seven weeks, but you can condense or expand the timeline to suit your personal schedule. It is vital that you adhere to a structured plan and set aside ample time each day to study. The more time you devote to studying, the more prepared and confident you will be on the day of the test.

Study Schedule

Week 1	After having read this first chapter to understand the format and content of this exam, take the first practice test for each of the three subject areas. Your scores will help you pinpoint your strengths and weaknesses. Make sure you simulate real exam conditions when you take the tests. Afterward, score them and review the explanations, especially for questions you answered incorrectly.
Week 2	Review the explanations for the questions you missed, and review the appropriate chapter sections. Useful study techniques include highlighting key terms and information, taking notes as you review each section, and putting new terms and information on note cards to help retain the information.
Weeks 3 and 4	Reread all your note cards, refresh your understanding of the competencies and skills included in the exam, review your college textbooks, and read over notes you took in your college classes. This is also the time to consider any other supplementary materials that your counselor or the Georgia Department of Education suggests. Review the department's website at *http://www.gace.nesinc.com*.
Week 5	Begin to condense your notes and findings. A structured list of important facts and concepts, based on your note cards and the GACE Basic Skills competencies, will help you thoroughly review for the test. Review the answers and explanations for any questions you missed.
Week 6	Have someone quiz you using the note cards you created. Take the second set of practice tests, adhering to the time limits and simulated test day conditions.
Week 7	Using all your study materials, review areas of weakness revealed by your score on the second set of practice tests. Then retake sections of the practice tests as needed.

Format of the GACE Basic Skills Test

What Types of Questions Are on the Test?

- The Reading test has approximately 42 selected-response (multiple-choice) questions.

- The Mathematics test has approximately 48 selected-response questions.

- The Writing test has approximately 42 selected-response questions and one constructed-response question.

Can I Take the Test Online?

The GACE Basic Skills Test is now offered on computer. Register online on the GACE Website. To verify this, go to *www.gace.nesinc.com/GA3_internet_based_testing.asp*.

Test-Taking Tips

Although you may not be familiar with tests like the GACE, this book will acquaint you with this type of exam and help alleviate your test-taking anxieties. By following the seven suggestions listed here, you can become more relaxed about taking the GACE, as well as other tests.

Tip 1. Acquaint yourself with the format of the GACE. When you are practicing, stay calm and pace yourself. After simulating the test only once, you will boost your chances of doing well, and you will be able to sit down for the actual GACE with much more confidence.

Tip 2. Read all the possible answers. Just because you think you have found the correct response, do not automatically assume that it is the best answer. Read through each choice to be sure that you are not making a mistake by jumping to conclusions.

Tip 3. Use the process of elimination. Go through each answer to a question and eliminate as many of the answer choices as possible. If you can eliminate two answer choices, you have given yourself a better chance of getting the item correct, because only two choices are left from which to make your guess. Do not leave an answer blank; it is better to guess than not to answer a question on the GACE test because there is no penalty for guessing.

Tip 4. Place a question mark in your answer booklet next to the answers you guessed, and then recheck them later if you have time.

Tip 5. Work quickly and steadily. You will have four hours to complete the entire test, so the amount of time you spend will depend upon whether you take all three subarea tests in one test session. Taking the practice tests in this book will help you learn to budget your precious time.

Tip 6. Learn the directions and format of the test. This will not only save time but also will help you avoid anxiety (and the mistakes caused by being anxious).

Tip 7. When taking the multiple-choice portion of the test, be sure that the answer oval you fill in corresponds to the number of the question in the test booklet. The multiple-choice test is graded by machine, and marking one wrong answer can throw off your answer key and your score. Be extremely careful.

The Day of the Test

Before the Test

On the morning of the test, be sure to dress comfortably so you are not distracted by being too hot or too cold while taking the test. Plan to arrive at the test center early. This will allow you to collect your thoughts and relax before the test and will also spare you the anguish that comes with being late. You should check your GACE Registration Bulletin to find out what time to arrive at the center.

What to Bring

Before you leave for the test center, make sure that you have your admission ticket. Your admission ticket lists your test selection, test site, test date, and reporting time. See the Test Selection options at *www.gace.nesinc.com/GA3_testselection.asp*.

You must also bring personal identification that includes one piece of current, government-issued identification, in the name in which you registered, bearing your photograph and signature and one additional piece of identification (with or without a photograph). If the name on your identification differs from the name in which you are registered, you must bring official verification of the change (e.g., marriage certificate, court order).

If for any reason you do not have proper identification or your admission ticket, you will need to report immediately and directly to the Information Table at the test site. You may be required to complete additional paperwork, which may reduce your available testing time.

You must bring several sharpened No. 2 pencils with erasers, because none will be provided at the test center. If you like, you can wear a watch to the test center. However, you cannot wear one that makes noise, because it might disturb the other test takers. Dictionaries, textbooks, notebooks, calculators, cell phones, beepers, PDAs, scratch paper, listening and recording devices, briefcases, or packages are not permitted. Drinking, smoking, and eating during the test are prohibited.

You may bring a water bottle into the testing room, as long as it is clear (without a label) but with a tight lid. During testing, you will have to store your bottle under your seat.

Security Measures

As part of the identity verification process, your thumbprint will be taken at the test site. Thumbprints will be used only for the purpose of identity verification. If you do not provide a thumbprint, you will not be allowed to take the test. No refund or credit of any kind will be given. This thumbprint does not take the place of the complete fingerprint set requirement for Georgia teacher certification.

Enhanced security measures, including additional security screenings, may be required by test site facilities. If an additional screening is conducted, only screened persons will be admitted to the test site. If you do not proceed through the security screening, you will not be allowed to take the test and you will not receive a refund or credit of any kind.

Late Arrival Policy

If you are late for a test session, you may not be admitted. If you are permitted to enter, you will not be given any additional time for the test session. You will be required to sign a statement acknowledging this.

If you arrive late and are not admitted, you will be considered absent and will not receive a refund or credit of any kind. You will need to register and pay again to take the test at a future administration.

Absentee Policy

If you are absent, you will not receive a refund or credit of any kind. You will need to register and pay again to take the test at a future administration.

During the Test

The GACE Basic Skills Test is given in one sitting, with no breaks. However, during testing, you may take restroom breaks. Any time that you take for restroom breaks is considered part of the available testing time. Procedures will be followed to maintain test security. Once you enter the test center, follow all the rules and instructions given by the test supervisor. If you do not, you risk being dismissed from the test and having your score canceled.

When all the materials have been distributed, the test instructor will give you directions for completing the informational portion of your answer sheet. Fill out the sheet carefully, because the information you provide will be printed on your score report.

Once the test begins, mark only one answer per question, completely erase unwanted answers and marks, and fill in answers darkly and neatly.

After the Test

When you finish your test, hand in your materials and you will be dismissed. Then, go home and relax—you deserve it!

Reading

The reading portion of the GACE Basic Skills Test **assesses critical reading and reading comprehension skills.** Test takers will be asked to read a passage and answer questions about the material included in that passage. It is comprised of 42 selected-response/multiple-choice questions.

This review is designed to prepare you for the reading section. You will be guided through a review of the content related to the test objectives. A step-by-step approach to help you analyze and answer questions about reading passages, as well as tips to help you quickly and accurately answer the questions, are also included. By studying this review, you will greatly increase your chances of achieving a good score on the reading section of the GACE.

I. GACE Reading Objectives

Remember, the more you know about the skills tested, the better you will perform on the test. The objectives on which you will be tested are contained in the following list:

- 0001 Understand the main idea and supporting details in written material.

- 0002 Identify a writer's purpose and point of view.

- 0003 Analyze the relationship among ideas in written material.

- 0004 Use critical reasoning skills to evaluate written material.

- 0005 Use reading strategies to comprehend written materials.

- 0006 Determine the meaning of words and phrases.

Now that you know what the objectives are, let's look at them more closely. This section will provide a review of the important information about each of the objectives.

Objective 0001: Understand the main idea and supporting details in written material.

The first objective deals with the main idea and the supporting details. The main idea is the topic discussed in the passage. Supporting details explain the main ideas providing support for the main idea statement. They illustrate or elaborate on the main idea of a paragraph. It is important to find the main idea of the passage because it helps you remember important information.

This is evident in the following passage.

Experienced lawyers know that most lawsuits are won or lost before they are ever heard in court. Thus, successful lawyers prepare their cases carefully, undertaking exhaustive research and investigation prior to going to court.

Interviews and statements taken from all available witnesses ascertain those who are likely to be called to support the other side. This time provides opportunities for strategy planning in the building of the case; decisions about which expert witnesses to call (such as doctors, chemists, or others who have special knowledge of the subject matter); books and articles to be read pertaining to the subject matter of the case; and meetings with witnesses to prepare them for possible questions by the opposing lawyers and to review the case.

Finally, a trial memorandum of law is handed to the judge at the outset of the trial. As a result of this thorough preparation, experienced lawyers know their strong and weak points and can serve their clients well.

The main idea expressed in this passage is the importance of pretrial preparation by lawyers. It is not explicitly stated, but it becomes apparent as you read the passage.

A description of the importance of conducting interviews and gathering statements from witnesses, the function of expert witnesses, and the importance of the trial memorandum are all details that support the main idea.

Objective 0002:   Identify a writer's purpose and point of view.

The second objective deals with a writer's purpose and point of view. The following questions are helpful in order to determine the author's purpose. Ask yourself if the relationship between the writer's main idea and the evidence the writer uses answers one of the following four questions:

- What is the writer's primary goal or overall objective?

- Is the writer trying to persuade me by using facts to make a case for an idea?

- Is the writer trying only to inform and enlighten me about an idea, object, or event?

- Is the writer attempting to amuse me or to keep me fascinated or laughing?

Read the following examples and see whether you can decide what the primary purpose of the statements might be.

Example 1   Jogging too late in life can cause more health problems than it solves. I will allow that the benefits of jogging are many: lowered blood pressure, increased vitality, better cardiovascular health, and better muscle tone. However, an older person may have a history of injury or chronic ailments that makes jogging counterproductive. For example: the elderly jogger may have hardening of the arteries, emphysema, or undiscovered aneurysms just waiting to burst and cause stroke or death. Chronic arthritis in the joints will only be aggravated by persistent irritation and use. Moreover, for those of us with injuries sustained in our youth—such as torn Achilles tendons or knee cartilage—jogging might just make a painful life more painful, canceling out the benefits the exercise is intended to produce.

Example 2   Jogging is a sporting activity that exercises all the main muscle groups of the body. That the voluntary muscles in the arms, legs, buttocks, and torso are engaged goes without question. Running down a path makes you move your upper body as well as your lower body muscles. People do not often take into account, however, how the involuntary muscle system is also put through its paces. The heart, diaphragm, and even the eye and facial muscles take part as we hurl our bodies through space at speeds up to five miles per hour over distances as long as 26 miles and more for some.

Example 3   It seems to me that jogging styles are as identifying as fingerprints! People seem to be as individual in the way they run as they are in personality. Here comes the Duck, waddling down the track, little wings going twice as fast as the feet in an effort to stay upright. At about the quarter-mile mark I see the Penguin, quite natty in the latest jogging suit, stiff as a board from neck to ankles and the ankles flexing a mile a minute to cover the yards. And down there at the half-mile post—there goes the Giraffe—a tall fellow in a spotted electric yellow outfit, whose long strides cover about a dozen yards each, and whose neck waves around under some old army camouflage hat that may have served its time in a surplus store in the Bronx or in the Arabian desert. If you see the animals in the jogger woods once, you can identify them from miles away just by seeing their gait. By the way, be careful whose hoof you step on; it may be mine!

GACE Tip

Good arguments are not just based on one's opinion.

In Example 1 the writer makes a statement that a number of people would debate and that isn't clearly demonstrated by science or considered common knowledge. In fact, common wisdom usually maintains the opposite. Many would say that jogging improves the health of the aging—even to the point of slowing the aging process. As soon as you see a writer point to or identify *an issue open to debate* that stands in need of proof, he or she is setting out to persuade you that one side or the other is the more justified position. You'll notice too that the writer takes a stand here. It's almost as if he or she is saying, "I have concluded that. ..." But a thesis or arguable idea is only a *hypothesis* until evidence is summoned by the writer to prove it. Effective arguments are based on serious, factual, or demonstrable evidence, not merely opinion.

In Example 2 the writer is just stating fact. This is not a matter for debate. From here, the writer's evidence is to *explain* and *describe* what is meant by the fact. This is accomplished by analyzing (breaking down into its constituent elements) the way the different muscle groups come into play or do work when jogging, thus explaining the fact stated as a main point in the opening sentence. The assertion that jogging exercises all of the muscle groups is not in question or a matter of debate. Besides taking the form of explaining how something works or what parts it comprises (for example, the basic parts of a bicycle are …), writers may show how the idea, object, or event functions. A writer may use this information to prove something. But if the writer doesn't argue to provide a debatable point one way or the other, then the purpose must be either to inform (as here) or to entertain.

In example 3 the writer is taking a stand yet not attempting to prove anything; a light-hearted observation is made and nothing more. In addition, all of the examples used to support the statement are fanciful, funny, odd, or peculiar to the writer's particular vision. Joggers aren't *really* animals, after all.

As you read the information regarding jogging, make sure you examine all of the facts that the author uses to support the main idea. This will allow you to decide whether or not the writer has made a case, and what sort of purpose it supports. Look for supporting details—facts, examples, illustrations, testimony, or research of experts—that are relevant to the topic in question and show what the writer says is so. In fact, paragraphs and theses consist of *show* and *tell*. The writer *tells* you something is so or not so and then *shows* you the facts, illustrations, expert testimony, or experiences to back up whatever is asserted.

It is also important to recognize the author's implied audience and the effect that the writer's language choices will have on that audience. The author's choice of style and content is affected by the intended audience. You will notice that Examples 1 and 2 are more formal, and include technical terms, whereas the third example is informal. Example 1 includes terms such as "arteries, emphysema, or undiscovered aneurysms," while Example 3 compares a jogger to a "duck, waddling down the track." The differences between the third passage and the first two suggest different audiences.

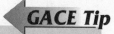

GACE Tip

The style an author uses is dependent upon her audience.

Objective 0003:   Analyze the relationship among ideas in written material.

The third objective deals with analyzing the relationship among ideas in written material. This objective includes various types of relationships such as cause and effect, analogies, or classification. It also involves analyzing relationships between or among similar ideas or ideas in opposition.

Other examples of content that may be covered under this objective include identifying a sequence of events or steps, predicting outcomes, and drawing conclusions based on the information stated or implied in the passage.

As you read, you should note the structure of the paragraphs. There are several common structures for passages some of which are included on the GACE. A number of these structures are described below.

Main Types of Paragraph Structures

1. Main idea plus supporting arguments

2. Main idea plus examples

3. Comparisons or contrasts

4. Pro and con structure

5. Cause and effect

6. Chronological or sequence of events

7. A structure that has several different aspects of one idea

For example, a paragraph on education in the United States in the 1600s and 1700s might define education, describe colonial education, give information about separation of church and state, and then outline the opposing and supporting arguments regarding taxation as a source of educational funding. Being able to recognize these structures will help you recognize how the author has organized the passage, and more easily determine the given facts.

If you see a writer using a transitional pattern that reflects a sequence moving forward in time, such as "In 1982 ... Then, in the next five years ... A decade later, in 1997, the ... ," chances are the writer is telling a story, history, or the like. Writers often use transitions of classification to analyze an idea, object, or event. They may say something like, "The first part ... Secondly ... Thirdly ... Finally ... " You may then ask yourself what the analysis is for. Is it to explain or to persuade you of something? These transitional patterns may also help reveal the relationship of one part of a passage to another. For example, a writer may be writing, "On the one hand ... On the other hand ... " This should alert you to the fact that the writer is comparing or contrasting two things. What for? Is one better than the other? Is one worse?

By understanding the relationship among the main point, transitions, and supporting information, you may more readily determine the pattern of organization as well as the writer's purpose in a given piece of writing.

As with the earlier paragraph showing the difference among possible purposes of education in the United States in the 1600s and 1700s, you must look at the relationship between the facts or information presented (that's the show part) and what the writer is trying to point out to you (that's the tell part) with that data. For example, a discussion presented about education in the 1600s might be used to:

1. Prove that it was a failure (a form of argument).

2. Show that it consisted of these elements (an analysis of the status of education during that time).

3. Show that education during that time was silly.

To understand the author's purpose, the main point and the supporting evidence must be considered together. To be meaningful, a controlling or main point is needed. You need to know if that main point is missing. You need to be able to distinguish between the writer showing data and the writer making a point.

Objective 0004:   Use critical reasoning skills to evaluate written material.

The fourth objective deals with the use of critical reasoning skills to evaluate written material. These skills are used in a number of possible ways. This might include evaluating the stated or implied assumptions upon which the validity of a writer's argument depends. The reader must judge the relevance or importance of facts, examples, or graphic data used by the writer to make a point. The reader must also evaluate the logic of a writer's argument and the validity of analogies, distinguish between fact and opinion, and assess the credibility or objectivity of a writer or source of written material.

Compare the two paragraphs that follow and note the different assumptions made by the authors. In the second paragraph the controlling statement changes the discussion from explanation to argument.

1. Colonial education was different than today's education and consisted of several elements. Education in those days meant primarily studying the three "R's" (Reading, 'Riting, and 'Rithmetic) and the Bible. The church and state were more closely aligned

with one another. Education was, after all, for the purpose of serving God better, not to make more money.

2. Colonial "education" was really just a way to create a captive audience for churches. Education in those days meant studying the three "R's" in order to learn God's word—the Bible—not commerce. The churches and the state were closely aligned with one another, and what was good for the church was good for the state—or else you were excommunicated, which kept you out of Heaven for sure.

The same informational areas are brought up in both paragraphs, but in paragraph 1 the writer treats it more analytically ("consisted of several elements"). However, the controlling statement in paragraph 2 puts forth a more volatile hypothesis, and then uses the same information to support that hypothesis.

It is also important to be able to recognize the difference between the statements of fact presented versus statements of the author's opinion. Look at the following examples. In each case ask yourself whether you are reading a fact or an opinion.

GACE Tip

It is important to be able to recognize the difference between fact and opinion.

1. Some roses are red.

2. Roses are the most beautiful flower on earth.

3. After humans smell roses they fall in love.

4. Roses are the worst plants to grow in your backyard.

Item 1 is a fact. All you have to do is look at the evidence. Go to a florist; you will see that Item 1 is true. A fact is anything that can be demonstrated to be objectively true in reality or which has been demonstrated to be true in reality and is documented by others. For example, the moon is orbiting about 250,000 miles from the earth.

Item 2 is an opinion. The writer claims this as truth but since it is a subjective quality (beauty), it remains to be seen. Others may hold different opinions. This is a matter of taste, not fact.

Item 3 is an opinion. There is probably some time-related coincidence between these two but there is no verifiable, repeatable, or observable evidence that this is always true. It is certainly not true in the way that if you throw a ball into the air, it will come back down to earth if left on its own without interference. Opinions have a way of sounding absolute; they are held by the writer with confidence, but are not facts that provide evidence.

Item 4, though perhaps sometimes true, is nevertheless a matter of opinion. Many variables contribute to the health of a plant in a garden: soil, temperature range, amount of moisture, and number and kinds of bugs. This is a debatable point for which the writer would have to provide evidence.

Objective 0005:   Use reading strategies to comprehend written materials.

Strategic reading is vital in comprehending what was read. This might include organizing and summarizing information, following directions or instructions, or interpreting visual information presented in charts, graphs, or tables.

Organizing and summarizing information is essential to the comprehension of passages. Read the following passage about water and, as you read, consider the topics that best organize the information in the passage.

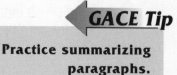

GACE Tip

Practice summarizing paragraphs.

Water

The most important source of sediment is earth and rock material carried to the sea by rivers and streams; glaciers and winds may also have transported the same materials. Other sources are volcanic ash and lava, shells and skeletons of organisms, chemical precipitates in seawater, and particles from outer space.

Water is a most unusual substance because it exists on the surface of the earth in its three physical states: ice, water, and water vapor. There are other substances that might exist in a solid, liquid, or gaseous state at temperatures normally found at the earth's surface, but there are fewer substances that occur in all three states.

Water is odorless, tasteless, and colorless. It is the only substance known to exist in a natural state as a solid, liquid, or gas on the surface of the earth. It is a universal solvent. Water does not corrode, rust, burn, or separate into its components easily. It is chemically indestructible. It can corrode almost any metal and erode the most solid rock. A unique property of water is that it expands and floats on water when frozen or in the solid state. Water has a freezing point of 0°C and a boiling point of 100°C. Water has the capacity for absorbing great quantities of heat with relatively little increase in temperature. When *distilled*, water is a poor conductor of electricity but when salt is added, it is a good conductor of electricity.

Sunlight is the source of energy for temperature change, evaporation, and currents for water movement through the atmosphere. Sunlight controls the rate of photosynthesis for all marine plants, which are directly or indirectly the source of food for all marine animals. Migration, breeding, and other behaviors of marine animals are affected by light.

Water, as the ocean or sea, is blue because of the molecular scattering of sunlight. Blue light, being of short wavelength, is scattered more effectively than light of longer wavelengths. Variations in color may be caused by particles suspended in water, water depth, cloud cover, temperature, and other variable factors. Heavy concentrations of dissolved materials cause a yellowish hue, while algae will cause the water to look green. Heavy populations of plant and animal materials will cause the water to look brown.

After reading the passage above you will recognize that it can be organized according to topics. The writer discusses the physical states of water, the properties of water, the effects of the sun on water, and the reasons for color variation in water. Organizing information in this manner will assist you in comprehending material.

GACE Tip

Reading directions correctly is a comprehension skill.

Comprehension also involves the ability to follow a set of directions or a list of instructions. Carefully read the following instructions for absentee voting.

Instructions for Absentee Voting

These instructions describe conditions under which voters were permitted to register for, or request absentee ballots to vote in, the November 4, 2008 election.

(1) If you moved on or prior to October 6, 2008, and did not register to vote at your new address, you are not eligible to vote in this election.

(2) If you move after this date, you may vote via absentee ballot or at your polling place, using your previous address as your address of registration for this election.

(3) You must register at your new address to vote in future elections.

(4) The last day to request an absentee ballot is October 31, 2008.

(5) You must be a registered voter in the county.

(6)   You must make a separate request for each election.

(7)   The absentee ballot shall be issued to the requesting voter in person or by mail.

After carefully reading the instructions for absentee voting, you should be able to answer questions regarding information presented. For example, consider the following item:

A voter will be able to participate in the November 4, 2008, election as an absentee if he or she

    A.   requested an absentee ballot on November 1, 2008

    B.   voted absentee in the last election.

    C.   moved as a registered voter on October 13, 2008.

    D.   moved on October 5, 2008.

Upon reading the passage, you will note that a voter will be able to participate as an absentee if he or she moved as a registered voter on October 13, 2008. Statement #1 and Statement #2 above provide the information that if you move after October 5, you may vote via absentee ballot.

Another important comprehension skill involves reading information presented in graphic form. Graphs are used to produce visual aids for sets of information. Often, the impact of numbers and statistics is diminished by an overabundance of tedious numbers. A graph helps a reader rapidly visualize or organize irregular information, as well as trace long periods of decline or increase. The following is a guide to reading the three main graphic forms that you may encounter when taking the GACE.

Line Graphs

Line graphs are used to track multiple elements of one or more subjects. One element is usually a time factor, over whose span the other element increases, decreases, or remains static. The lines that compose such graphs are connected points that are displayed on the chart through each integral stage. For example, look at the following immigration graph.

The average number of immigrants from 1820 to 1830 is represented at one point; the average number of immigrants from 1831 to 1840 is represented at the next. The line that connects these points is used only to ease the visual gradation between the points. It is not

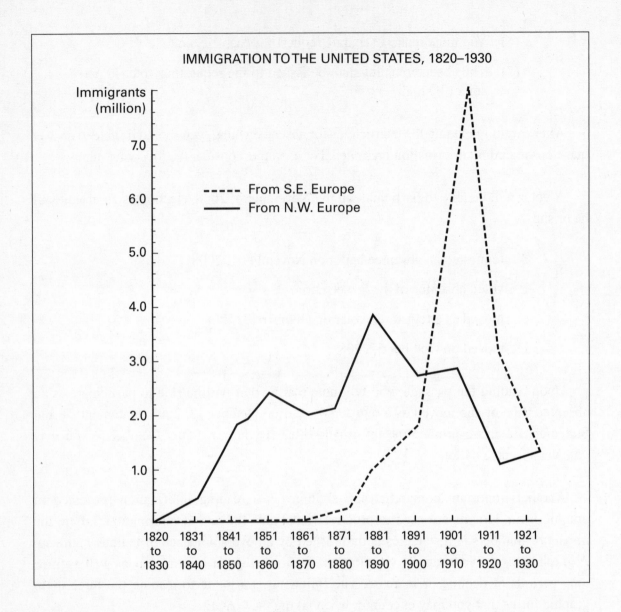

IMMIGRATION TO THE UNITED STATES, 1820–1930

meant to give a strictly accurate representation for every year between the two decades. If it were, the line would not be a straight, even progression from year to year as these lines demonstrate. The purpose of the graph is to plot the average increases or decreases from point to point. When dealing with more than one subject, a line graph must use either different colored lines or different types of lines if the graph is black-and-white. In the graph, the dark bold line represents immigration from Northwestern Europe and the broken line represents immigration from Southeastern Europe.

To read a line graph, find the point of change that interests you. For example, if you want to trace immigration from Northwestern Europe from 1861-1870, you would find the position of the dark line on that point. Next, trace the position to the vertical infor-mation on the chart. In this instance, one would discover that approximately two million immigrants arrived from Northwestern Europe in the period of time from 1861 to 1890. If you want to know when the number of immigrants reached four million, you would find four million on the vertical side of the graph and read across. Between 1881 and 1890, four million immigrants arrived from Northwestern Europe, and the same number arrived from Southeastern Europe between 1891 and 1910.

Bar Graphs

Bar graphs are also used to plot two dynamic elements of a subject. However, unlike a line graph, the bar graph usually deals with only one subject. The exception to this is when the graph is three-dimensional and the bars take on the dimension of depth. However, because we will only be looking at two-dimensional graphs, we will be working with only

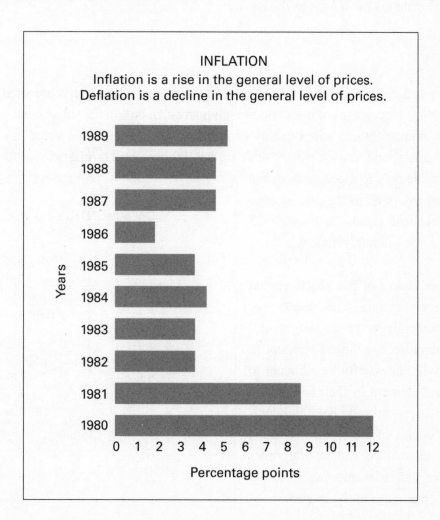

a single subject. The other difference between a line and a bar graph is that a bar graph usually calls for a single element to be traced in terms of another, whereas a line graph usually plots either of the two elements with equal interest. For example, in the bar graph, inflation and deflation are being marked over a span of years.

Percentage points are assigned to each year's level of prices, and that percentage decreases (deflation) from 1980 to 1981 and from 1981 to 1982. The price level is static from 1982 to 1983, then increases (inflation) from 1983 to 1984. Therefore, it is obvious that the bar graph is read strictly in terms of the changes exhibited over a period of time or against some other element. Conversely, a line graph is used to plot two dynamic elements of equal interest to the reader (e.g., either number of immigrants or the particular decade in question).

To read a bar graph, simply begin with the element at the base of a bar and trace the bar to its full length. Once you reach its length, cross-reference the other element of information that matches the length of the bar.

Pie Charts

Pie charts differ greatly from line graphs and bar graphs. Pie charts are used to help a reader visualize percentages of information with many elements to the subject. An entire "pie" represents 100 percent of a given quality of information. The pie is the sliced into measurements that correspond to each piece's share of the 100 percent. For example, in the pie chart that follows, Jason's rent occupies a slice greater than any other in the pie, because no other element equals or exceeds 25 percent of Jason's monthly budget.

Another aspect of pie charts is that the smaller-percentage elements are moved consecutively to the larger elements. Therefore, the largest element in the chart will necessarily be adjacent to the smallest element in the chart, while the line that separates them is the beginning or endpoint of the chart. From this point the chart fans out to the other elements of the chart, moving from the smallest percentages to the largest.

To read a pie chart, choose the element of the subject that interests you and compare its size to those of the other elements. In cases where the elements are similar in size, do not assume that they are equal. The exact percentage of the element will be listed within that slice of the chart. For example, Jason's utilities, clothes, and spending money are all similar in size, but it is clear when reading the chart that each possesses a different value.

Reading Tables

Tables are useful because they relate large bodies of information within a confined area. To read a table, cross-reference the column headings that run horizontally across the top of the table with the row headings that run vertically down the left side of the table.

Drug	Psychological Dependence	Physical Dependence	Physical Withdrawal Effects	Development of Tolerance
Depressants				
Alcohol	Mild to very strong	Very strong	Severe/ dangerous	Minimal
Barbiturates	Develops slowly	Develops slowly	Death possible	Minimal
Narcotics				
Opiates (heroin, morphine)	Very strong; develops rapidly	Rapid/ increases with dosage	Frightening symptoms but not dangerous	Very high; goes down quickly after withdrawal (Danger if user returns to original dose)
Stimulants				
Amphetamines	Strong	Not in formal sense, but body seeks "rush"	Mild	Extremely high
Cocaine	Very strong	None	None (can cause heart spasms and instant death even if healthy)	None
Crack	Strong	Strong	Mild	High
Psychedelics				
LSD	Unpredictable	None	None	Extremely high
Marijuana	Mild to strong	Some, in high doses	None	None (Some to high doses)

Scan the table for overall information to the appropriate headings of the table to interpret the information listed. Note that some tables possess horizontal subheadings, which further clarify the different areas of information.

To use the preceding table, one should simply choose a particular drug, and then find the appropriate information needed about that drug through the headings listed at the top of the table. For example, the physical withdrawal effects of amphetamines, a stimulant drug, are mild.

Objective 0006:   Determine the meaning of words and phrases.

Objective six deals with the use of context clues to determine the meaning of words, phrases, or figurative expressions. This involves using surrounding words in the sentence or passage in order to determine the meaning of an unknown word or phrase.

Consider again the third paragraph from the passage on water used earlier.

> Water is odorless, tasteless, and colorless. It is the only substance known to exist in a natural state as a solid, liquid, or gas on the surface of the earth. It is a universal solvent. Water does not corrode, rust, burn, or separate into its components easily. It is chemically indestructible. It can corrode almost any metal and erode the most solid rock. A unique property of water is that it expands and floats on water when frozen or in the solid state. Water has a freezing point of 0°C and a boiling point of 100° C. Water has the capacity for absorbing great quantities of heat with relatively little increase in temperature. When *distilled*, water is a poor conductor of electricity, but when salt is added, it is a good conductor of electricity.

You will notice that the last sentence includes the word *distilled*. As you read the sentence try to determine the meaning of the word from the surrounding context clues.

The words, "but when salt is added," give the reader a clue that distilled may best be defined as "free of salt content."

II. Strategies for Taking the Reading Test

To help you further master these skills, the remainder of this chapter provides practice using the types of passages and questions that you will encounter on the GACE reading test. Each question is tied directly to one of the six GACE objectives identified and explained in the previous section.

The Passages

The passages in the reading section of the GACE include very diverse subjects. Although you will not be expected to have prior knowledge of the information presented in the passages, you will be expected to know the fundamental reading comprehension techniques presented in this chapter. Only your ability to read and comprehend material will be tested.

The Questions

Each passage will be followed by a number of questions. The questions will ask you to make determinations based on what you have read. You will commonly encounter questions that will ask you to:

1. Determine which of the given answer choices best expresses the main idea of the passage. (objective 0001)

2. Determine which details best support the writer's main idea. (objective 0001)

3. Determine the author's purpose in writing the passage. (objective 0002)

4. Analyze cause-and-effect relationships based on information in the passage. (objective 0003)

5. Use critical reasoning skills to evaluate the validity of an argument. (objective 0004)

6. Know the difference between fact and opinion in a statement. (objective 0004)

7. Determine the organization of the information in the passage. (objective 0005)

8. Determine which of the answer choices best summarizes the information presented in the passage. (objective 0005)

9. Answer a question based on information presented in a graphic form. (objective 0005)

10. Determine the definition of a word as it is used in the passage. (objective 0006)

Test-Taking Strategies and Tips

In order to make the most out of the time allotted, it is important to read strategically. The following is a recommended plan of attack to follow when reading the passages and answering the questions in the reading section.

1. Read over the *questions* (the questions only, not the possible answers) before reading the passage. This will help you to focus on the purpose for reading.

2. Read the passage while keeping the questions in mind.

3. Uncover the main idea or theme of the passage. It is often contained within the first few lines of the passage.

4. Uncover the main idea of each paragraph. Usually it is contained in either the first or last sentence of the paragraph.

5. Skim over the detailed points of the passage while circling key words or phrases. These are words or phrases such as *but, on the other hand, although, however, yet,* and *except.* These key words give clues to the organization of the information and important points to recall.

6. When answering the questions, approach each question one at a time. Read each carefully, selecting the one "best answer."

7. If the question is asking for an answer that can only be found in a specific place in the passage, save it for last since this type of question requires you to go back to the passage and therefore takes more of your time.

Additional Tips

- Look over all the passages first and then attack the passages that seem easiest and most interesting.

- Read the directions carefully.

- Identify and underline what sentences are the main ideas of each paragraph.

- If a question asks you to draw inferences, your answer should reflect what is implied in the passage, rather than what is directly stated.

- Use the context of the sentence to find the meaning of an unfamiliar word.

- Identify what sentences are example sentences and label them with an "E."

- Determine whether or not the writer is using facts or opinions.

- Circle key transitions and identify dominant patterns of organization.

- Make your final response and move on. Don't linger over or get frustrated by the really difficult passages. If you haven't gotten answers after two attempts, answer as best you can and move on. You are not penalized for guessing.

- If you have time at the end, go back to the passages that were difficult and review them again.

A Four-Step Approach

When you take the reading section of the GACE, you will have two basic tasks: 1) to read the passage and 2) to answer the questions.

Carefully reading the passage is the more important of the two. Answering the questions is based on an understanding of the passage. What follows is a four-step approach to reading:

Step 1:   Preview the passage.

Step 2:   Read actively.

Step 3:   Review the passage.

Step 4:   Answer the questions.

The following exercises will help prepare you to use these four steps when you complete the reading section of the GACE.

Step 1: Preview the Passage

A preview of the reading passage will give you a purpose and a reason for reading. It is a good strategy to use when taking a test. Before beginning to read the passage, you should take about 30 seconds to look over the passage and questions. An effective way to preview the passage is to quickly read the first sentence of each paragraph, the concluding sentence of the passage, and the questions (but not the answers) following the passage. The sample passage below will allow you to practice this skill. Practice previewing the passage by reading the first sentence of each paragraph and the last line of the passage.

Passage

That obscenity and pornography are difficult areas for the Supreme Court is well documented. The Court's numerous attempts to define obscenity have proven unworkable and left the decision to the subjective preferences of the justices. Perhaps Justice Stewart put it best when, after refusing to define obscenity, he declared, but "I know it when I see it." Does the Court literally have to see it to know it? Specifically, what role does the fact-pattern, including the materials' medium, play in the Court's decisions?

Several recent studies employ fact-pattern analysis in modeling the Court's decision making. These studies examine the fact-pattern or case characteristics, often with ideological and attitudinal factors, as a determinant of the decision reached by the Court. In broad terms, these studies owe their theoretical underpinnings to attitude theory. As the name suggests, attitude theory views the Court's attitudes as an explanation of its decisions.

These attitudes, however, do not operate in a vacuum. As Spaeth explains, "the activation of an attitude involves both an object and the situation in which that object is encountered." The objects to which the court directs its attitudes are litigants. The situation—the subject matter of the case—can be defined in broad or narrow terms. One may define the situation as an entire area of the law (e.g., civil liberties issues). On an even broader scale, the situation may be defined as the decision to grant certiorari or whether to defect from a minimum-winning coalition.

Defining the situation with such broad strokes, however, does not allow one to control for case content. In many specific issue areas, the cases present strikingly similar patterns. In examining the Court's search and seizure decisions, Segal found that a relatively small number of situational and case characteristic variables explain a high proportion of the Court's decisions.

Despite Segal's success, efforts to verify the applicability of fact-pattern analysis in other issue areas and using broad-based factors have been slow. Renewed interest in obscenity and pornography by federal and state governments as a result of lobbying campaigns by fundamentalist groups, the academic community, and other anti-pornography interest groups pro and con indicate that the Court's decisions in this area deserve closer examination.

The Court's obscenity and pornography decisions also present an opportunity to study the Court's behavior in an area where the Court has granted significant decision-making authority to the states. In *Miller v. California* (1973), the Court announced the importance of local community standards in obscenity determinations. The Court's subsequent behavior may suggest how the Court will react in other areas where it has chosen to defer to the states (e.g., abortion).

Questions

1. The main idea of the passage is best stated in which of the following?

   A. The Supreme Court has difficulty convicting those who violate obscenity laws.

   B. The current definitions for obscenity and pornography provided by the Supreme Court are unworkable.

   C. Fact-pattern analysis is insufficient for determining the attitude of the Court toward the issues of obscenity and pornography.

   D. Despite the difficulties presented by fact-pattern analysis, Justice Segal found the solution in the patterns of search-and-seizure decisions.

2. Of the following, which fact best supports the writer's contention that the Court's decisions in the areas of obscenity and pornography deserve closer scrutiny?

   A. The fact that a Supreme Court Justice said, "I know it when I see it."

   B. Recent studies that employ fact-pattern analysis in modeling the Court's decision-making process

C. The fact that attitudes do not operate in a vacuum

D. The fact that federal and state governments, interested groups, and the academic community show renewed interest in the obscenity and pornography decisions by the Supreme Court

3. The writer's main purpose in this passage is to

A. convince the reader that the Supreme Court is making decisions about obscenity based on their subjective views alone.

B. explain to the reader how fact-pattern analysis works with respect to cases of obscenity and pornography.

C. define obscenity and pornography for the layperson.

D. demonstrate the role fact-pattern plays in determining the Supreme Court's attitude about cases in obscenity and pornography.

4. Based on the data in the passage, what would most likely be the major cause for the difficulty in pinning down the Supreme Court's attitude toward cases of obscenity and pornography?

A. The personal opinions of the Court justices

B. The broad nature of the situations of the cases

C. The ineffective logistics of certiorari

D. The inability of the Court to resolve the variables presented by individual case content

5. Based on the passage, the rationale for fact-pattern analyses arises out of what theoretical groundwork?

A. Subjectivity theory

B. The study of cultural norms

C. Attitude theory

D. Cybernetics

6. Which of the following statements express the writer's opinion rather than a fact?

A. It is well documented that the area of obscenity and pornography is a difficult one for the Supreme Court.

B. The objects to which a court directs its attitudes are the litigants.

C. In many specific issue areas, the cases present strikingly similar fact-patterns.

D. The Court's subsequent behavior may suggest how it will react in other legal areas.

7. Which group of topics best reflects the organization of the passage?

A. I. The difficulties of the Supreme Court

II. Several recent studies

III. Spaeth's definition of *attitude*

IV. The similar patterns of cases

V. Other issue areas

VI. The case of *Miller v. California*

B. I. The Supreme Court, obscenity, and fact-pattern analysis

II. Fact-pattern analyses and attitude theory

III. The definition of *attitude* for the Court

IV. The definition of *situation*

V. The breakdown in fact-pattern analysis

VI. Studying Court behavior

C. I. Justice Stewart's view of pornography

II. Theoretical underpinnings

III. A minimum-winning coalition

IV. Search-and-seizure decisions

V. Renewed interest in obscenity and pornography

VI. The importance of local community standards

D. I. The Court's numerous attempts to define obscenity

II. Case characteristics

III. The subject matter of cases

IV. The Court's proportion of decisions

V. Broad-based factors

VI. Obscenity determination

8. Which of the following paragraphs is the best summary of the passage?

A. The Supreme Court's decision-making process with respect to obscenity and pornography has become too subjective. Fact-pattern analyses used to determine the overall attitude of the Court reveal only broad-based attitudes on the part of the Court toward the situations of obscenity cases. But these patterns cannot fully account for the Court's attitudes toward case content. Research is not conclusive on whether fact-pattern analyses work when applied to legal areas. Renewed public and local interest suggests continued study and close examination of how the Court makes decisions. Delegating authority to the states may reflect patterns for Court decisions in other socially sensitive areas.

B. Though subjective, the Supreme Court decisions are well documented. Fact-pattern analyses reveal the attitude of the Supreme Court toward its decisions in cases. Spaeth explains that an attitude involves both an object and a situation. For the Court, the situation may be defined as the decision to grant certiorari. Cases present strikingly similar patterns, and a small number of variables explain a high proportion of the Court's decisions. Segal has made an effort to verify the applicability of fact-pattern analysis with some success. The Court's decisions on obscenity and pornography suggest weak Court behavior, such as in *Miller v. California*.

C. To determine what obscenity and pornography mean to the Supreme Court, we must operate in a vacuum. The litigants and the subject matter of cases are defined in broad terms (such as an entire area of law) to reveal the Court's decision-making process. Search-and-seizure cases reveal strikingly similar patterns, leaving the Court open to grant certiorari effectively. Renewed public interest in the Court's decisions proves how the Court will react in the future.

D. Supreme Court decisions about pornography and obscenity are under examination and are out of control. The Court has to see the case to know it. Fact-pattern analyses reveal that the Court can only define cases in narrow terms, thus revealing individual egotism on the part of the Justices. As a result of strikingly similar patterns in search-and-seizure cases, the Court should be studied further for its weakness in delegating authority to state courts, as in the case of *Miller v. California*.

9.   In the context of the passage, *subjective* might be more closely defined as

   A.   personal.
   B.   wrong.
   C.   focused.
   D.   objective.

By previewing the passage you should have read the following:

- It is well documented that the areas of obscenity and pornography are difficult ones for the Supreme Court.

- Several recent studies employ fact-pattern analysis in modeling the Court's decision making.

- These attitudes, however, do not operate in a vacuum.

- Defining the situation with such broad strokes, however, does not allow one to control for case content.

- Despite Segal's success, efforts to verify the applicability of fact-pattern analysis in other issue areas and using broad-based factors have been slow in coming.

- The Court's obscenity and pornography decisions also present an opportunity to study the Court's behavior in an area where the Court has granted significant decision-making authority to the states.

- The Court's subsequent behavior may suggest how the Court will react in other areas where it has chosen to defer to the states (e.g., abortion).

These few sentences tell you much about the entire passage. As you begin to examine the passage, you should first determine the main idea of the passage and underline it so you can easily refer to it if a question requires you to do so (see question 1). *The main idea should be found in the first paragraph of the passage, and may even be the first sentence.* From what you have read thus far, you now know that the main idea of this passage is that the Supreme Court has difficulty in making static decisions about obscenity and pornography.

In addition, there are many details that support the main idea (see question 2). By reading further in the passage you know that recent studies have used fact-pattern analysis in modeling the Court's decision. You have learned that attitudes do not operate independently and that case content is important. The feasibility of using fact-pattern analysis in other areas and using broad-based factors has not been quickly verified. To study the behavior of the Court in an area in which they have granted significant decision-making authority to the states, one has only to consider the obscenity and pornography decisions. In summary, the author suggests that the Court's subsequent behavior may suggest how the Court will react in those other areas in which decision-making authority has previously been ceded to the states. As you can see, having this information will make the reading of the passage much easier.

You should have also looked at the stem of the question in your preview. You do not need to spend time reading the answers to each question in your preview. The stem alone can help to guide you as you read.

The stems in this case are as follows:

1. The main idea of the passage is best stated in which of the following?

2. Of the following, which fact best supports the writer's contention that the Court's decisions in the areas of obscenity and pornography deserve closer scrutiny?

3. The writer's main purpose in this passage is to _____.

4. Based on the data in the passage, what would most likely be the major cause for the difficulty in pinning down the Supreme Court's attitude toward cases of obscenity and pornography?

5. Based on the passage, the rationale for fact-pattern analyses arises out of what theoretical groundwork?

6. Which of the following statements express the writer's opinion rather than a fact?

7. Which group of topics best reflect the organization of the passage?

8. Which of the following paragraphs is the best summary of the passage?

9. In the context of the passage, *subjective* might be more closely defined as _____.

Step 2: Read Actively

After you preview you are now ready to read actively. This means that, as you read, you will be engaged in such things as underlining important words, topic sentences, main ideas, and words denoting the tone of the passage. If you think underlining can help you save time and help you remember the main ideas, feel free to use your pencil.

Read the first sentence of each paragraph carefully, since this often contains the topic of the paragraph. You may wish to underline each topic sentence.

During this stage you should also determine the writer's purpose in writing the passage (see question 3), as this will help you focus on the main points and the writer's key points in the organization of a passage.

Step 3: Review the Passage

After you finish reading actively, take 10 or 20 seconds to look over the main idea and the topic sentences that you have underlined, and the key words and phrases you have marked. Now you are ready to enter Step 4 and answer the questions.

Step 4: Answer the Questions

In Step 2, you gathered enough information from the passage to answer questions dealing with the objectives. Let's look again at these questions.

Main Idea Questions (Objective 0001)

Looking back at the questions that followed the passage, you should see that question 1 is a main idea question.

1. The main idea of the passage is best stated in which of the following?

    A. The Supreme Court has difficulty convicting those who violate obscenity laws.

    B. The current definitions for obscenity and pornography provided by the Supreme Court are unworkable.

    C. Fact-pattern analysis is insufficient for determining the attitude of the Court toward the issues of obscenity and pornography.

    D. Despite the difficulties presented by fact-pattern analysis, Justice Segal found the solution in the patterns of search-and-seizure decisions.

In answering the question, you see that choice C is the correct answer. The writer uses the second, third, fourth, and fifth paragraphs to show how fact-pattern analysis is an ineffective determinant of the Supreme Court's attitudes toward obscenity and pornography.

Choice A is incorrect. Nothing is ever said directly about *convicting* persons accused of obscenity, only that the Court has difficulty defining it.

Choice B is also incorrect. Though the writer states it as a fact, it is only used as an effect that leads the writer to examine how fact-pattern analysis does or does not work to reveal the "cause" or attitude of the Court toward obscenity and pornography.

Also, answer choice D is incorrect. The statement is contrary to what Segal found when he examined search-and-seizure cases.

Supporting Details Questions (Objective 0001)

Question 2 requires you to analyze the author's supporting details.

2.   Of the following, which fact best supports the writer's contention that the Court's decisions in the areas of obscenity and pornography deserve closer scrutiny?

   A.   The fact that a Supreme Court Justice said, "I know it when I see it."

   B.   Recent studies that employ fact-pattern analysis in modeling the Court's decision-making process

   C.   The fact that attitudes do not operate in a vacuum

   D.   The fact that federal and state governments, interested groups, and the academic community show renewed interest in the obscenity and pornography decisions by the Supreme Court.

Look at the answer choices to answer this question. Choice D must be correct. In the fifth paragraph, the writer states that the "renewed interest"—a real and observable fact—from these groups "indicates the Court's decisions ... deserve closer examination," another way of saying scrutiny.

Choice A is incorrect. The writer uses this remark to show how the Court cannot effectively define obscenity and pornography, relying on "subjective preferences" to resolve issues.

In addition, choice B is incorrect because the writer points to the data in D, not fact-pattern analyses, to prove this. Choice C is also incorrect. Although it is true, the writer makes this point to show how fact-pattern analysis doesn't help clear up the real-world situations in which the Court must make its decisions.

As you determine where the author's supporting details are, you may want to label them with an "S" so that you can refer back to them easily when answering questions.

Purpose Questions (Objective 0002)

In examining question 3 you will see that you must determine the author's purpose in writing the passage.

3. The writer's main purpose in this passage is to

    A. convince the reader that the Supreme Court is making decisions about obscenity based on their subjective views alone.

    B. explain to the reader how fact-pattern analysis works with respect to cases of obscenity and pornography.

    C. define obscenity and pornography for the layperson.

    D. demonstrate the role fact-pattern plays in determining the Supreme Court's attitude about cases in obscenity and pornography.

Looking at the answer choices you should see that choice D is correct. Though the writer never states it directly, the data is consistently summoned to show that fact-pattern analysis only gives us part of the picture, or "broad strokes" about the Court's attitude, but cannot account for the attitude toward individual cases.

Choice A is incorrect. The writer doesn't try to convince us of this fact, but merely states it as an opinion resulting from the evidence derived from the "well-documented" background of the problem.

B is also incorrect. The writer not only explains the role of fact-pattern analysis but also rather shows how it cannot fully apply.

The passage is about the Court's difficulty in defining these terms, not the man or woman on the street. Nowhere do definitions for these terms appear. Therefore, choice C is incorrect.

Cause and Effect Questions (Objective 0003)

Question 4 requires you to analyze a cause-and-effect relationship.

4. Based on the data in the passage, what would most likely be the major cause for the difficulty in pinning down the Supreme Court's attitude toward cases of obscenity and pornography?

    A. The personal opinions of the Court justices

    B. The broad nature of the situations of the cases

    C. The ineffective logistics of certiorari

    D. The inability of the Court to resolve the variables presented by individual case content

Choice D is correct, as it is precisely what fact-pattern analyses cannot resolve.

Response A is incorrect because no evidence is presented for it; all that is mentioned is that they do make personal decisions. Answer choice B is incorrect because it is one way in which fact-pattern analysis can be helpful. Finally, C is only a statement about certiorari being difficult to administer. The author never claimed this about it in the first place.

Critical Reasoning Questions (Objective 0004)

To answer question 5 you must be able to recall information from the passage as you use critical reasoning skills to evaluate written material.

5. Based on the passage, the rationale for fact-pattern analyses arises out of what theoretical groundwork?

    A. Subjectivity theory

    B. The study of cultural norms

    C. Attitude theory

    D. Cybernetics

The easiest way to answer this question is to refer back to the passage. In the second paragraph the writer states that recent studies using fact-pattern analyses—"owe their theoretical underpinnings to attitude theory." Therefore, we can conclude that response C is correct.

Answer choices A, B, and D are incorrect, as they are never mentioned or discussed by the writer.

Fact vs. Opinion Questions (Objective 0004)

By examining question 6, you can see that you are required to know the difference between fact and opinion.

6.   Which of the following statements express the writer's opinion rather than a fact?

    A.   It is well documented that the area of obscenity and pornography is a difficult one for the Supreme Court.

    B.   The objects to which a court directs its attitudes are the litigants.

    C.   In many specific issue areas, the cases present strikingly similar fact-patterns.

    D.   The Court's subsequent behavior may suggest how the Court will react in other legal areas.

Keeping in mind that an opinion is something that is yet to be proven to be the case, you can determine that choice D is correct. It is the only statement among the four for which evidence is yet to be gathered. It is the writer's opinion that this may be a way to predict the Court's attitudes.

Choices A, B, and C are all derived from verifiable data or documentation, and are therefore incorrect.

Organization Questions (Objective 0005)

Question 7 asks you to organize given topics to reflect the organization of the passage.

7.   Which group of topics best reflect the organization of the passage?

    A.   I.   The difficulties of the Supreme Court

        II. Several recent studies

       III. Spaeth's definition of *attitude*

       IV. The similar patterns of cases

       IV. Other issue areas

       V. The case of *Miller v. California*

B. I.   The Supreme Court, obscenity, and fact-pattern analysis.

II. Fact-pattern analyses and attitude theory

III. The definition of *attitude* for the Court

IV. The definition of *situation*

V.   The breakdown in fact-pattern analysis

VI. Studying Court behavior

C. I.   Justice Stewart's view of pornography

II. Theoretical underpinnings

III. A minimum-winning coalition

IV. Search-and-seizure decisions

V.   Renewed interest in obscenity and pornography

VI. The importance of local community standards

D. I.   The Court's numerous attempts to define obscenity

II. Case characteristics

III. The subject matter of cases

IV. The Court's proportion of decisions

V.   Broad-based factors

VI. Obscenity determination

After examining all of the choices you will determine that choice B is the correct response. These topical areas lead directly to the implied thesis that the "role" of fact-pattern analysis is insufficient to determine the attitude of the Supreme Court in the areas of obscenity and pornography.

Choice A is incorrect because the first topic stated in the list is not the topic of the first paragraph. It is too global. The first paragraph is about the difficulties the Court has with defining obscenity and how fact-pattern analysis might be used to determine the Court's attitude and clear up the problem.

Choice C is incorrect because each of the items listed in this topic list represents supporting evidence or data for the real topic of each paragraph. (See the list in B for correct topics.) For example, Justice Stewart's statement about pornography is only cited to indicate the nature of the problem the Court has with obscenity. It is not the focus of the paragraph itself.

Finally, choice D is incorrect. As with choice C, these are all incidental pieces of information or data used to support broader points.

Summarization Questions (Objective 0005)

To answer question 8 you must be able to summarize the passage.

8. Which of the following paragraphs is the best summary of the passage?

   A. The Supreme Court's decision-making process with respect to obscenity and pornography has become too subjective. Fact-pattern analyses used to determine the overall attitude of the Court reveal only broad-based attitudes on the part of the Court toward the situations of obscenity cases. But these patterns cannot fully account for the Court's attitudes toward case content. Research is not conclusive on whether fact-pattern analyses work when applied to legal areas. Renewed public and local interest suggests continued study and close examination of how the Court makes decisions. Delegating authority to the states may reflect patterns for Court decisions in other socially sensitive areas.

   B. Though subjective, the Supreme Court decisions are well documented. Fact-pattern analyses reveal the attitude of the Supreme Court toward its decisions in cases. Spaeth explains that an attitude involves both an object and a situation. For the Court, the situation may be defined as the decision to grant certiorari. Cases present strikingly similar patterns, and a small number of variables explain a high proportion of the Court's decisions. Segal has made an effort to verify the applicability of fact-pattern analysis with some success. The Court's decisions on obscenity and pornography suggest weak Court behavior, such as in *Miller v. California.*

   C. To determine what obscenity and pornography mean to the Supreme Court, we must operate in a vacuum. The litigants and the subject matter of cases are defined in broad terms (such as an entire area of law) to reveal the Court's decision-making process. Search-and-seizure cases reveal strikingly similar patterns, leaving the Court open to grant certiorari effectively. Renewed public interest in the Court's decisions proves how the Court will react in the future.

   D. Supreme Court decisions about pornography and obscenity are under examination and are out of control. The Court has to see the case to know it. Fact-pattern analyses reveal that the Court can only define cases in narrow terms, thus revealing individual egotism on the part of the justices. As a result of strikingly similar patterns in search-and-seizure cases, the Court should be studied further for its weakness in delegating authority to state courts, as in the case of *Miller v. California.*

The paragraph that best and most accurately reports what the writer demonstrated based on the implied thesis is choice C. That is the correct answer to question 8.

Choice A is incorrect. It reflects some of the evidence presented in the passage, but the passage does not imply that all Court decisions are subjective, just the ones about pornography and obscenity. Similarly, the writer does not suggest that ceding authority to the states (as in *Miller v. California*) is a sign of some weakness, but merely that it is worthy of study as a tool for predicting or identifying the Court's attitude.

Response B is also incorrect. The writer repeatedly shows how fact-pattern analysis cannot pin down the Court's attitude toward case content.

D is incorrect. Nowhere does the writer say or suggest that the justice system is "out of control" or that the justices are "egotists," only that they are liable to be reduced to being "subjective" rather than having a cogent and identifiable shared standard.

Definition Questions (Objective 0006)

Question 9 requires you to determine the meaning of words in context.

9.   In the context of the passage, *subjective* might be more closely defined as

   A.   personal.
   B.   wrong.
   C.   focused.
   D.   objective.

Choice A is the best answer. We can see from the example that Justice Stewart's comment is not an example of right or wrong. Most of the time if we are talking about people's "preferences," they are usually about taste or quality. They are usually not a result of scientific study and sometimes not even clear reasoning. They arise out of personal taste, idiosyncratic intuitions, etc. Thus, A is the most likely choice.

Choice C is incorrect because the Court's focus is already in place: on obscenity and pornography. Choice B is incorrect. Nothing is implied or stated about the rightness or wrongness of the decisions themselves. Rather it is the definition of obscenity that seems "unworkable." D is also incorrect. Objective is an antonym of subjective in this context.

To reason based on the object of study is the opposite of reasoning based upon the beliefs, opinions, or ideas of the one viewing the object rather than the evidence presented by the object.

You may not have been familiar with the word *subjective*, but from your understanding of the writer's intent, you should have been able to figure out what was being sought. Surrounding words and phrases almost always offer you some clues in determining the meaning of a word. In addition, any examples that appear in the text may also provide some hints.

Interpretation of Graphic Information Questions (Objective 0005)

Graphs, charts, and tables may also play a large part on the GACE, and you should be familiar with them. More than likely, you will encounter at least one passage that is accompanied by some form of graphic information. You will then be required to answer any question(s) based on the interpretation of the information presented in the graph, chart, or table as described in section one of this chapter.

Helpful Hints for Reading Graphic Information

You should approach any graphic information you encounter as a key to a larger body of information in abbreviated form. Be sure to use the visual aids of the graphics (e.g., the size of slices on pie charts) *as aids only*; do not ignore the written information listed on the graph or table, etc.

Note especially the title and headings so that you know exactly at what you are looking. Also, be aware of the source of the information, where applicable. Know what each element of the graphic information represents; this will help you compare how drastic or subtle any changes are, and over what span of time they take place. Be sure you realize what the actual numbers represent: whether it is dollars, so many thousands of people, millions of shares, and so forth. Finally, note the way in which the graphic information relates to the text it seeks to illustrate. Know in what ways the graphic information supports the arguments of the author of the given passage.

Conclusion

This review was designed to prepare you for the reading section of the GACE Basic Skills Test. **You were guided through a review of content related to the GACE reading objectives.** When taking the test you should utilize the step-by-step approach from this chapter. It will help you as you analyze the reading passages and answer the questions about those passages.

Remember, the more you know about the skills tested, the better you will perform on the test. By studying this review, you have greatly increased your chances of achieving a good score on the reading section of the GACE.

Mathematics

The mathematics portion of the GACE Basic Skills Test reviews **basic math skills for teachers**. Test takers will be required to answer 48 selected-response/multiple-choice questions.

This review is designed to prepare you for the mathematics section with a healthy review of the content related to the test objectives. Helpful tips are also included. By studying this review, you will greatly increase your chances of achieving a good score on the mathematics section of the GACE.

2. GACE Mathematics Objectives

0007 Understand number properties and number operations.

For example:

- identifying mathematically equivalent ways of representing numbers

- performing operations on integers, fractions, decimals, and percents

- applying number properties (e.g., distributive, order of operations) to simplify numerical expressions

0008   Understand measurement concepts and principles of geometry.

For example:

- applying knowledge of measurement concepts (e.g., time, space, and money)

- selecting and converting units within and between standard and metric measurement

- applying knowledge of the language of geometry (e.g., points, lines, angles, and distance) in various situations

- analyzing fundamental properties of basic geometric shapes

- determining the length, perimeter, area, and volume of geometric shapes or figures

0009   Understand statistical concepts and data analysis and interpretation.

For example:

- interpreting information presented in tables

- interpreting information presented in line graphs, scatter plots, pictographs, bar graphs, histograms, and pie graphs

- determining the theoretical probability of simple events

- demonstrating knowledge of measures of central tendency (e.g., mean, median) and variability (e.g., range, deviation from the mean)

- demonstrating knowledge of the use of statistical concepts in real-world situations

0010   Understand problem-solving principles and techniques.

For example:

- identifying missing terms in numerical and graphical patterns

- solving problems and drawing conclusions using deductive reasoning

- solving word problems involving integers, fractions, decimals, and percents

- applying number properties and geometric principles to solve a variety of problems

- following a set of instructions to perform a given computation

- evaluating an algebraic expression by substituting numbers for variables

- solving algebraic equations and inequalities

- estimating results and determining reasonableness

0007   Number Properties and Operations

This section includes: mathematically equivalent ways of representing numbers; adding, subtracting, multiplying, and dividing fractions, decimals, and integers; number properties such as the distributive property and order of operations; applying number properties to simplify and solve numerical expressions; solving problems with percents and ratios; performing computation with exponents and scientific notation; estimating solutions to problems; and using the concepts of "less than" and "greater than."

Computation with Fractions

There are three steps involved in adding and subtracting fractions. First, make sure that the denominators of both fractions are the same. Then, add the numerators and write that answer over the denominator. Finally, simplify the fraction if needed.

When adding and subtracting fractions that have unlike denominators, a common denominator must be obtained by changing the given fractions to equivalent fractions with the same denominator. These equivalent fractions will have the same value as the original fractions, and they can be easily added or subtracted because they have the same denominator.

For example, to add $\frac{1}{2}$ and $\frac{2}{3}$, the lowest common denominator is 6, because the least common multiple of the denominators (2 and 3) is 6. Therefore, $\frac{1}{2}$ can be written as $\dfrac{3}{6}$, and $\dfrac{2}{3}$ can be written as $\dfrac{4}{6}$. After changing $\dfrac{1}{2} + \dfrac{2}{3}$ to $\dfrac{3}{6} + \dfrac{4}{6}$, we can easily add the numerators together, arriving at the answer of $\dfrac{7}{6}$, or $1\dfrac{1}{6}$.

To add mixed numbers (those made up of a whole number and a fraction), add the fractions first, then the whole numbers. If the fractions sum to more than 1, add the 1 to the whole number sum (as if you were "carrying" to the next column when adding).

Subtracting fractions is much the same as adding. If the denominators are the same, simply subtract the numerators and simplify the fraction. If the denominators are not the same, a common denominator must be obtained. One challenge occurs when subtracting mixed numbers such as $3\dfrac{2}{5}$ and $1\dfrac{4}{5}$. Because $\dfrac{4}{5}$ cannot be subtracted from $\dfrac{2}{5}$, we must rename $3\dfrac{2}{5}$ to $2\dfrac{7}{5}$. We arrive at this renamed number by "borrowing" one whole, or $\dfrac{5}{5}$ from the 3, and adding the $\dfrac{5}{5}$ to the existing $\dfrac{2}{5}$. The new problem, then, is $2\dfrac{7}{5}$ minus $1\dfrac{4}{5}$, which equals $1\dfrac{3}{5}$.

GACE Tip

You don't need common denominators to multiply or divide fractions.

Multiplying and dividing fractions does not require the use of common denominators. When multiplying fractions, simply multiply the numerators together, multiply the denominators together, and then simplify the resulting fraction. For example, $\dfrac{2}{5} \times \dfrac{3}{4}$ equals $\dfrac{6}{20}$, or $\dfrac{3}{10}$.

To multiply whole numbers, change the whole numbers to improper fractions, such as $\dfrac{10}{3}$, and then follow the procedure described above.

To divide fractions, "flip," or invert, the divisor (2nd fraction), and multiply. For example, in the case of $\dfrac{1}{2}$ divided by $\dfrac{3}{8}$, change the problem to read $\dfrac{1}{2} \times \dfrac{8}{3}$. After multiplying, the answer is $\dfrac{8}{6}$ or $1\dfrac{1}{3}$.

Computation with Decimals

Decimal numbers are another way of representing fractions in which denominators are powers of ten (tenths, hundredths, and thousandths). For example, $\frac{12}{100}$ is written as 0.12, $\frac{4}{1000}$ is written as 0.004, and so on.

To add or subtract decimal numbers, simply arrange them vertically, with the decimal points aligned. Then add or subtract as with whole numbers. Remember that a whole number can be written as a decimal number by placing a decimal point at the end of the number, and then adding zeroes as needed. Therefore, 3 becomes 3.0, or 3.00, etc.

GACE Tip

When you add or subtract decimal numbers, align the decimals.

To multiply decimal numbers, arrange the numbers vertically, with alignment on the right side (or "right justified"). Multiply the numbers as if they were whole numbers. Count the number of digits to the right of the decimal point in each of the two factors. Starting at the right side of the product, move the decimal point that many places to the left (ensuring that there are the same number of digits to the right of the decimal in the answer as there were in the factors together). Here is an example:

$$\begin{array}{r} 1.64 \\ \times\ 0.3 \\ \hline .492 \end{array}$$

Multiply the numbers as if they were whole numbers. Since there are 3 digits to the right of the decimal in the factors, make sure that the decimal in the product also has 3 digits to the right of the decimal.

To divide decimal numbers, set up the problem as a traditional whole-number division problem. In the divisor, move the decimal all the way to the right, making it appear as a whole number. Count the number of "places" the decimal was moved. Now, in the dividend, move the decimal the same number of places to the right. Move the decimal directly upward, and write it into the quotient spot. Finally, divide the numbers as if they were whole numbers to arrive at the answer. Here is an example:

$$0.3\overline{)1.44}$$

Move the decimal point in the divisor one place to the right, so it appears as a whole number. Then move the decimal point in the dividend one place to the right as well.

$$0.3\overline{)1.44}\ \ \overset{4.8}{}$$

Write the decimal point in the quotient above where it appears in the dividend. Divide as if the numbers were whole numbers.

Careful placement of digits and decimal points when writing the problem and the quotient help ensure a correct answer.

Computation with Integers

The rules for performing operations on integers (positive and negative whole numbers), and on fractions and decimal numbers in which at least one is negative, are typically the same as the rules for performing operations on non-negative numbers. Pay close attention to the sign (positive or negative value) of each number, and the answer. The rule for multiplication and division is that two positives or two negatives result in a positive answer, whereas "mixing" a positive and a negative gives a negative answer ($-5 \times 3 = -15$, for example). Adding and subtracting with positive and negative numbers is somewhat different. When negative numbers are involved, think of the values as money, with "adding" being thought of as "gaining" and "subtracting" being thought of as "losing." Further, positive numbers can be seen as "credits" and negative numbers, "debts." (Be careful: adding or "gaining" -5, is like *losing* 5).

Percent

Percent is a way of representing a number "out of 100." In fact, the word "percent" literally means "per 100." It is easy to write a percent number as a fraction or a decimal. For example, 25% is the same as $\dfrac{25}{100}$ and 0.25.

GACE Tip

Percent means *per 100*.

There are three types of percent problems: finding a percent of a number, finding what percent one number is of another number, and finding the total when the percentage is known.

Finding a percent of a number

First, write the percent as a decimal. To do this, simply replace the % sign with a decimal, and move it two places to the left. For example, 25% would be written as .25.

Second, multiply the decimal and the given number. Place the decimal point as described in the multiplying decimals section above.

Example   What is 60% of 24?

Write the percent as a decimal.   .60

Multiply the decimal and the given number. $.60 \times 24$

Place the decimal point in the correct place. 14.40

Finding what percent one number is of another number

Set up an equation: __ percent times the total number is the smaller number? It helps to write the percent number as a fraction or decimal.

Example   What percentage of 120 is 48?

Write the equation: $\dfrac{n}{100} \times 120 = 48$

Solve the equation: $1.2n = 48$

$n = 40$

Therefore, 48 is 40% of 120.

Finding the total when the percent is known

Write a proportion. (Percentage is $\dfrac{n}{100}$; set it equal to the given number over the unknown number.)

Solve the proportion.

Example   15 is 6% of what number?

Write the proportion: $\dfrac{15}{n} = \dfrac{6}{100}$

Solve the proportion by cross-multiplying: $6n = 15 \times 100$

$6n = 1500$

$n = 250$

Therefore, 15 is 6% of 250.

Solving and Simplifying Equations

Mathematical expressions and equations often include several operations. When simplifying those expressions and equations, there is a specific order in which each operation is done. The steps in the "order of operations" are:

1. Perform the operations inside parentheses and brackets.

2. Clear the exponents.

3. Multiply and divide, from left to right.

4. Add and subtract, from left to right.

GACE Tip

To simplify equations, use the mnemonic: *Please Excuse My Dear Aunt Sally.*

The mnemonic "Please Excuse My Dear Aunt Sally" (which stands for "parentheses, exponents, multiply, divide, add, subtract") is a device that helps with remembering the order of operations. Here is an example:

Example 1 $4 + 9 \times 3 - 2 = 29$ Multiply 9 by 3 *before* doing the addition and subtraction.

Example 2 $3(4 + 1)^2 = 75$ Add the numbers inside the parentheses, which is 5; clear the exponent next by squaring 5 to equal 25; then multiply left to right so that $3 \times 25 = 75$.

Sometimes, mathematical expressions are represented in a shortened form. *Exponential notation* is a way to show repeated multiplication. For example, $3 \times 3 \times 3$ may be written as 3^3, which is equal to 27. Be mindful that 3^3 does not mean 3×3, but the use of 3 as a factor 3 times.

Scientific notation is a way to show numbers using exponents, particularly very large or very small numbers. A number is in scientific notation when it is shown as a number between 1 and 10 times a power of 10. Therefore, the number 75,000 in scientific notation is shown as 7.5×10^4.

Other common mathematical notation symbols include the following:

Symbol	Meaning	Examples		
<	less than	$.412 < .43$	$-35 < -7$	$\dfrac{1}{3} < \dfrac{1}{2}$
>	greater than	$.792 > .692$	$5 > -3$	$\dfrac{4}{5} > \dfrac{2}{3}$
≠	not equal to	$.5 \neq .4$	$-7 \neq 7$	$\dfrac{2}{5} \neq \dfrac{1}{3}$

0008   Geometry and Measurement

This section involves applying knowledge of measurement concepts (such as time, space, and money) to solve problems; selecting and converting units within and between the standard and metric measurement systems; using the language of geometry (such as points, lines, angles, and distance) with a variety of problems; analyzing fundamental properties of basic geometric shapes; and finding the length, perimeter, area, and volume of geometric shapes and figures.

When you take the GACE, a page of mathematical definitions and formulas will be provided. This section is a review of the information needed to address geometry and measurement questions.

Definitions

π	pi	This symbol indicates the ratio between a circle's circumference and its diameter, and is commonly rounded to 3.14.
$\angle$	angle	There are three types of angles: (a) acute, in which the degree measure is less than 90°, (b) right, in which the degree measure is exactly 90°, and (c) obtuse, in which the degree measure is greater than 90°.
$\angle$ABC	angle ABC	In this notation, the angle has vertex B, and is formed by rays BA and BC.
∟	right angle	This symbol indicates a right angle, which measures exactly 90°.
$\overline{AB}$	line segment AB	The line over AB indicates a line segment, which has two endpoints.
$\overleftrightarrow{AB}$	line AB	The line with arrows on both ends over AB indicates a line that continues forever.
$\overrightarrow{AB}$	ray AB	This ray starts at endpoint A, continues through point B, and continues forever.
$\cong$	congruent	Figures, angles, or line segments that are congruent are exactly the same shape and the same size.
$\sim$	similar	Figures that are similar have the same shape, but not the same size. The corresponding sides of similar figures are proportional.

The following are formulas for finding the areas of basic polygons (informally defined as closed, coplanar geometric figures with three or more straight sides). Abbreviations used are as follows: *A* stands for area, *l* stands for length, *w* stands for width, *h* stands for height, and *b* stands for length of the base.

Triangle (a three-sided polygon): $A = \dfrac{b \times h}{2}$. (Note that, as shown in the figure that follows, the height of a triangle is not necessarily the same as the length of any of its sides.)

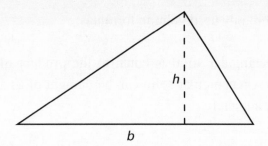

Rectangle (a four-sided polygon with four right angles): $A = l \times w$

Parallelogram (a four-sided polygon with two pairs of parallel sides): $A = l \times w$. (Note that, as with triangles, and as shown in the figure below, the height of a parallelogram is not necessarily the same as the length of its sides.)

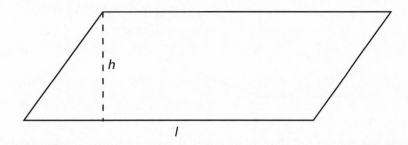

The area of a circle can be found by squaring the length of its radius, then multiplying that product by π. The formula is given as $A = \pi r^2$. (π, or pi, is the ratio of a circle's circumference to its diameter. The value of π is the same for all circles; approximately 3.14159. The approximation 3.14 is adequate for many calculations.) The approximate area of the circle shown below can be found by squaring 6 (giving 36), then multiplying 36 by 3.14, giving an area of about 113 square units.

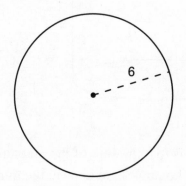

Here are several commonly used volume formulas:

The volume of a rectangular solid is equal to the product of its length, width, and height—$A = l \times w \times h$. (A rectangular solid can be thought of as a box, wherein all intersecting edges form right angles.)

A prism is a polyhedron with two congruent, parallel faces (called bases) and whose lateral (side) faces are parallelograms. The volume of a prism can be found by multiplying the area of the prism's base by its height. The volume of the triangular prism shown hereafter is 60 cubic units. (The area of the triangular base is 10 square units, and the height is 6 units.)

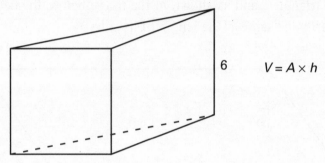

$V = A \times h$

A cylinder is like a prism in that it has parallel faces, but its rounded "side" is smooth. The formula for finding the volume of a cylinder is the same as the formula for finding the volume of a prism: The area of the cylinder's base is multiplied by the height. The volume of the cylinder in the following figure is approximately 628 cubic units. $(5 \times 5 \times \pi \times 8)$.

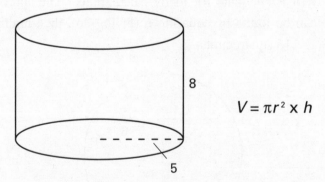

$V = \pi r^2 \times h$

A property of all triangles is that the sum of the measures of the three angles is 180°. If, therefore, the measures of two angles are known, the third can be deduced using addition, and then subtraction.

Right triangles (those with a right angle) have several special properties. A chief property is described by the Pythagorean Theorem, which states that in any right triangle with legs (shorter sides) a and b, and hypotenuse (the longest side) c, the sum of the squares of the sides will be equal to the square of the hypotenuse ($a^2 + b^2 = c^2$). Note that in the right triangle shown here, $3^2 + 4^2 = 5^2$.

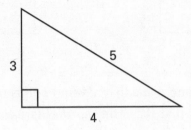

Applying Reasoning Skills

Geometric figures are *similar* if they have the exact same shapes, even if they do not have the same sizes. In transformational geometry, two figures are said to be similar if and only if a similarity transformation maps one figure onto the other. In the figure that follows, triangles A and B are similar.

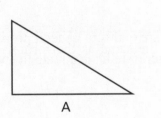

A

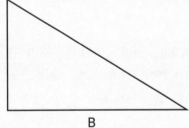

B

Corresponding angles of similar figures have the same measure, and the lengths of corresponding sides are proportional. In the similar triangles below, $\angle A \cong \angle D$ (meaning "angle A is congruent to angle D"), $\angle B \cong \angle E$, and $\angle C \cong \angle F$. The corresponding sides of the triangles below are proportional, meaning that:

$$\frac{AB}{DE} = \frac{BC}{EF} = \frac{CA}{DF}$$

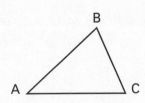

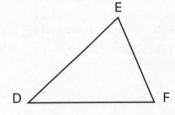

Figures are *congruent* if they have the same shape *and* size. (Congruent figures are also similar.) In the figure below, rectangles A and B are congruent.

Straight lines within the same plane that have no points in common (that is, they never cross) are parallel lines. Note that the term *parallel* is used to describe the relationship between two coplanar lines that do not intersect. Lines that are not coplanar—although they never cross—are not considered to be parallel. Coplanar lines crossing at right angles (90°) are perpendicular.

When presented with math or logic problems, including geometry problems, *deductive reasoning* may be helpful. Deductive reasoning is reasoning from the general to the specific, and is supported by deductive logic. Here is an example of deductive reasoning:

> All humans who have walked on the moon are males (a general proposition). Neil Armstrong walked on the moon, therefore he is a male (a specific proposition).

Note that conclusions reached via deductive reasoning are sound only if the original assumptions are actually true.

With *inductive* reasoning, a general rule is inferred from specific observations (which may be limited). Moving from the statement "All fish I have ever seen have fins" (specific but limited observations) to "All fish have fins" (a general proposition) is an example of inductive reasoning. Conclusions arrived at via inductive reasoning are not necessarily true.

An example of how logical reasoning can be used to solve a geometry problem is given hereafter. (In this case *deductive* reasoning is used to find the measure of ∠J.)

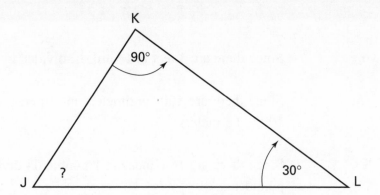

The sum of the measures of the three angles of any triangle is 180° (a general proposition). The sum of the measures of ∠K and ∠L is 120°; therefore, the measure of ∠J is 60° (a specific proposition).

Some problems may require you to make conversions for units of measurement (distance, volume, and mass) in both the standard system and the metric system. These are the most common conversions:

Distance		**Volume**	
1 foot = 12 inches		1 gallon = 4 quarts	
1 yard = 3 feet		1 quart = 2 pints (32 ounces)	
1 mile = 5280 feet			
		1 liter = 1000 milliliters	
1 kilometer = 1000 meters		1 cubic centimeter = 1 milliliter	
1 meter = 100 centimeters			
1 centimeter = 10 millimeters		1 quart = 0.95 liters	
1 inch = 2.54 centimeters			
Mass		**Time**	
1 pound = 16 ounces		1 minute = 60 seconds	
1 ton = 2000 pounds		1 hour = 60 minutes	
		1 day = 24 hours	
1 gram = 1000 milligrams		1 year = 365 days	
1 kilogram = 1000 grams		1 year = 52 weeks	
1 kilogram = 2.2 pounds			

Examples:

12 ft. = _____ yd.   Since there are 3 feet in 1 yard, 12 divided by 3 = 4 yards.

450 cm = _____ m   Since there are 100 centimeters in 1 meter, 450 divided by 100 = 4.5 meters.

64 oz. = _____ lbs.   Since there are 16 ounces in 1 pound, 64 divided by 16 = 4 pounds.

7200 g = _____ kg   Since there are 1000 grams in 1 kilogram, 7200 divided by 1000 = 7.2 kilograms.

7 gal. = _____ qt.   Since there are 4 quarts in 1 gallon, $7 \times 4 = 28$ quarts.

8300 ml = _____ l   Since there are 1000 milliliters in 1 liter, 8300 divided by 1000 = 8.3 liters.

7 hours = _____ min.   Since there are 60 minutes in 1 hour, $7 \times 60 = 420$ minutes.

45 min. = _____ hr.   There are 60 minutes in one hour. 45 minutes is less than one hour, so set up a fraction to show 45 out of 60 minutes $\left(\frac{45}{60} = \frac{3}{4}\right)$. Therefore, 45 minutes is $\frac{3}{4}$ of an hour.

0009   Data Analysis and Statistics

This section includes interpreting information presented in tables, line graphs, scatter plots, pictographs, bar graphs, histograms, and pie charts; determining the theoretical probability of simple events; demonstrating knowledge of measures of central tendency (mean, median), and variability (range, deviation from the mean); and demonstrating knowledge of the use of statistical concepts to solve real-world problems.

Graphs, tables, and charts come in many different forms; most of these represent numerical data in easy-to-read visual formats. A bar graph, like the one below, typically shows "how much" for each category.

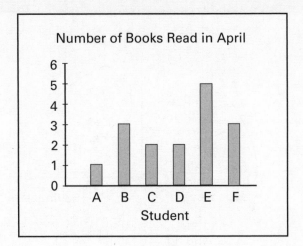

Line graphs, like the one below, are well suited to indicate *change over time*. These graphs indicate time (in months, years, etc.) on the bottom or horizontal axis. We use line graphs to show trends in data.

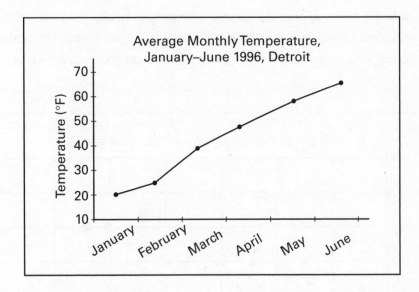

Pie graphs (also called circle graphs or pie charts) show how a quantity is "split up." As with the example below, pie graphs may not necessarily be accompanied by specific numeric values. These graphs are particularly effective for showing relative amounts at a glance.

Scatter plots are used to investigate relationships between two variables. The scatter plot below shows height (in centimeters) in relation to arm span (in centimeters). As might be expected, as a person's height increases, their arm span tends to increase as well.

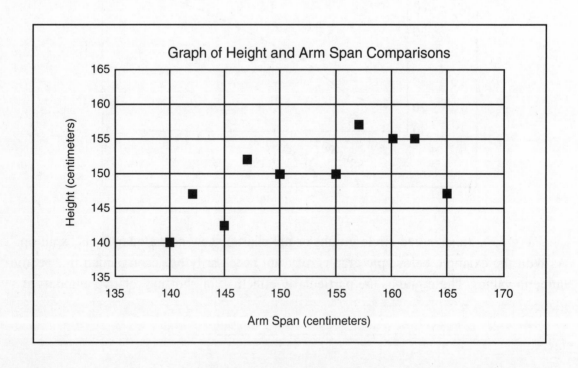

Histograms are graphs that use vertical columns to show frequencies. The histogram below shows the number of students who made particular scores on a quiz.

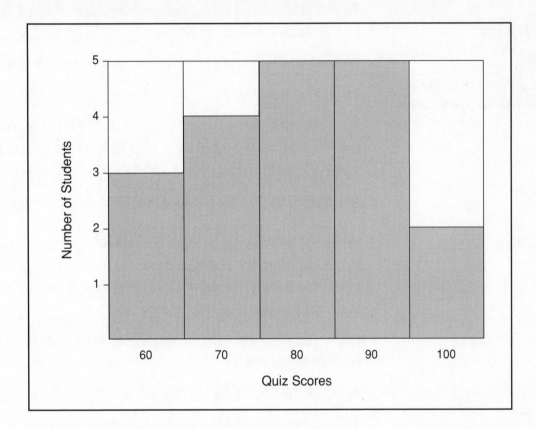

Statistical Concepts

Data can be represented in *discrete* or *continuous* form, depending on what they represent. Discrete data have gaps between them. A bar graph is a common way to show discrete data. For example, the bar graph above shows the number of students who made particular scores on a test. Discrete data are usually obtained by counting. Continuous data are usually represented by an unbroken line on a graph, and usually are obtained by measuring. The line graph on page 65, shows the average monthly temperature over time. The data are continuous, because there are no gaps in the months or in the temperatures.

There are a number of statistical terms and concepts that you may need to know for the test:

Mean

Commonly known as the "average," the mean is the sum of a set of numbers divided by the quantity of numbers in the set. To find the mean, add all of the numbers together, and divide by how many numbers are given.

GACE Tip

**Mean: average
Median: center number
Mode: occurs most often**

For example, suppose you are given the following data set:

16, 9, 11, 19, 12, 16, 22

To find the mean, add all the numbers together $(16 + 9 + 11 + 19 + 12 + 16 + 22 = 105)$. Then, divide the sum (105) by the quantity of numbers in the data set (7).

105 divided by 7 = 15. The mean of this data set is 15.

Median

The median is the center value in a set of numbers; to find the median, list the numbers from smallest to largest, and locate the number in the middle. If there are two middle numbers, compute their average.

Given the same data set as above, list the numbers from smallest to largest.

9, 11, 12, 16, 16, 19, 22

The number in the middle is 16, which is the median.

Mode

A measure of central tendency, the mode is the value in a set of numbers that occurs most often.

Given the same data set as above, we see that 16 occurs twice in the data set, and all of the other numbers occur once. Therefore, 16 is the mode.

Range

The range is the measure of the variation (spread) that is the difference between the largest value and smallest value in a set of data. To find the range, subtract the smallest number in the set from the largest number.

Sample
A sample is a survey of the population made by taking a set that is judged to be representative of the population. Choosing the sample in a randomized way is essential for validity and believability.

Standard Deviation
Standard deviation is the most commonly used expression of spread, or variation, of data. The higher the standard deviation, the higher is the degree of spread around the center of the data (that is, the data are more inconsistent with each other).

Percentiles
A percentile is a ranking or measure of where a piece of data stands in relation to the other data in the set. Percentiles tell how many other data are lower in value. For example, a person might score 75% on a test, but rank in the 90 percentile. This means that 89% of all other test takers received a lower score. The median occurs at the 50 percentile.

Frequency Distributions
Frequency distributions represent the likelihood that a statistic of interest will fall in a certain interval; for example, the height of a person chosen at random may follow the normal distribution (also called a standard distribution, or "bell-shaped curve"). These are some types of distributions:

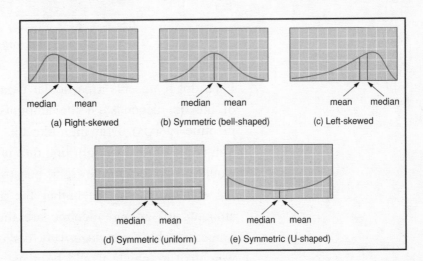

median mean
(a) Right-skewed

median mean
(b) Symmetric (bell-shaped)

mean median
(c) Left-skewed

median mean
(d) Symmetric (uniform)

median mean
(e) Symmetric (U-shaped)

Figure (b) is the normal distribution, on which tests are often said to be graded. In this figure, more scores fall in the middle than on the high or low ends. In the right-skewed distribution in Figure (a), more of the scores are low, and in the left-skewed distribution in Figure (c), more of the scores are high. The distribution in Figure (d) shows that all scores are distributed equally from high to low, and Figure (e) shows a distribution in which most scores were either high or low, with fewer in the average range. Notice the location of the mean and median in each figure.

Correlation

Correlation is the relationship between two variables. For example, a graph of tar and nicotine in cigarettes might look like this:

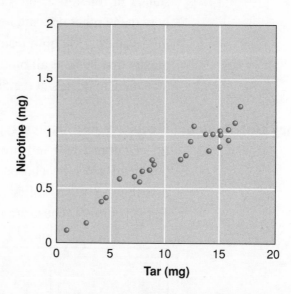

Each dot represents a particular cigarette, and the placement of the dot depends on the amounts of its tar (*x*-axis) and nicotine (*y*-axis). Drawings like this are called *scatter plots*. You could draw a straight line through this scatter plot, and it would go up and to the right, because, in general, the higher the amount of tar, the higher the amount of nicotine. The amounts of tar and nicotine are thus *positively correlated*. Some variables are *negatively correlated*; for instance, the weight of a vehicle would be negatively correlated with gas mileage if several models of vehicle were plotted in a scatter plot.

Here are some other scatter plots with varying kinds of correlation:

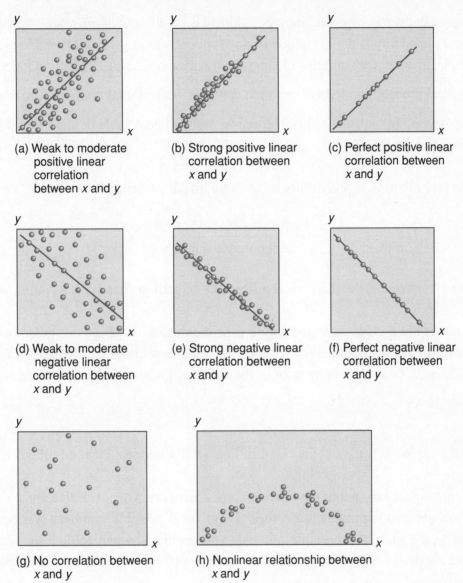

(a) Weak to moderate positive linear correlation between x and y

(b) Strong positive linear correlation between x and y

(c) Perfect positive linear correlation between x and y

(d) Weak to moderate negative linear correlation between x and y

(e) Strong negative linear correlation between x and y

(f) Perfect negative linear correlation between x and y

(g) No correlation between x and y

(h) Nonlinear relationship between x and y

When a correlation is linear or almost linear, you can use the graph to make predictions. For example, in the graph of tar and nicotine above, you could predict with a fair amount of certainty that a cigarette with 10 mg of tar would have between 0.7 and 0.8 mg of nicotine. In scatterplots without a linear correlation [(g) and (h) above], it's much harder to predict the value of y, given the value of x, in fact, in graph (g) it's nearly impossible.

Probability

One probability concept that may be addressed on the test is *theoretical probability.* Theoretical probability is the likelihood of an event occurring, given all possible outcomes. For example, given the possibilities of choosing a red candy, a blue candy, or a green candy, the theoretical probability of choosing a red candy is $\frac{1}{3}$. The total possible outcomes of an event are required for calculations of theoretical probability. A table or chart that shows the possibilities may be helpful.

To find the theoretical probability of an event, make a fraction:

$$\frac{\text{number of ways the event can occur}}{\text{total possible outcomes}}$$

Example 1   What is the theoretical probability of getting "heads" if a coin is tossed?

When you flip a coin, there are only 2 possible outcomes—heads or tails. Two is the denominator of the fraction. The number of ways that you could get "heads" is 1 (only 1 side is a "head"). One is the numerator of the fraction. Therefore, the theoretical probability is $\frac{1}{2}$ or 50%.

Example 2   What is the likelihood of rolling a "7" when two dice are rolled?

First, determine how many possible outcomes there are when two dice are rolled. The chart below shows the possible outcomes. There are 6 possible numbers you could roll when rolling die #1, and 6 possible numbers you could roll when rolling die #2. Therefore, there are 36 possible combinations or outcomes (6 × 6 = 36). This is the denominator of the fraction.

Second, find the number of ways the event can occur. In this case, the sum of "7" appears 6 times. Six is the numerator of the fraction. Therefore, the theoretical probability is $\frac{6}{36}$, or $\frac{1}{6}$, or 16.6%.

Possible Outcomes – Die #2	Possible Outcomes – Die #1						
		1	**2**	**3**	**4**	**5**	**6**
	1	2	3	4	5	6	7
	2	3	4	5	6	7	8
	3	4	5	6	7	8	9
	4	5	6	7	8	9	10
	5	6	7	8	9	10	11
	6	7	8	9	10	11	12

Example 3 Look at the spinner below. Assume that each section in the spinner is equal in area. What is the likelihood of getting a 1 on the first spin and a 2 on the second spin?

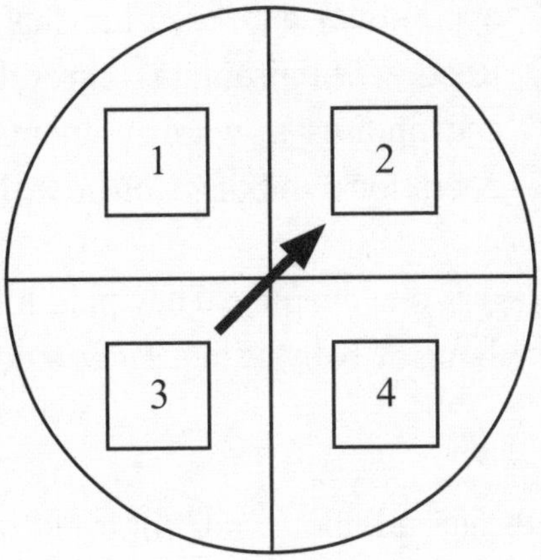

First, determine the number of possible outcomes when spinning a spinner twice. The ordered pairs below show the possibilities (outcome of spin 1, outcome of spin 2).

(1, 1)	(2, 1)	(3, 1)	(4, 1)
(1, 2)	(2, 2)	(3, 2)	(4, 2)
(1, 3)	(2, 3)	(3, 3)	(4, 3)
(1, 4)	(2, 4)	(3, 4)	(4, 4)

Sixteen possible outcomes exist. This is the denominator of the fraction.

Only *one* of the outcomes (1, 2) illustrates the possibility of getting a 1 with the first spin and a 2 with the second spin. One is the numerator of the fraction.

Therefore, the theoretical probability of getting a 1 with the first spin and a 2 with the second spin is $\frac{1}{16}$ or 6.25%.

0010   Problem-Solving Principles and Techniques

This section includes identifying missing terms in numerical and graphic patterns; solving word problems involving integers, fractions, decimals, and percents; solving problems and drawing conclusions using a variety of problem-solving techniques; evaluating and solving algebraic expressions, equations, and inequalities; and estimating results and determining whether the answer is reasonable.

GACE Tip

When you have finished a problem, always check to see that your answer makes sense.

There are two keys to successfully solving word problems: setting up the problem correctly (using the correct operations) and ensuring that your answer is reasonable. Read word problems carefully; often, particular words and phrases in word problems translate into numbers and operation symbols. Consider this word problem:

Roberto babysat for the Yagers one evening. They paid him $5 just for coming over to their house, plus $7 for every hour of babysitting. How much was he paid if he babysat for 4 hours?

In this problem, "plus" indicates addition, and "for every hour" suggests multiplication. Thus, the equation for this problem can be set up like this: $5 + (7 \times 4)$ = Roberto's earnings.

There are a number of "clue words" that suggest which operations should be used. The chart below contains a sample of these words.

Addition Clue Words	Subtraction Clue Words
add altogether in all plus sum total	difference have left how much/many more less than remain
Multiplication Clue Words	**Division Clue Words**
for every multiplied by product of times	as much divided equally parts separated split sharing something

Although these clue words suggest which operation is appropriate, each word problem requires an individual approach. Keeping in mind the reasonableness of the computational setup should be helpful.

It may also be helpful to use a variety of problem-solving strategies. These may include drawing a picture, making a chart or table, looking for a pattern, logical reasoning, or working backwards.

Writing

The writing portion of the GACE Basic Skills Test **assesses the test-taker's ability to recognize well-written compositions and Standard American English usage as well as to compose a written response to a given topic.** When you take this test, you will be asked to read a passage and answer questions about the words or punctuation included in that passage. You may also be asked to fill in the blank with a sentence or phrase that makes the passage more effective.

The GACE Writing Test is divided into two sections. The first section includes approximately 42 selected-response (multiple-choice) test items. The second Section requires you to demonstrate the ability to prepare an essay (constructed-response) on a given prompt.

When you take the second section of the Writing Test you will be directed to write a written response on a given topic. Your composition will be evaluated on the following criteria: **appropriateness** (how well your response addresses the topic and is appropriate for the audience, purpose, and occasion); your **focus** and **organization** (logical sequence of thoughts and ideas, and overall clarity); your **support** (how well you have used details to support your thesis statement); your **grammar**, **sentence structure**, and **usage** (the extent to which your response has no errors in usage, and the precision of your word choice); and your **use of conventions** (the extent to which your response has no errors in spelling, capitalization, and punctuation). Your responses will be rated on a four-point scale from "4" to "1." Other possible scores you could receive would be: "unscorable" or "blank."

This review is designed to prepare you for the multiple-choice questions in the Test III (Writing) subarea. The review will help you to recognize good writing and give you pointers on how to write a well-developed composition on a given subject. Tips to help you quickly and accurately answer the questions are also included. By studying this review, you will greatly increase your chances of achieving a good score on the GACE.

3. GACE Writing Skills Objectives

Skills Covered in Selected-Response Questions

0011   Recognize unity, focus, and development in writing

For example:

- recognizing unnecessary shifts in point of view or distracting details that impair the development of the main idea in a piece of writing

- recognizing revisions that improve the unity and focus of a piece of writing

- recognizing thesis statements, topic sentences, and supporting elements

0012   Recognize effective organization in writing

For example:

- recognizing methods of paragraph organization

- recognizing the use of transitional words or phrases

- reorganizing sentences to improve cohesion and the effective sequence of ideas

0013   Recognize effective sentences

For example:

- recognizing redundancy

- identifying structures (e.g., sentences, fragments, run-on sentences)

- identifying standard subject-verb agreement

- identifying double negatives, parallel structure, and standard placement of modifiers

0014   Recognize Standard American English usage

For example:

- recognizing the standard use of verb forms and cases

- recognizing the standard use of pronouns/antecedents and plural and possessive forms of nouns

- recognizing the standard use and formations of adverbs and adjectives

- recognizing standard punctuation and capitalization

Skills Covered in Constructed-Response Questions

0015   Demonstrate the ability to prepare a developed composition on a given topic using language and style appropriate to a given audience, purpose, and occasion

- composing a coherent, focused, and sustained composition on a given topic using language and style appropriate to a specified audience, purpose, and occasion

- stating and maintaining a clear thesis statement using organizational strategies to enhance meaning and clarity

- providing reasoned support and/or specific examples to maintain the thesis statement

- using effective sentence structure, word choice, and mechanics (e.g., grammar, syntax)

- using spelling, capitalization, and punctuation according to the conventions of Standard American English

The Passages

The reading passages in this part of your test will be based on many different subjects. Although you will not be expected to know the content presented in the passages, you will be expected to recognize correct writing techniques and select appropriate revisions to sections that are not grammatically correct. Each passage will be followed by a number of questions. Some questions may ask you to find mistakes in Standard American English usage; others may ask you to supply appropriate words or phrases in blanks.

Objective 0011   Recognize unity, focus and development in writing

Recognizing unnecessary shifts in point of view or distracting details that impair the development of the main idea in a piece of writing

Point of view is the relationship of the writer to the written piece. The point of view in a particular passage must be consistent throughout the passage. Unnecessary shifts in the point of view come about by the change in the number of the noun or pronoun. Points of view may be considered one of three *persons:*

- First person singular or plural (*I*, *we*): the narrator is part of the composition

- Second person singular or plural (*you*): the narrator is addressing the reader

- Third person singular or plural (*he*, *she*, *it*, *they*): the narrator is not a part of the composition, but an observer of it

For example, this text is written in *second person* (*you*) which addresses the reader directly. Generally, it is best to stay in the point of view, or the correct person, in which you begin the passage. The most common shift in point of view in college writing is from first or third person to second person. Consider the following:

GACE Tip

Stay with the same person that you started with.

"Just trying to figure out which college to attend is a big challenge. The prospective college student must take into consideration cost and available majors, as well as location of the school. Once the list has been narrowed down by these factors, you might want to take into account where your parents might like you to go."

Because the writer began in the third person, in this instance the point of view should remain in the third person. The writer could make the following changes to correct the unnecessary shift in point of view. The second sentence could be changed:

"You, the prospective college student, must take into consideration cost and available majors, as well as location of the school."

Or the *third:*

> "Once the list has been narrowed down by these factors, he or she might want to take into account where his or her parents might like him or her to go." OR "Once the list has been narrowed down by these factors, students might want to take into account where their parents might like them to go."

You can see that the replacement to third person singular in this instance can be somewhat stilted, but selection of the point of view is more dependent on the audience and the purpose of the passage.

On the test, you will be asked to recognize these inconsistencies in point of view and select corrections that provided consistency across the passage. In this example, as you will see in the test, it is necessary to read the entire passage to determine the appropriate point of view.

This descriptive statement that accompanies Objective 0011 also focuses on the importance of being able to recognize *distracting details*. These are sentences or phrases within the passage that do not address the main idea. Again, it is essential to read the entire passage to be able able to recognize information that does not fit into the passage.

Recognizing revisions that improve the unity and focus of a piece of writing

You will be asked to select answers that will provide revisions to the passages given. You need to be able to identify revisions that improve the *unity and focus* of a piece of writing. The unity of a composition is that quality in which all the sentences support the main idea and the parts fit together in a complete, self-contained whole. The focus of a composition is that quality in which the position or proposition of the writer is clearly evident. Consider this passage:

GACE Tip

All of the sentences in a composition need to support the main idea.

> In 1867 Congress passed the Fourteenth Amendment, which granted citizenship to "all persons born or naturalized in the United States." This included former slaves recently freed. The Fourteenth Amendment

also gave "equal protection of the laws" to all citizens and declared that no state could deny anyone "life, liberty or property" without due process. Due process means that everyone has equal protection under the law, and people may not be treated differently, or discriminated against. The 14th Amendment made it illegal for states to discriminate against anyone based on race. However, a number of white southerners did not want to give African Americans real freedom and, as a result, most southern states adopted black codes to limit the freedoms of African Americans.

This passage has both unity and focus because all of the sentences are supportive of the main idea of the historical delivery of equal rights under the law to African Americans. The passage addresses the constitutional law and the measures taken to violate that law.

Recognizing thesis statements, topic sentences, and supporting elements

A **thesis statement** is a position or proposition advanced by a writer and all the information in an essay supports or elaborates on this idea. The **topic sentence** is one that states the main idea of a paragraph, while the **supporting elements** are facts, examples, details, illustrations, testimony, or the research of experts that verify or add credence to a main idea.

A successful thesis statement can be recognized by asking these questions about the passage:

1. What was the central idea that guided the passage?

2. What questions were answered in the passage?

3. What significant ideas surfaced in the passage?

4. What did I find out after I read the passage?

When you are reading to locate the thesis statements, topic sentences, and supporting elements, look for the main idea and be wary of irrelevant ideas. Take the following example:

[1]After 1870, many northerners grew tired of trying to force change on the South. [2]They felt that it was time to forget the Civil War and let southerners run their own governments, even if that meant African Americans might lose the rights they had so recently gained. [3]Many changes occurred during Reconstruction that were meant to help the former slaves and

freedmen. [4]Without federal protection, the Reconstruction governments that were supportive of African American civil rights fell in 1877.

Sentence 3 is not a supporting element of this passage. While sentence 4 does mention Reconstruction, the thesis of this passage does not focus on the changes that occurred during Reconstruction, but rather how those changes were abandoned. The proposition advanced by this writer within the passage is that when northerners grew tired of supporting the Reconstruction governments in the south, these governments fell. The reasons why the northerners no longer supported the Reconstruction governments, such as they grew tired of trying to force change and that they felt it was time to forget the Civil War, act as supporting elements.

Objective 0012   Recognize effective organization in writing

Recognizing methods of paragraph organization

Good writing is evidenced by a coherent composition, which has a systematic order of ideas. Coherent writing is recognized by the connections between one sentence or paragraph and the next. Sentences and paragraphs should be arranged in such a way that it is easy to determine the intent of the writer. This arrangement should be clear and logical so that the flow of the information is easy to follow.

Different types of compositions use different orders of paragraphs, but usually there is an introductory paragraph followed by supporting paragraphs that further describe the supporting elements, and a concluding paragraph. The order in which the information is presented may be affected by the content of the composition. Some paragraphs will be written in chronological order, some in spatial order, and some compositions may be written to compare or contrast objects and events, and this order will be presented.

GACE Tip

Well-organized writing includes an introductory paragraph, supporting paragraphs, and a concluding paragraph.

The following example uses **spatial order** in the first paragraph, **chronological order** in the second, and **compare and contrast** in the third.

1. My best friend and I handed over our tickets and headed into the stadium. Immediately in front of us was the concession stand, but we headed up the long ramp on our right to

the upper level. Once on the upper level, another concession stand stood in front of us, but we went instead to the stairs between the concession stand and the restrooms to get to our seats.

2. Before we arrived at our assigned row, we first greeted other season ticket holders who we had seen at previous games. We then inched our way to our seats while trying not to step on anyone's toes. When we got to our seats, we once again greeted familiar faces and then adjusted our seat cushions. Before we sat down, we got the vendor's attention for some hot dogs and cold drinks. Finally we were ready.

3. This game was unlike any game last season: we could feel the excitement in the air. Last year we rarely saw the stadium filled before kickoff, but at this game, every seat was filled by the time the team hit the field for warm-ups. This game reminded me of games during the season when we won the national championship, which meant that everyone was up and cheering from the beginning to the end. Unlike last year when some fans left at halftime, this year fans stayed after the game to continue to show support for the team.

Recognizing the use of transitional words or phrases

A **transition** is a connecting word or phrase that clarifies the relationship of other words or ideas. Transitional words and phrases show the relationship between details and help make these relationships clear. Consider these commonly used transitions and the relationships they illustrate:

Time: *after, always, before, finally, first, immediately, later, meanwhile, now, sometimes, soon, until*

Place: *above, ahead, around, below, down, far, here, inside, near, next, opposite, outside, over, parallel, there, under, vertically, within*

Order of importance: *first, latter, primarily, secondarily*

Cause and effect: *as a result, because, by, so, then, therefore*

Comparison and contrast: *but, even more, however, just as, like, on the other hand, unlike*

Example: *for example, for instance, namely, that is*

In the previous passages, note the words and phrases in the first paragraph that identify the place (in front, between), the second paragraph that illustrate the order in which the events occurred (before, first), and the third paragraph that compare and contrast (unlike, but).

Reorganizing sentences to improve cohesion and the effective sequence of ideas

The key to cohesion is **organization**. The logical sequence of ideas, coupled with transitional words and phrases to keep connections clear, is the mainstay of coherent writing. It is a sign of good writing when paragraphs are arranged so that one leads logically to the next and sentences within paragraphs are ordered so that readers can easily follow the flow of ideas. Consider the following example:

> LBJ pushed to have the civil rights bill passed. It had passed in the House of Representatives, in February 1964, but was stalled in the Senate where southern segregationists intended to kill it. After President Kennedy's assassination on November 22, 1963, President Lyndon Johnson was determined to continue Kennedy's civil rights policies. Johnson was aided in his goal to pass the civil rights bill by national remorse over Kennedy's assassination. President Johnson took advantage of the public mood and on July 2, 1964, he signed into law the Civil Rights Act of 1964. Even though Johnson was from the South, he had broken with the segregationists.

While the content and ideas are presented within the example, it is difficult to follow chronologically or through the order of importance. Here is the passage reorganized with the ideas more effectively sequenced:

> After President Kennedy's assassination on November 22, 1963, President Lyndon Johnson was determined to continue Kennedy's civil rights policies. He pushed to have the civil rights bill passed. Though it had passed in the House of Representatives in February 1964, it was stalled in the Senate, where southern segregationists intended to kill it. Even though Johnson was from the South, he had broken with the segregationists. Johnson was aided in his goal to pass the civil rights bill by national remorse over Kennedy's assassination. President Johnson took advantage of public mood and on July 2, 1964, he signed into law the Civil Rights Act of 1964.

The rearrangement of the sentences, and the addition of one transition word, helps the reader to understand the progression of the information.

Objective 0013   Recognize effective sentences

Recognizing redundancy

Often in college writing, the same point will be restated in more than one question. You will encounter test questions that will gauge your ability to detect redundancies (unnecessary repetitions). These questions require you to select sentences that use only those necessary words to convey a message clearly. Effective writing is concise writing, but this doesn't mean that short sentences are better than long ones simply because they are brief. Repetition of words, sounds, and phrases should be used only for emphasis. Consider the following example:

GACE Tip

Effective writing is concise writing.

> Often, anxiety before a competition can promote poor performance in football players, especially quarterbacks. Being nervous can cause players to forget plays, throw to covered receivers, and move too quickly from behind center.

"Anxiety" in the first sentence and "being nervous" in the second means essentially the same thing, as do "quarterbacks" and "players." These two sentences can be combined and reworked to offer a more concise thesis and supporting details.

> "Anxiety in quarterbacks can have disastrous results when their nervousness promotes poor performance like forgetting plays, throwing to covered receivers, and moving too quickly from behind center."

Identifying structures (e.g., sentences, fragments, run-on sentences)

A **sentence** is a group of words that expresses a complete thought and can be classified by structure (simple, compound, complex, compound-complex). Every sentence has two basic parts, a subject and a predicate.

Sentence fragments are incomplete sentences that either 1) lack a subject or a verb or 2) are preceded by a subordinating conjunction (e.g., *after*, *before*, *since*, *until*). A **run-on sentence** is two or more complete sentences written as though they were one sentence.

Consider how sentences can be identified from existing fragments or run-on sentences:

Fragment that lacks a subject:

Incorrect   Kitty has several ideas about teaching reading to young children. That won't cost much to implement.

Correct   Kitty has several ideas that won't cost much to implement about teaching reading to young children.

Fragment that is a subordinate clause:

Incorrect   Jemella went to the later show. Because it was a romance.

Correct   Jemella went to the later show because it was a romance. OR

Jemella went to the later show. It was a romance.

Run-on sentence as a comma splice (two main clauses separated only by a comma)**:**

Incorrect   I did not see her come in, she was late.

Correct   I did not see her come in. She was late. OR

I did not see her come in; she was late. OR

I did not see her come in, but she was late.

Two main clauses without a comma before the coordinating conjunction:

Incorrect   I usually buy my airplane ticket early but I thought I would wait this year.

Correct   I usually buy my airplane ticket early, but I thought I would wait this year.

Identifying standard subject-verb agreement

There are **two basic rules of subject and verb agreement** that govern all the other rules:

1. a singular subject must have a singular verb.

2. a plural subject must have a plural verb.

A verb must agree with its subject in person and number, and this is often where students make mistakes. It is good practice to identify the real subject of a sentence and then determine whether the verb form should be singular or plural.

Every English verb has five forms, two of which are the bare form (plural and the –s form (singular). In other words, singular verb forms end in –s; plural forms do not.

Here are the **rules governing subject verb agreement in action**:

Intervening Phrases and Clauses

A verb must agree with the subject of the sentence, not with the object of the preposition. Do not mistake a word in an intervening clause for the subject of a sentence.

Example   The collection of baseball cards *was* very valuable. (The subject is *collection*, a singular noun. *Of baseball cards* is a prepositional phrase with a plural object. The verb *was* agrees with the singular noun *collection*.)

Prepositional phrases beginning with compound prepositions such as *along with, together with, in addition to,* and *as well as* introduce phrases that modify the subject without changing the number. Although their meaning is similar to that of *and*, these expressions don't form compound sentences.

Example   The newspapers, together with the aluminum, are ready to be recycled. (The subject is *newspapers*, a plural noun. *Together with the aluminum* is a prepositional phrase with a singular object. The verb *are* agrees with the plural noun *newspapers*.)

Appositives and adjective clauses give information about the subject but don't change its number. Make sure you don't mistake a word in an appositive of an adjective clause for the subject of the sentence.

Example   *Sharon*, one of my sisters, *cooks* for the entire family during the holidays. (singular)

Example   The *states* that border Florida *are* Alabama and Georgia. (plural)

Compound Subjects

A compound subject is joined by *and* or *both*. It takes a plural verb unless its parts belong to one unit or they both refer to the same thing.

| Examples | The *Tigris* and the *Euphrates flow* through southwestern Asia. (plural) |

Both *rivers* and *streams provide* irrigation for farmland. (plural)

| Examples | *Peanut butter* and *jelly is* my favorite sandwich. (singular) |

Her *lord* and *master is* the dog. (singular)

When compound subjects are joined by *or* or *nor* (or by *either . . . or* or *neither . . . nor*), the verb agrees with the subject closer to it.

| Examples | *Raisins* or an *apple makes* a good snack. (singular) |

Neither the *equipment* nor the *uniforms have arrived* yet. (plural)

Collective Nouns

When a **collective noun refers to a group as a whole**, it requires a singular verb. When a collective noun refers to each member of a group individually, it requires a plural verb.

| Examples | The *chorus performs* beautifully. (singular) |

The *chorus are staying* at different hotels. (plural)

When deciding the number of the verb needed for a collective noun, it is helpful to look for the pronouns *its* and *their*. When a collective noun is referred to by *its*, the collective noun requires a singular verb. When a collective noun is referred to by *their*, the collective noun needs a plural verb.

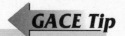

GACE Tip

***Its* takes a singular verb; *their* requires a plural verb.**

Some nouns ending in *–s,* such as *mumps, measles, news,* and *mathematics,* take singular verbs. Other nouns ending in *–s, like scissors, pants, binoculars,* and *eyeglasses,*

GACE BASIC SKILLS

take plural verbs. Many nouns that end in *–ics* are either singular or plural, depending on the context. In general, if the noun refers to a whole, like a disease or science, it requires a singular verb. If it is referring to qualities, activities, or individual items, it requires a plural verb.

Examples   *Measles is* usually a childhood disease. (singular)

His *pants were wrinkled* from sitting for so long. (plural)

Statistics is one of my favorite courses. (singular)

Statistics are the basis of much research. (plural)

Nouns of Amount

When a plural noun of amount refers to one unit, it acts as a singular subject. When it refers to individual units, it acts as a plural subject.

Examples   Two *weeks is* not enough time to see China. (singular)

Your five *days* of quarantine *are* up. (plural)

When a fraction or a percentage refers to a singular word, it requires a singular verb. When it refers to a plural word, it requires a plural verb.

Examples   Fifty *percent* of the *money was used* for bribes. (singular)

Fifty *percent* of the *voters are* in line. (plural)

A unit of measurement usually requires a singular verb.

Examples   Sixteen by twenty *inches is* a standard size for a picture frame. (singular)

Ten *yards is needed* for a first down. (singular)

Indefinite Pronouns

Some indefinite pronouns are always singular, some are always plural, and others may be singular or plural depending on their use.

Indefinite Pronouns

Singular	Another, anyone, anybody, anything, each, either, everybody, everyone, everything, neither, nobody, no one, nothing, one, other, somebody, someone, something
Plural	Both, few, many, others, several
Singular or Plural	All, any, enough, most, much, none, some

Singular indefinite pronouns require singular verbs and **plural indefinite pronouns** require plural verbs. For those indefinite pronouns that can be either singular or plural, subject-verb agreement depends on the nouns to which they refer.

Examples

Everyone wants a ticket to the concert. (singular)

Few of us *believe* we will get tickets. (plural)

Most of the stadium *was* completely full. (*Most* refers to the singular noun *stadium*.)

Most of the attendees *were* young adults. (*Most* refers to the plural noun *attendees*.)

Phrases and Clauses as Subjects

Whenever a phrase or a clause acts as a subject, the verb must be singular.

Examples

Running laps is good exercise. (The gerund phrase *running laps* functions as the subject and agrees with the singular verb *is*.)

To worry about grades is ineffectual. (The infinitive phrase *to worry about grades* functions as the subject and agrees with the singular verb *is*.)

Whoever makes the most pies wins the blue ribbon. (The noun clause *whoever makes the most pies* functions as the subject and agrees with the singular verb *wins*.)

Adjective Clauses

When the subject of an adjective clause is a relative pronoun, the verb in the clause must agree with the word to which the relative pronoun refers.

If the relative pronoun is the subject of the clause and it refers to a singular word, the verb in the adjective clause must be singular.

Example   The woman who teaches my cooking class dresses in white. (singular)

If the relative pronoun is the subject of the adjective clause and it refers to a plural word, then the verb in the adjective clause must be plural

Example   Coffee shops that have the Internet are convenient. (plural)

If an adjective clause is preceded by *the only one of* (plural word), the relative pronoun will refer to the word *one*, and the verb in the clause must be singular.

Example   Dennis is the only one of my brothers who has children. (The antecedent of *who* is *one*, not *brothers*, because only one brother has children. Since *one* is singular, *who* is considered singular, and the verb in the adjective clause, *has,* must also be singular.)

If an adjective clause is preceded by *one of* (plural word), then the relative pronoun will refer to the plural word, and the verb in the clause must be plural.

Example   Beijing was one of my favorite places that were included on our itinerary. (The antecedent of *that* is *places*, not *one*, because there were other places on the itinerary. Since *places* is plural, *that* is considered plural and the verb in the adjective clause, *were*, must also be plural.)

Identifying double negatives, parallel structure, and standard placement of modifiers

A double negative is two or more negative words used to express the same idea. Use only one negative word to express a negative idea.

Incorrect	I don't have no cell phone service in this area.
Correct	I don't have any cell phone service in this area. OR
Correct	I have no cell phone service in this area.

Some sentences can correctly contain more than one negative word. Notice in the example below, however, that each clause only contains one negative word.

Examples   The girls *didn't* go to the movie because they had *no* money.

Parallel Structure

Parallel structure is expressing similar details using similar grammatical structures. Parallel structures often contain conjunctions and words, phrases or sentences that have similar grammatical form. Parallel structure refers to the grammatical balance of a series of any of the following:

Phrases. The boy rode *up the street, toward the town*, and *away from his incomplete chores*.

Adjectives. The university has been *historically nondiscriminatory, traditionally liberal*, and *unconventionally civil*.

Nouns. The luncheon consisted of *casseroles, a meat dish*, and *dessert*.

Verbs. The contestant *bit, chewed,* and *swallowed* the hot dog in less than five seconds.

Verbals. *Collaborating, planning*, and *implementing* are all parts of a successful team goal.

Correlative Conjunctions. *Either* we will finish this tonight, *or* we will come back tomorrow and complete it.

Sometimes a **string of grammatical structures** seem to be parallel because they address the same type of thought. Remember to look for structures that are similar, not the thought behind the structure.

| Incorrect | The man was heroic and a credit to his division. |
| Correct | The man was a hero and a credit to his division. |

Modifiers

Modifiers are words used to describe other words in sentences. Modifiers that modify the wrong word or seem to modify more than one word in a sentence are called misplaced modifiers. Modifiers should be placed as close as possible to the words they modify in order to make the meaning of the sentence clear.

Incorrect	At the last meeting, the governor discussed the cost of filling potholes in the interstate with members of his budgetary team. (prepositional phrase incorrectly modifying *filling potholes)*
Correct	At the last meeting, the governor discussed with members of his budgetary team the cost of filling potholes in the interstate. (prepositional phrase correctly modifying *discussed*)
Incorrect	Swimming effortlessly and easily, the coach cheered the relay team. (participial phrase incorrectly modifying *the coach*)
Correct	The coach cheered the relay team swimming effortlessly and easily. (participial phrase correctly modifying *the relay team*)

Dangling modifiers seem logically to modify no word at all. To correct a sentence that has a dangling modifier, you must supply a word that the dangling modifier can sensibly modify.

Incorrect	Sailing the ship to the north, a storm was avoided.
Correct	A storm was avoided because the captain sailed the ship to the north. OR
Correct	Sailing the ship to the north, the captain avoided the storm.

Objective 0014   Recognizing Standard American English usage

Recognizing the standard use of verb forms and cases

Most college writers can identify the regular verbs that form the past tense by adding the suffix *–ed*. Irregular verbs seem to offer up the most problem because there is no rule to determine how the past and past participle forms are created.

Base Form	**Past Form**	**Past Participle** (have, has, had)
be, am, are, is	was, were	been
swim	swam	swum
put	put	put
write	wrote	written
lie	lay	lain

Strategies for the Essay

To give yourself the best chance of writing a good constructed response, it is important to understand the assignment directions and have a pretty good idea of what the graders are looking for. Since you have four hours to complete all sections of the GACE Basic Skills Assessment, you should set aside approximately 60 minutes to complete this task. Remember this time schedule is only a suggestion and each writer should adjust this based on his or her own strengths.

0015   Demonstrate the ability to prepare a developed composition on a given topic using language and style appropriate to a given audience, purpose, and occasion.

For example:

- Composing a coherent, focused, and sustained composition on a given topic using language and style appropriate to a specified audience, purpose, and occasion

The writing prompts on the GACE are designed to measure your knowledge of expository writing. Expository writing is that writing which informs an audience by presenting information and explaining concepts and ideas. Effective expository writing enables readers to understand information by taking them down a logical step-by-step path. When you write your answer you should pay special attention to the following criteria:

1. Respond directly to the prompt.

2. Make your writing thoughtful and interesting.

3. Vary word and sentence choice for the purpose and audience named in the response.

4. Choose a method of organization that allows you to present details in a logical sequence.

5. Stay focused on your purpose for writing by appraising whether every sentence you write is a worthy contribution to your composition.

6. Use appropriate transitions to support the flow of ideas.

7. Elaborate through effective use of detail.

8. Communicate your response effectively by using correct spelling, capitalization, punctuation, grammar, usage, and sentence structure.

It is important that you know exactly what a writing prompt of the constructed-response assignment asks for. After reading the prompt, quickly jot down the ideas that immediately occur to you. Look for the exact words within the prompt that specify audience and purpose.

There are particular strategies that will be helpful in composing a well developed essay for the constructed-response assignment. These steps are prewriting, drafting, and revising, editing, and proofreading. You should carefully consider these steps and practice using them before you take the test.

Prewriting

Prewriting is beginning to gather and organize details before you write. Allow close to one-fourth of your time for prewriting.

- Consider your audience. Some questions you might ask are: What does the reader need and want to know? What information will require more explanation? What details will interest or influence my audience. Because your audience may be unfamiliar with your perspective on the topic, it is important to provide an explanation to guarantee that your audience will understand your ideas.

- Consider your purpose. Does the writing prompt ask you to inform the audience? Persuade the audience? Entertain the audience? Your purpose should factor into the planning of your writing just as the audience does.

- Organize the information you want to include in your response. Identify how you want to present the information: compare-and-contrast, cause-and-effect, problem-and solution.

- Plan a structure before you draft your essay. This will keep you on track and help you address all points you want to discuss in your response. Remember your outline is not part of your grade, so do not spend time creating an elaborate structure, but instead strive to get the ideas down and leave yourself enough time to develop a strong response. For each section of your outline, jot down the main ideas you want to include, using key words or details.

- You may do your prewriting on scratch paper but you must use the booklet provided to submit your complete response.

The next objective listed for the constructed-response assignment addresses formulating a thesis and supporting statements. It will help you if you think of this as the actual drafting of the essay.

- **Stating and maintaining a clear thesis statement using organizational strategies to enhance meaning and clarity**

- **Providing reasoned support and/or specific examples to maintain the thesis statement**

Drafting

Drafting is getting your ideas down in roughly the format you intend. Allow about half of your time for drafting.

- Once you have chosen your organization, identify a focus for your response. Consider the type of writing you are creating and draft a simple statement to direct your writing.

- Your essay should have three parts: an introduction that addresses the question and states the thesis; a body which should present at least two main points to support your thesis; and a conclusion that will restate the answer expressed in the thesis and sum up the main points in the body of the essay.

- Your opening paragraph should include a thesis statement to focus the attention of your audience immediately. Remember that the introduction foreshadows the basic structure of the constructed-response assignment.

- Explain your points clearly and in logical order. The types of paragraphs you write depend on the topic and the purpose for writing. Back up your thesis with support from your memory or your own personal experience, Here are some types of details you can use in your response:

  ○ Facts, incidents or trends

  ○ Specific examples

  ○ Descriptive details

- Your conclusion should reemphasize the main points of the essay, and it should also explore their implications.

The next step in preparing your structured-response answer is the nuts-and-bolts of writing. In this step you will revise, edit, and proofread your response before you submit it. When you view this as a process, you will be able to strengthen your response to the writing prompt. Remember, the organization of your writing is the framework for the entire submission. You may decide to strengthen the structure by reordering or adding paragraphs.

- Using effective sentence structure, word choice, and mechanics (i.e., grammar, syntax)

- Using spelling, capitalization, and punctuation according to the conventions of Standard American English

Revising, editing, and proofreading

Revising is correcting any major errors and proofreading is fixing errors in grammar, spelling and grammar. Allow almost one fourth of your time to revise and edit. Use the last few minutes to proofread your work.

- Review your response. Decide whether everything is clearly defined. Neatly cross out any details that do not support your purpose.

- Make sure that you have used transitions to show the connections among your ideas and help the reader in following your line of thinking. You may use transitions either at the beginnings of paragraphs, or you may use them to show the connections among ideas within a single paragraph.

- Check for errors in spelling, grammar, and punctuation. To help with spelling, consider looking at each word, starting with the last word in each paragraph and moving toward the first. If you are unsure of the spelling, consider replacing the word in question with a word you know how to spell correctly.

- Look for common grammar errors in your writing. For example, check subject-verb agreement, make sure each sentence expresses a complete thought and verify that you have used pronouns correctly.

- When making changes, place one line through the text you want eliminated. Use a carat [^] to indicate the placement of added words.

- Since this constructed-response assignment may be hand-written, make sure that each word is legible.

Practice Test 1
Part 1: Reading

GACE Basic Skills

ANSWER SHEET
PRACTICE TEST 1, PART 1: READING

1 _____

2 _____

3 _____

4 _____

5 _____

6 _____

7 _____

8 _____

9 _____

10 _____

11 _____

12 _____

13 _____

14 _____

15 _____

16 _____

17 _____

18 _____

19 _____

20 _____

21 _____

22 _____

23 _____

24 _____

25 _____

26 _____

27 _____

28 _____

29 _____

30 _____

31 _____

32 _____

33 _____

34 _____

35 _____

36 _____

37 _____

38 _____

39 _____

40 _____

41 _____

42 _____

PART 1:   **Reading**
              42 questions

Read the passage below; then answer the two questions that follow.

America's national bird, the mighty bald eagle, is being threatened by a new menace. Once decimated by hunters and loss of habitat, this newest danger is suspected to be from the intentional poisoning by livestock ranchers. Authorities have found animal carcasses injected with restricted pesticides. These carcasses are suspected to have been placed to attract and kill predators such as the bald eagle in an effort to preserve young grazing animals. It appears that the eagle is being threatened again by the consummate predator, humans.

1. One can conclude from this passage that

    A.   the pesticides used are detrimental to the environment.

    B.   the killing of eagles will protect the rancher's rangeland.

    C.   ranchers must obtain licenses to use the pesticides.

    D.   the poisoning could result in the extinction of the bald eagle.

2. The author's attitude is one of

    A.   detached observation.

    B.   concerned interest.

    C.   informed acceptance.

    D.   unbridled anger.

Questions 3, 4, and 5 refer to the graph below.

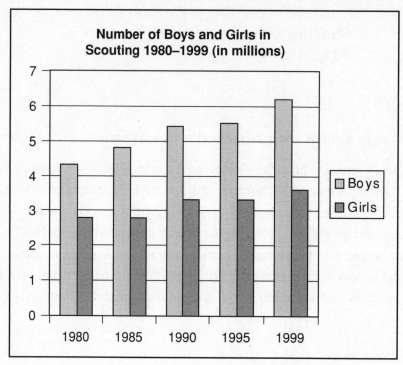

**Number of Boys and Girls in
Scouting 1980–1999 (in millions)**

Source: United States Census Bureau

3. In what year was the involvement in scouting closest to being equal between girls and boys?

   A. 1980

   B. 1985

   C. 1990

   D. 1995

4. What was the difference (in millions) between the number of boys and the number of girls involved in scouting in 1999?

   A. 1.6 million

   B. .9 million

   C. 2.6 million

   D. 2.0 million

5. What year had the greatest discrepancy between the involvement of boys and the involvement of girls in scouting?

    A.   1980

    B.   1985

    C.   1990

    D.   1999

Read the passage below; then answer the six questions that follow.

Frederick Douglass

1   Frederick Douglass was born Frederick Augustus Washington Bailey in 1817 to a white father and a slave mother. Frederick was raised by his grandmother on a Maryland plantation until he was eight. It was then that he was sent to Baltimore by his owner to be a servant to the Auld family. Mrs. Auld recognized Frederick's intellectual acumen and defied the law of the state by teaching him to read and write. When Mr. Auld warned that education would make the boy unfit for slavery, Frederick sought to continue his education in the streets. When his master died, Frederick was returned to the plantation to work in the fields at age 16. Later, he was hired out to work in the shipyards in Baltimore as a ship caulker. He plotted an escape but was discovered before he could get away. Five years later he was able to pay his way to New York City and then to New Bedford, Massachusetts. He eluded slave hunters by changing his name to Douglass.

2   At an 1841 antislavery meeting in Massachusetts, Douglass was invited to give a talk about his experiences under slavery. His impromptu speech was so powerful and so eloquent that it thrust him into a career as an agent for the Massachusetts Anti-Slavery Society.

3   Douglass wrote his autobiography in 1845 primarily to counter those who doubted his authenticity as a former slave. This work became a classic in American literature and a primary source about slavery from the point of view of a slave. Douglass went on a two-year speaking tour abroad to avoid recapture by his former owner and to win new friends for the abolition movement. He returned with funds to purchase his freedom and to start his own antislavery newspaper. He became a consultant to Abraham Lincoln and throughout Reconstruction fought doggedly for full civil rights for freedmen. He also supported the women's rights movement.

6. According to the passage, Douglass's autobiography was motivated by

   A. the desire to make money for his antislavery movement.

   B. the desire to start a newspaper.

   C. his interest in authenticating his life as a slave.

   D. his desire to educate people about slavery.

7. The central idea of the passage is that Frederick Douglass

   A. was influential in changing the laws regarding the education of slaves.

   B. was one of the most eminent human rights leaders of the century.

   C. was a personal friend and confidant to a president.

   D. wrote a classic in American literature.

8. According to the author of this passage, Mrs. Auld taught Frederick to read because

   A. Frederick wanted to learn like the other boys.

   B. she recognized his natural ability.

   C. he needed to read to work in the home.

   D. she obeyed her husband's wishes in the matter.

9. The title that best expresses the ideas of this passage is

   A. The History of the Anti-Slavery Movement.

   B. The Dogged Determination of Frederick Douglass.

   C. Frederick Douglass's Contributions to Freedom.

   D. The Oratorical and Literary Brilliance of Frederick Douglass.

10. In the context of the passage, impromptu is closest in meaning to

   A. unprepared.

   B. in a quiet manner.

   C. forceful.

   D. elaborate.

11. This passage is most likely written for an audience of

    A. textbook publishers.

    B. general readers.

    C. biographers.

    D. feminists.

Read the passage below; then answer the three questions that follow.

1 One of the many tragedies of the Civil War was the housing and care of prisoners. The Andersonville prison, built by the Confederates in 1864 to accommodate 10,000 Union prisoners, was not yet completed when prisoners began arriving. Five months later, the total number of men incarcerated there had risen to 31,678.

2 The sounds of death and dying were not diminished by the surrender of weapons to a captor. Chances of survival for prisoners in Andersonville were not much better than in the throes of combat. Next to overcrowded, inadequate shelter caused unimaginable suffering. The Confederates were not equipped with the manpower, tools or supplies necessary to house such a population of captives. Prisoners themselves gathered lumber, logs, anything they could find to construct some sort of protection from the elements. Some prisoners dug holes in the ground, risking suffocation from cave-ins, but many hundreds were left exposed to the wind, rain, cold, and heat.

3 Daily food rations were exhausted by the sheer numbers that had to be served, resulting in severe dietary deficiencies. The overcrowding, meager rations, and deplorable unsanitary conditions resulted in rampant disease and a high mortality rate. The consequences of a small scratch or wound could result in death in Andersonville. During the prison's 13-month existence, more than 12,000 prisoners died and were buried in the Andersonville cemetery. Most of the deaths were caused by diarrhea, dysentery, gangrene, and scurvy that could not be treated due to inadequate staff and supplies.

12. What is the central idea of the passage?

   A. The prison was never fully completed.

   B. Prison doctors were ill-equipped to handle emergencies.

   C. Andersonville prison was not adequate to care for three times as many prisoners as it could hold.

   D. Many prisoners died as a result of shelter cave-ins.

13. From this passage the author's attitude toward the Confederates is one of

   A. impartiality.

   B. contempt.

   C. indifference.

   D. denial.

14. In the context of the passage, the word *throes* is closest in meaning to

   A. area.

   B. midst.

   C. times.

   D. vicinity.

Read the passage below; then answer the three questions that follow.

1   To the Shakers, perfection was found in the creation of an object that was both useful and simple. Their Society was founded in 1774 by Ann Lee, an Englishwoman from the working classes, who arrived in New York with eight followers. "Mother Ann" established her religious community on the belief that worldly interests were evil.

2   To gain entrance into the Society, believers had to remain celibate, have no private possessions, and avoid contact with outsiders. The order came to be called "Shakers" because of the feverish dance the group performed at their meetings. Another characteristic of the group was the desire to seek perfection in their work.

3   Shaker furniture was created to exemplify specific characteristics: simplicity of design, quality craftsmanship, harmony of proportion, and usefulness. While the Shakers did not create any innovations in furniture designs, they were known for fine craftsmanship. In their work, the major emphasis was on function, and not on excessive or elaborate decorations that they believed contributed nothing to the product's usefulness.

15. The passage indicates that members of the religious order were called the Shakers because

   A.   they shook hands at their meetings.

   B.   they did a shaking dance at their meetings.

   C.   they took their name from the founder.

   D.   they were named after the township where they originated.

16. Which of the following is the most appropriate substitute for the use of the term innovations in the third paragraph?

   A.   corrections

   B.   changes

   C.   functions

   D.   brocades

17. Which of the following does the passage suggest about the Shakers?

   A.   Shakers believed in form over function in their designs.

   B.   Shaker furniture has seen a surge in popularity.

   C.   Shakers appeared to believe that form follows function.

   D.   Shaker furniture is noted for the use of brass hardware.

Read the passage below; then answer the three questions that follow.

Benjamin Franklin began writing his autobiography in 1771, but he set it aside to assist the colonies in gaining independence from England. After a hiatus of 13 years, he returned to chronicle his life, addressing his message to the younger generation. In this significant literary work of the early United States, Franklin portrays himself as benign, kindhearted, practical, and hardworking. He established a list of ethical conduct and recorded his transgressions when he was successful in overcoming temptation. Franklin wrote that he was unable to arrive at perfection, ". . . yet I was, by the endeavor, a better and happier man then I otherwise should have been if I had not attempted it."

18. Which of the following is the LEAST appropriate substitute for the use of the term <u>ethical</u> near the end of the passage?

    A. moral

    B. depraved

    C. virtuous

    D. qualified

19. The passage suggests which of the following about Franklin's autobiography?

    A. It was representative of early American literature.

    B. It fell short of being a major work of literary quality.

    C. It personified Franklin as a major political figure.

    D. It was a notable work of early American literature.

20. Which of the following slogans best describes Franklin's assessment of the usefulness of attempting to achieve perfection?

    A. Cleanliness is next to Godliness.

    B. Nothing ventured, nothing gained.

    C. Ambition is its own reward.

    D. Humility is everything.

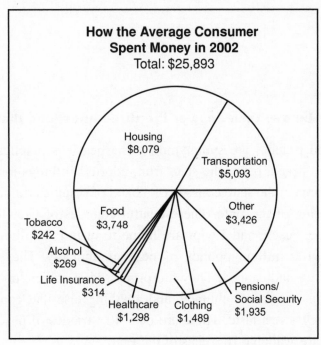

How the Average Consumer Spent Money in 2002
Total: $25,893

Housing $8,079
Transportation $5,093
Food $3,748
Other $3,426
Tobacco $242
Alcohol $269
Life Insurance $314
Healthcare $1,298
Clothing $1,489
Pensions/ Social Security $1,935

Source: Census Bureau's Statistical Abstract of the U.S.

21. According to the graph, the average consumer spent approximately 50 percent of her/his earnings on

   A.   housing and healthcare costs.

   B.   transportation and housing.

   C.   food.

   D.   transportation and pensions.

22. After transportation, the next greatest amount of money was spent on

   A.   clothing.

   B.   other.

   C.   food.

   D.   pensions/social security.

23. According to the graph, expenditure on health care was approximately equal to

    A. clothing.
    B. pensions.
    C. food.
    D. other.

Read the passage below; then answer the three questions that follow.

Georgia and peaches are synonymous. The peach is practically a symbol of Georgia. The peach, being the state fruit, adorns all things in the state. The main growing area in the state consists of a band of counties running diagonally through the center of the state. These central counties of Crawford, Houston, Macon, Monroe, Peach, and Taylor are home to over 1½ million peach trees. They produce 100 million pounds of peaches annually. These peaches are sold as fresh fruit and canned. They are processed as jellies, preserves, peach cider, ice cream, hot sauce, chutney, and anything else that can benefit from the peach's tangy, sweet taste. There are over 40 varieties of peaches grown in Georgia. They are available 16 weeks of the year.

24. The central idea of the passage is that the Georgia peach

    A. is practically a symbol of Georgia.
    B. is available 16 weeks of the year.
    C. is grown in 6 central counties of Georgia.
    D. is processed in a variety of ways.

25. In the passage, the word synonymous is closest in meaning to

    A. the same.
    B. the opposite.
    C. equivalent in connotation.
    D. alike.

26. According to the passage, how many varieties of peaches are grown in Georgia?

    A. Less than 30

    B. More than 100

    C. Over 40

    D. A dozen

Read the passage below; then answer the five questions that follow.

1   Spa water quality is maintained through a filter to ensure cleanliness and clarity. Wastes such as perspiration, hairspray, and lotions, which cannot be removed by the spa filter, can be controlled by shock treatment or super chlorination every other week. Although the filter traps most of the solid material to control bacteria and algae and to oxidize any organic material, the addition of disinfectants such as bromine or chlorine is necessary.

2   As all water solutions have a pH that controls corrosion, proper pH balance is also necessary. A pH measurement determines if the water is acid or alkaline. Based on a 14-point scale, a pH reading of 7.0 is considered neutral while a lower reading is considered acidic, and a higher reading indicates alkalinity or basic. High pH (above 7.6) reduces sanitizer efficiency, clouds water, promotes scale formation on surfaces and equipment, and interferes with filter operation. When pH is high, add a pH decrease more rapidly. A weekly dose of a stain and scale fighter also will help to control this problem. Low pH (below 7.2) is equally damaging, causing equipment corrosion, water that is irritating, and rapid sanitizer dissipation. To increase pH, add sodium bicarbonate (e.g., *Spa Up*).

3   The recommended operating temperature of a spa (98°–104°) is a fertile environment for the growth of bacteria and viruses. This growth is prevented when appropriate sanitizer levels are continuously monitored. Bacteria can also be controlled by maintaining a proper bromine level of 3.0 to 5.0 parts per million (ppm) or a chlorine level of 1.0–2.0 ppm. As bromine tablets should not be added directly to the water, a bromine floater will properly dispense the tablets. Should chlorine be the chosen sanitizer, a granular form is recommended, as liquid chlorine or tablets are too harsh for the spa.

27. Although proper chemical and temperature maintenance of spa water is necessary, the most important condition to monitor is the

    A. prevention of the growth of bacteria and viruses.

    B. prevention of the corrosion of equipment.

    C. prevention of the formation of scales.

    D. prevention of cloudy water.

28. Of the chemical and temperature conditions in a spa, the condition most dangerous to one's health is

    A. spa water temperature above 104°.

    B. bromine level between 3.0 and 5.0.

    C. pH level below 7.2.

    D. spa water temperature between 90° and 104°.

29. The primary purpose of the passage is to

    A. relate that maintenance of a spa can negate the full enjoyment of the spa experience.

    B. convey that the maintenance of a spa is expensive and time consuming.

    C. explain the importance of proper spa maintenance.

    D. detail proper spa maintenance.

30. The spa filter can be relied upon to

    A. control algae and bacteria.

    B. trap most solid material.

    C. assure an adequate level of sanitation.

    D. maintain clear spa water.

31. Which chemical should one avoid when maintaining a spa?

A. liquid chlorine

B. bromine

C. sodium bisulfate

D. baking soda

Read the passage below; then answer the three questions that follow.

1   There is an importance of learning communication and meaning in language. Yet the use of notions such as communication and meaning as the basic criteria for instruction, experiences, and materials in classrooms may misguide a child in several respects. Communication in the classroom is vital. The teacher should use communication to help students develop the capacity to make their private responses become public responses. Otherwise, one's use of language would be in danger of being what the younger generation refers to as mere words, mere thoughts, and mere feelings.

2   Learning theorists emphasize specific components of learning; behaviorists stress behavior in learning; humanists stress the affective in learning; and cognitivists stress cognition in learning. All three of these components occur simultaneously and cannot be separated from each other in the learning process. In 1957, Festinger referred to dissonance as the lack of harmony between what one does (behavior) and what one believes (attitude). Attempts to separate the components of learning either knowingly or unknowingly create dissonances wherein language, thought, feeling, and behavior become diminished of authenticity. As a result, ideas and concepts lose their content and vitality, and the manipulation and politics of communication assume prominence.

32. Which of the following best describes the author's attitude toward the subject discussed?

A. A flippant disregard

B. A mild frustration

C. A passive resignation

D. An informed concern

33. The primary purpose of the passage is to

    A. discuss the relationships between learning and communication.

    B. assure teachers that communication and meaning are the basic criteria for learning in classrooms.

    C. stress the importance of providing authentic communication in classroom learning.

    D. address the role of communication and meaning in classrooms.

34. Which of the following is the most complete and accurate definition of the term <u>mere</u> as used in the passage?

    A. small

    B. minor

    C. little

    D. insignificant

Read the passage below; then answer the five questions that follow.

The Beginnings of the Submarine

A submarine was first used as an offensive weapon during the American Revolutionary War. The *Turtle*, a one-man submersible designed by an American inventor named David Bushnell and hand-operated by a screw propeller, attempted to sink a British man-of-war in New York Harbor. The plan was to attach a charge of gunpowder to the ship's bottom with screws and explode it with a time fuse. After repeated failures to force the screws through the copper sheathing of the hull of the H.M.S. *Eagle*, the submarine gave up and withdrew, exploding its powder a short distance from the *Eagle*. Although the attack was unsuccessful, it caused the British to move their blockading ships from the harbor to the outer bay.

On February 17, 1864, a Confederate craft, a hand-propelled submersible, carrying a crew of eight men, sank a Federal corvette that was blockading Charleston Harbor. The hit was accomplished by a torpedo suspended ahead of the Confederate *Hunley* as she rammed the Union frigate *Housatonic*, and is the first recorded instance of a submarine sinking a warship.

The submarine first became a major component in naval warfare during World War I, when Germany demonstrated its full potential. Wholesale sinking of Allied shipping by the German U-boats almost swung the war in favor of the Central Powers. Then, as now, the submarine's greatest advantage was that it could operate beneath the ocean surface where detection was difficult. Sinking a submarine was comparatively easy, once it was found—but finding it before it could attack was another matter.

During the closing months of World War I, the Allied Submarine Devices Investigation Committee was formed to obtain from science and technology more effective underwater detection equipment. The committee developed a reasonably accurate device for locating a submerged submarine. This device was a trainable hydrophone, which was attached to the bottom of the ASW ship, and used to detect screw noises and other sounds that came from a submarine. Although the committee disbanded after World War I, the British made improvements on the locating device during the interval between then and World War II, and named it *ASDIC* after the committee.

American scientists further improved on the device, calling it SONAR, a name derived from the underlined initials of the words **so**und **na**vigation and **r**anging.

At the end of World War II, the United States improved the snorkel (a device for bring air to the crew and engines when operating submerged on diesels) and developed the *Guppy* (short for greater underwater propulsion power), a conversion of the fleet-type submarine of World War II fame. The superstructure was changed by reducing the surface area and streamlining the metal fairing. Performance increased greatly with improved electronic equipment, additional battery capacity, and the addition of the snorkel.

35. The passage implies that one of the most pressing modifications needed for the submarine was to

    A.   streamline its shape.

    B.   enlarge the submarine for accommodating more torpedoes and men.

    C.   reduce the noise caused by the submarine.

    D.   add a snorkel.

36. It is inferred that

    A. ASDIC was formed to obtain technology for underwater detection.

    B. ASDIC developed an accurate device for locating submarines.

    C. the hydrophone was attached to the bottom of the ship.

    D. ASDIC was formed to develop technology to define U.S. shipping.

37. SONAR not only picked up the sound of submarines moving through the water but also

    A. indicated the speed at which the sub was moving.

    B. gave the location of the submarine.

    C. indicated the speed of the torpedo.

    D. placed the submarine within a specified range.

38. According to the passage, the submarine's success was due in part to its ability to

    A. strike and escape undetected.

    B. move swifter than other vessels.

    C. submerge to great depths while being hunted.

    D. run silently.

39. From the passage, one can infer that

    A. David Bushnell was indirectly responsible for the sinking of the Federal corvette in Charleston Harbor.

    B. David Bushnell invented the *Turtle*.

    C. the *Turtle* was a one-man submarine.

    D. the *Turtle* sank the *Eagle* on February 17, 1864.

Read the passage below; then answer the three questions that follow.

1   In 1975, Sinclair observed that it had often been supposed that the main factor in learning to talk is being able to imitate. Schlesinger (1975) noted that at certain stages of learning to speak, a child tends to imitate everything an adult says to him or her, and it therefore seems reasonable to accord to such imitation an important role in the acquisition of language.

2   Moreover, various investigators have attempted to explain the role of imitation in language. In his discussion of the development of imitation and cognition of adult speech sounds, Nakazema (1975) stated that although the parent's talking stimulates and accelerates the infant's articulatory activity, the parent's phoneme system does not influence the child's articulatory mechanisms. Slobin and Welsh (1973) suggested that imitation is the reconstruction of the adult's utterance and that the child does so by employing the grammatical rules that he has developed at a specific time. Schlesinger proposed that by imitating the adult the child practices new grammatical constructions. Brown and Bellugi (1964) noted that a child's imitations resemble spontaneous speech in that they drop inflections, most function words, and sometimes other words. However, the word order of imitated sentences usually was preserved. Brown and Bellugi assumed that imitation is a function of what the child attended to or remembered. Shipley et al. (1969) suggested that repeating an adult's utterance assists the child's comprehension. Ervin (1964) and Braine (1971) found that a child's imitations do not contain more advanced structures than his or her spontaneous utterances; thus, imitation can no longer be regarded as the simple behavioristic act that scholars assumed it to be.

40.   The author of the passage would tend to agree with which of the following statements?

   A.   Apparently, children require practice with more advanced structures before they are able to imitate.

   B.   Apparently, children only imitate what they already do, using whatever is in their repertoire.

   C.   Apparently, the main factor in learning to talk remains being able to imitate.

   D.   Apparently, children cannot respond meaningfully to a speech situation until they have reached a stage at which they can make symbol-orientation responses.

41. The primary purpose of the passage is to

    A. explain the role of imitation in language acquisition.

    B. assure parents of their role in assisting imitation in language acquisition.

    C. relate the history of imitation in language acquisition.

    D. discuss relationships between psychological and physiological processes in language acquisition.

42. An inference that parents may make from the passage is that they should

    A. be concerned when a child imitates their language.

    B. focus on developing imitation in their child's language.

    C. realize that their child's imitations may reflect several aspects of language acquisition.

    D. realize that their talking may over-stimulate their child's articulatory activity.

ANSWER KEY – READING PRACTICE TEST 1

Question	Answer	Objective	
1	D	0001	Understand the main idea and supporting details in written material.
2	B	0002	Identify a writer's purpose and point of view.
3	A	0004	Use critical reasoning skills to evaluate written material.
4	C	0004	Use critical reasoning skills to evaluate written material.
5	D	0004	Use critical reasoning skills to evaluate written material.
6	C	0003	Analyze the relationship among ideas in written material.
7	B	0001	Understand the main idea and supporting details in written material.
8	B	0003	Analyze the relationship among ideas in written material.
9	C	0001	Understand the main idea and supporting details in written material.
10	A	0006	Determine the meaning of words and phrases.
11	B	0002	Identify a writer's purpose and point of view.
12	C	0001	Understand the main idea and supporting details in written material.
13	A	0002	Identify a writer's purpose and point of view.
14	B	0006	Determine the meaning of words and phrases.
15	B	0003	Analyze the relationship among ideas in written material.
16	B	0006	Determine the meaning of words and phrases.

Question	Answer	Objective	
17	C	0004	Use critical reasoning skills to evaluate written material.
18	B	0006	Determine the meaning of words and phrases.
19	D	0004	Use critical reasoning skills to evaluate written material.
20	B	0004	Use critical reasoning skills to evaluate written material.
21	B	0001	Understand the main idea and supporting details in written material.
22	C	0001	Understand the main idea and supporting details in written material.
23	A	0001	Understand the main idea and supporting details in written material.
24	A	0001	Understand the main idea and supporting details in written material.
25	C	0006	Determine the meaning of words and phrases.
26	C	0005	Use reading strategies to comprehend written materials.
27	A	0005	Use reading strategies to comprehend written materials.
28	A	0005	Use reading strategies to comprehend written materials.
29	C	0001	Understand the main idea and supporting details in written materials.
30	B	0005	Use reading strategies to comprehend written materials.
31	A	0005	Use reading strategies to comprehend written materials.
32	D	0002	Identify a writer's purpose and point of view.

Question	Answer	Objective	
33	C	0001	Understand the main idea and supporting details in written material.
34	D	0006	Determine the meaning of words and phrases.
35	A	0004	Use critical reasoning skills to evaluate written material.
36	D	0004	Use critical reasoning skills to evaluate written material.
37	D	0005	Use reading strategies to comprehend written materials.
38	A	0005	Use reading strategies to comprehend written materials.
39	A	0004	Use critical reasoning skills to evaluate written material.
40	B	0002	Identify a writer's purpose and point of view.
41	A	0001	Understand the main idea and supporting details in written material.
42	C	0004	Use critical reasoning skills to evaluate written material.

Practice Test 1, Part 1 Progress Chart

0001 Understand the Main Idea and Supporting Details in Written Material —/11

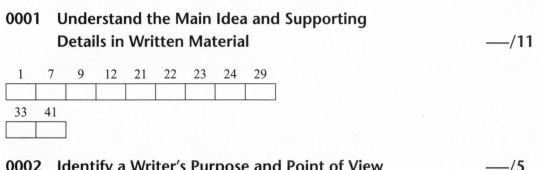

0002 Identify a Writer's Purpose and Point of View —/5

**0003   Analyze the Relationship Among Ideas
in Written Material**   ——/3

6   8   15

**0004   Use Critical Reasoning Skills to Evaluate
Written Material**   ——/10

3   4   5   17   19   20

35   36   39   42

**0005   Use Reading Strategies to Comprehend
Written Materials**   ——/7

26   27   28   30   31   37   38

0006   Determine the Meaning of Words and Phrases   ——/6

10   14   16   18   25   34

Detailed Explanations for Practice Test 1, Part 1: Reading

1. **D**

   It is implied that the poisoning of animal carcasses in the habitat of bald eagles presents a new danger of extinction for America's symbol. Choices A and C are not mentioned in the passage. Choice B suggests a reason for the poisoning; however, the overall focus of the passage does not support this answer.

2. **B**

   The author's use of words such as "mighty bald eagle" and "threatened by a new menace" supports concern for the topic. Therefore, choices A and C are not applicable. The author appears for the most part to be objective. Choice D is too strong to be correct.

3. **A**

   In 1980, the difference between the number of boys and girls involved in scouting was 1.5 million. This represents the closest margin.

4. **C**

   In 1999, the difference between the number of boys and girls involved in scouting was 2.6 million.

5. **D**

   The greatest difference between the number of boys and the number of girls involved in scouting was in 1999, at 2.6 million. There were almost twice as many boys as there were girls.

6. **C**

   Douglass was interested in raising social consciousness about slavery. The passage stresses his interest in refuting those who doubted his claim to have been a slave.

7. **B**

   Choice A is not supported by the text. Choices C and D, while true, are irrelevant to the question.

8. **B**

    This choice is supported by the statement, "Mrs. Auld recognized Frederick's intellectual acumen. . . ." Choice D contradicts information in the passage. The passage does not support choices A and C.

9. **C**

    Choices A and B are either too broad or too general. Choice D is too specific and limited to cover the information in the passage.

10. **A**

    An *impromptu* speech is one given off-the-cuff.

11. **B**

    The writer's accessible style, use of easy-to-understand supporting details and examples, and avoidance of technical language indicate that the passage was most likely written for an audience of general readers.

12. **C**

    The passage states that housing of prisoners was "one of the many tragedies of the Civil War," and that "overcrowding, meager rations… resulted in rampant disease and a high mortality rate," implying that the prison facility was inadequate for the number of prisoners. All other choices are discussed, but the main issue is overcrowded conditions.

13. **A**

    The author emphasizes a lack of supplies and manpower to care for the prisoners, not a lack of interest in doing so by the Confederates. Hence, choices B, C, and D are not appropriate.

14. **B**

    In the *midst* of combat is closest in meaning to *throes*. The area and the vicinity of combat are not as close to the meaning of *throes*. The time of combat is not as important as actually being in the midst of battle.

15. **B**

    This choice is supported by the second paragraph of the passage. All other choices are irrelevant to information in the passage.

16. **B**

    Innovations means changes or new features that have been introduced.

17. **C**

    The passage discusses the importance of usefulness as well as simplicity to the Shakers; therefore, the function of the piece of furniture would be more important than the particular form. Choices A and D are contradictory to the information given, while choice B is beyond the information given in the text.

18. **B**

    Depraved means "corrupted" or "perverted." All other choices have to do with accepted standards of conduct.

19. **D**

    The author states that Franklin's work was a "significant literary work of early United States." Each of the other choices is not supported by the text.

20. **B**

    The final sentence of the paragraph supports this choice. Choice C might apply, but choice B is closest to the overall mood of the passage. Choices A and D are not relevant to the question.

21. **B**

    Transportation and housing total about half of the $25,892.

22. **C**

    According to the graph, food is next, after transportation, in amount of money spent by the consumer.

23. **A**

    According to the graph, healthcare was closest to clothing in total amount spent.

24. **A**

    The central idea of the passage is that the Georgia peach is practically a symbol of Georgia. Choices B, C, and D do not reflect the central idea. They are details in the passage.

25. **C**

    Synonymous is closest in meaning to *equivalent* in connotation.

26. **C**

    This choice is clearly stated in the passage.

27. **A**

    Choices B, C, and D present minor problems in spa maintenance. If bacteria and viruses are allowed to grow, they can become a possible source of health problems. They are controlled by both temperature and chemicals.

28. **A**

    Choices B, C, and D are correct levels or degrees.

29. **C**

    Choices A and B represent an inference that goes beyond the scope of the passage and would indicate a bias on the part of the reader. Although the passage explains spa maintenance, in choice D, the information is not adequate to serve as a detailed guide.

30. **B**

    The other choices, A and C, refer to chemical or temperature maintenance. Although choice D helps to ensure clarity, choice B is explicitly stated in the passage.

31. **A**

    Choices B, C, and D are appropriate chemicals. Although chlorine is an alternative to bromine, this passage indicates it should be granular as indicated in choice A.

32. **D**

    Choices A, B, and C all connote extreme or inappropriate attitudes not expressed in the passage. The author presents an informed concern—choice D.

33. **C**

> For the other choices, A, B, and D, the criteria, the role, the discussion, and the assurance for communication or learning are not provided in the passage. The passage stresses the importance of authenticity in communication—choice C.

34. **D**

> Each of the choices is a possible definition, but the passage overall suggests that communication needs to be developed so that students' responses may become more significant and authentic—choice D.

35. **A**

> Answer A is correct because of the importance of streamlining mentioned in the final paragraph. B and C are not suggested in the paragraph, and D is secondary in importance to A.

36. **D**

> Since it may be inferred from the general purpose of underwater detection equipment, D is correct. While A and B are true statements, they are not inferences. C is not implied in the passage.

37. **D**

> Answer D is correct because the "R" in SONAR stands for "Ranging." A, B, and C are neither mentioned nor implied by the passage.

38. **A**

> As was mentioned in the third sentence of the third paragraph, A is correct. B, C, and D are not mentioned in the passage.

39. **A**

> It may be inferred that Bushnell's invention led to the success of the later version of the submarine. B and C are true, but are not inferences because they are directly stated in the first paragraph. D is not a true statement; the *Turtle* had no direct link to the 1864 incident.

40. **B**

Choices A and D are not supported by the passage. Choice C represents an incorrect conclusion. Choice B is supported by the various investigators' explanations.

41. **A**

As stated explicitly in the passage, the various investigators have attempted to explain the role of imitation in language—choice A. The other choices go beyond the scope of the passage.

42. **C**

As the investigators studied different aspects of language while attempting to explain the role of imitation in language, choice C is correct. The other choices go beyond the scope of the passage.

Practice Test 1
Part 2: Mathematics

GACE Basic Skills

1 _____	13 _____	25 _____	37 _____
2 _____	14 _____	26 _____	38 _____
3 _____	15 _____	27 _____	39 _____
4 _____	16 _____	28 _____	40 _____
5 _____	17 _____	29 _____	41 _____
6 _____	18 _____	30 _____	42 _____
7 _____	19 _____	31 _____	43 _____
8 _____	20 _____	32 _____	44 _____
9 _____	21 _____	33 _____	45 _____
10 _____	22 _____	34 _____	46 _____
11 _____	23 _____	35 _____	47 _____
12 _____	24 _____	36 _____	48 _____

DEFINITIONS AND FORMULAS

Measurement

U.S. Standard Metric

Distance

1 inch = 2.54 centimeters
12 inches = 1 foot
3 feet = 1 yard
5280 feet = 1 mile
1 centimeter = 10 millimeters
1 meter = 100 centimeters
1 kilometer = 1000 meters

Volume (liquid)

1 quart = 32 ounces
1 quart $\approx$ 0.95 liters
1 gallon = 4 quarts
1 liter = 1000 milliliters
1 cubic centimeter = 1 milliliter

Mass

1 pound = 16 ounces
1 ton = 2000 pounds
2.2 pounds $\approx$ 1 kilogram
1 gram = 1000 milligrams
1 kilogram = 1000 grams

Time

1 minute = 60 seconds
1 hour = 60 minutes
1 day = 24 hours
1 year = 365 days
1 year = 52 weeks

Definitions

=	equal to
>	greater than
<	less than
$\geq$	greater than or equal to
$\leq$	less than or equal to
π	$\approx$ 3.14
$\angle$	angle
$m\angle$	measure of angle
$\llcorner$	right angle
$\overline{AB}$	line segment
AB	length of line segment AB
$\angle ABC$	angle with vertex B formed by rays BA and BC

Formulas

Square
Area $= s^2$
Perimeter $= 4s$

Rectangle
Area $= bw$
Perimeter $= 2b + 2w$

Triangle
Area $= \frac{1}{2}bh$
Sum of the interior angles $= 180°$

Right triangle
Pythagorean formula: $c^2 = a^2 + b^2$

Circle
Area $= \pi r^2$
Circumference $= 2\pi r$
Diameter $= 2r$

Right cylinder
Surface area $= 2\pi rh + 2\pi r^2$
Volume $= \pi r^2 h$

Cube
Surface area $= 6s^2$
Volume $= s^3$

Rectangular solid
Surface area $= 2bw + 2bh + 2wh$
Volume $= bwh$

PART 2:   **Mathematics**
                     48 questions

1. Multiply $\frac{2}{3}$ by $\frac{4}{5}$. Show your answer in simplified (reduced) form.

    A. $\frac{6}{8}$

    B. $\frac{6}{15}$

    C. $\frac{8}{15}$

    D.   1

2. Add $2\frac{3}{4}$ and $1\frac{1}{2}$.

    A. $3\frac{4}{6}$

    B. $3\frac{1}{2}$

    C. $3\frac{5}{4}$

    D. $4\frac{1}{4}$

3. Subtract $3\frac{2}{3}$ from $7\frac{1}{2}$.

    A. $4\frac{1}{6}$

    B. $3\frac{5}{6}$

    C.   4

    D. $3\frac{1}{6}$

4. Divide $\dfrac{2}{3}$ by $\dfrac{4}{5}$. Choose the answer in simplest form.

   A. $\dfrac{8}{15}$

   B. $\dfrac{2}{15}$

   C. $\dfrac{10}{12}$

   D. $\dfrac{5}{6}$

5. Perform the indicated operation.

   $$(-16) - (-5)$$

   A. -11

   B. 11

   C. 21

   D. -21

6. Divide 8.2 by 0.05.

   A. 1.64

   B. 164

   C. 16.4

   D. .164

7. The number 14 is approximately 22% of which of the following numbers?

   A. 56

   B. 60

   C. 308

   D. 64

8. Simplify to a single term in scientific notation.

$$(2 \times 10^3) \times (6 \times 10^4)$$

    A. 12×10^7
    B. 12×10^{12}
    C. 1.2×10^8
    D. 1.2×10^{12}

9. Simplify: $3 + 2 \times 5 - 4$

    A. 21
    B. 9
    C. 5
    D. −5

10. Select the number that is missing in the problem below.

$$1,806 - \underline{\hspace{2cm}} = 358$$

    A. 2,164
    B. 1,552
    C. 1,458
    D. 1,448

11. Bob gets $6 an hour for babysitting. His sister Jana gets $7 an hour. One evening Bob babysat for 4 hours, while Jana babysat for half that long. How much money did they earn altogether for the evening?

    A. $24
    B. $38
    C. $14
    D. $19

12. The population of the city of Fairview increased by approximately 0.5% last year. If the population at the beginning of the year was 2,460, what was the approximate population at the end of the year?

    A. 2,472

    B. 2,960

    C. 2,465

    D. 2,510

13. A red rose bush is 39 inches tall and a yellow rose bush is $36\frac{3}{4}$ inches tall. The red rose bush is growing at a rate of $\frac{1}{2}$ of an inch per week, and the yellow rose bush is growing at a rate of $\frac{3}{4}$ of an inch per week. How long will it be before they are the same height?

    A. 6 weeks

    B. 8 weeks

    C. 9 weeks

    D. 12 weeks

14. Sarah began studying at 11:20 a.m. She took a break from 2:05 to 2:20, then studied until 3:15. How much time did she spend studying?

    A. 3 hours 55 minutes

    B. 2 hours 50 minutes

    C. 3 hours 45 minutes

    D. 3 hours 40 minutes

15. Convert: 120 mg = _____ g

    A. 0.12

    B. 1.20

    C. 12

    D. .012

16. Convert: 5.6 km = _____ cm

    A.   560

    B.   5,600

    C.   56,000

    D.   560,000

17. Convert: 14 feet = _____ inches

    A.   42 inches

    B.   520 inches

    C.   168 inches

    D.   84 inches

18. Convert: 4 feet 3 inches = _____ inches

    A.   48 inches

    B.   51 inches

    C.   54 inches

    D.   16 inches

19. Use the figure below to answer the question.

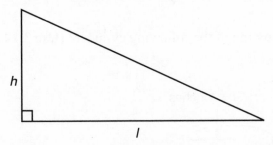

    Which formula can be used to find the area of the triangle?

    A. $A = \dfrac{(l \times h)}{2}$

    B. $A = \dfrac{(l + h)}{2}$

    C. $A = 2(l + h)$

    D. $A = 2(l \times h)$

20. What is the area of a triangle with a base length of 20 inches and a height of 8 inches?

   A.   80 square inches

   B.   120 square inches

   C.   40 square inches

   D.   28 square inches

21. You have a square piece of paper that has a perimeter of 20 cm. What is the area of the paper?

   A.   400 square cm

   B.   25 square cm

   C.   16 square cm

   D.   24 square cm

22. A circle has a radius of 4 cm. What is the area of the circle? (Use 3.14 as an approximation for pi.)

   A.   12.56 square centimeters

   B.   25.12 square centimeters

   C.   37.68 square centimeters

   D.   50.24 square centimeters

23. What is the approximate volume of the following cylinder? (Use 3.14 as an approximation for pi.)

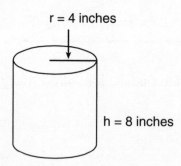

r = 4 inches

h = 8 inches

   A.   401.92 cubic inches

   B.   3215.36 cubic inches

   C.   37.68 cubic inches

   D.   100.48 cubic inches

24. Use the figures given to answer the question that follows.

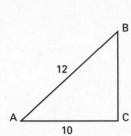
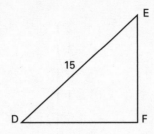

If the two triangles are similar, what is the length of side DF?

A. 12.5 units

B. 13 units

C. 12 units

D. 13.5 units

25. Use the figure given to answer the question that follows. Assume that AD is a line.

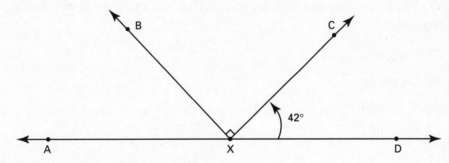

What is the measure of angle AXB?

A. 48°

B. 90°

C. 42°

D. There is not enough information to answer the question.

26. The daily high temperatures in Frostbite, Minnesota, for one week in January were as follows:

Sunday:	−2°F
Monday:	3°F
Tuesday:	0°F
Wednesday:	−4°F
Thursday:	−5°F
Friday:	−1°F
Saturday:	2°F

What was the average (mean) daily high temperature for that week?

A. 7

B. −7

C. −1

D. 1

27. In 4 practice runs on a 100 m track, a sprinter has times of 12.4 seconds, 11.95 seconds, 12.25 seconds, and 13.0 seconds. What was the average practice time of the sprinter?

A. 12.6 seconds

B. 12.4 seconds

C. 12.55 seconds

D. 12.3 seconds

28. James has 15 pennies in his pocket. The mint date on 3 of the pennies is 2003. If James randomly chooses one penny out of his pocket, what is the probability that the penny will have the date of 2003?

A. 15%

B. 20%

C. 25%

D. 3%

29. A bag contains 9 red chips, 7 blue chips, and 8 white chips. Without looking at the color, you choose one marble from the bag. What is the approximate likelihood that the marble is white?

    A. 50%

    B. 38%

    C. 33%

    D. 29%

30. The following table lists the gross income and profit for the Bailey Company.

Year	2000	2001	2002	2003	2004	2005	2006
Gross Income	1,315	1,625	2,018	2,758	3,566	4,459	5,034
Profit	143	172	222	1,327	1,464	1,562	2,709

    In which year was the difference between gross income and profit the greatest?

    A. 2001

    B. 2003

    C. 2005

    D. 2006

31. Use the graph to answer the question that follows.

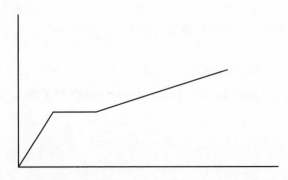

    Which of the following scenarios could be represented by the graph above?

    A. Mr. Cain mowed grass at a steady rate for a while, then took a short break, and then finished the job at a steady but slower rate.

    B. Mr. Cain mowed grass at a steady rate for a while, and then mowed at a steady slower rate, then he took a break.

C.   Mr. Cain mowed grass at a variable rate for a while, then took a short break, and then finished the job at a variable rate.

D.   Mr. Cain mowed grass at a steady rate for a while, then took a short break, and then finished the job at a steady but faster pace.

32.   Use the bar graph that follows to answer the question.

MS. PATTON'S EARNINGS, 1998–2002

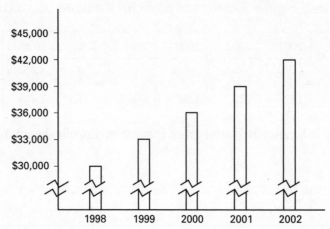

Only one of the statements below is necessarily true. Which one?

A.   The range of Ms. Patton's earnings for the years shown is $15,000.

B.   Ms. Patton's annual pay increases were consistent over the years shown.

C.   Ms. Patton earned $45,000 in 2003.

D.   Ms. Patton's average income for the years shown was $38,000.

33. The scatter plot below shows the relationship between grade level and hours of reading each week. Which statement describes this relationship?

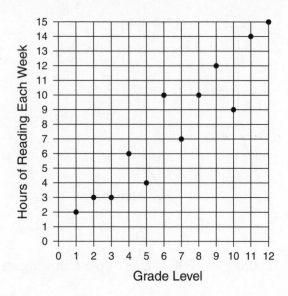

A. As grade level goes down, the number of reading hours goes up.

B. As grade level goes up, the number of reading hours goes down.

C. As grade level goes up, the number of reading hours goes up.

D. Grade level and reading hours are unrelated.

34. Use the pie chart below to answer the question that follows.

VOTES FOR CITY COUNCIL

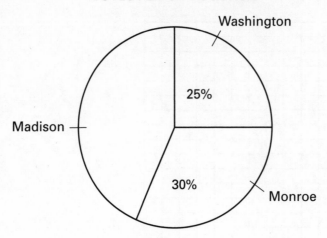

If the total number of people voting was 600, which of the following statements are true?

I. Madison received more votes than Monroe and Washington combined.

II. Madison received 45% of the votes.

III. Monroe received 180 votes.

IV. Madison received 330 votes.

A. I and III only

B. I and IV only

C. II and III only

D. II and IV only

35. The following plot represents an individual's shoe size and height.

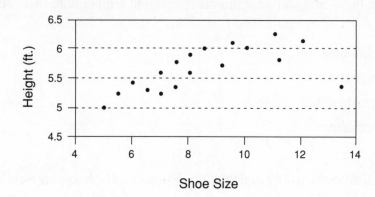

Which of the following best describes the relationship between shoe size and height?

A. There appears to be no relationship between shoe size and height.

B. An increase in height causes an increase in shoe size.

C. There appears to be a negative relationship between shoe size and height.

D. There appears to be a positive relationship between shoe size and height.

36. What is the next number in this sequence?

4096, 1024, 256, 64, _____

A. 4

B. 8

C. 16

D. 32

37. What is the next number in this sequence?

60, 57, 53, 48, _____

A. 45

B. 44

C. 43

D. 42

38. To convert from a Celsius temperature to a Fahrenheit temperature, multiply the Celsius temperature by $\frac{9}{5}$ and add 32. Find the Fahrenheit temperature that is equal to $-20°$ Celsius.

   A. -4 degrees Fahrenheit

   B. 0 degrees Fahrenheit

   C. 4 degrees Fahrenheit

   D. 8 degrees Fahrenheit

39. Bridal Veil Falls in California is 189 meters high. Niagara Falls, between New York and Ontario, is $\frac{2}{7}$ the height of Bridal Veil Falls. How high is Niagara Falls?

   A. 378 meters

   B. 54 meters

   C. 60 meters

   D. 108 meters

40. Camille bought a bracelet from her favorite store. The price of the bracelet was $31.99, and sales tax was 6.5%. She paid for her purchase with $35.00. How much change did Camille receive?

   A. $0.93

   B. $0.78

   C. $1.12

   D. $1.03

41. A survey was taken to determine the amount of time children spent watching TV each day. The results were 1 hour or less (18.4%), between 1 and 5 hours (68.8%), and 5 or more hours (12.8%). If you considered 415 children, about how many would you expect to watch television for 1 hour or less each day?

   A. 72

   B. 76

   C. 80

   D. 84

42. Bev, Kim, Lee, Ron, and Sue each have a favorite sport. No two of them have the same favorite sport. Using the following clues, find Bev's favorite sport.

- Ron's favorite sport is not basketball.
- Bev does not like basketball or soccer.
- Sue's favorite sport is volleyball.
- Kim does not like golf.
- Lee's favorite sport is the sport that Kim does not like.
- Three of the sports are basketball, soccer, and tennis.

   A. Bev's favorite sport is volleyball.
   B. Bev's favorite sport is golf.
   C. Bev's favorite sport is tennis.
   D. It is impossible to determine Bev's favorite sport from the information given.

43. Simplify the following expression. Then evaluate it when $x = 3$.
$$5x + 3 + (-8) + (-3x)$$

   A. 1
   B. 17
   C. 19
   D. 35

44. Evaluate the following expression using the following values: $x = 3$, $y = 4$, and $z = 6$.
$$2x\,(z + 3y)$$

   A. 108
   B. 120
   C. 216
   D. 432

45. Solve for q:

$$\frac{1}{4}q - 9 = 3$$

A. $q = 12$
B. $q = 27$
C. $q = 48$
D. $q = 108$

46. What are the solutions of this equation?

$$3x^2 - 11 = 1$$

A. 2 and –2
B. 3 and –3
C. 4 and –4
D. 1 and –1

47. Solve the following inequality:

$$2(x + 1) \geq 3x - 2$$

A. $x \geq 2$
B. $x \geq 4$
C. $x \leq 2$
D. $x \leq 4$

48. Which equation could be used to solve the following problem?

"Three consecutive odd numbers add up to 117. What are they?"

A. $x + (x + 2) + (x + 4) = 117$
B. $x + 3x + 5x = 117$
C. $x + x + x = 117$
D. $x + (x + 1) + (x + 3) = 117$

ANSWER KEY – MATHEMATICS PRACTICE TEST 1

Question	Answer	Objective	
1	C	0007	Understand number properties and number operations.
2	D	0007	Understand number properties and number operations.
3	B	0007	Understand number properties and number operations.
4	D	0007	Understand number properties and number operations.
5	A	0007	Understand number properties and number operations.
6	B	0007	Understand number properties and number operations.
7	D	0007	Understand number properties and number operations.
8	C	0007	Understand number properties and number operations.
9	B	0007	Understand number properties and number operations.
10	D	0007	Understand number properties and number operations.
11	B	0010	Understand problem-solving principles and techniques.
12	A	0010	Understand problem-solving principles and techniques.
13	C	0010	Understand problem-solving principles and techniques.
14	D	0010	Understand problem-solving principles and techniques.

Question	Answer	Objective	
15	A	0008	Understand measurement concepts and principles of geometry.
16	D	0008	Understand measurement concepts and principles of geometry.
17	C	0008	Understand measurement concepts and principles of geometry.
18	B	0008	Understand measurement concepts and principles of geometry.
19	A	0008	Understand measurement concepts and principles of geometry.
20	A	0008	Understand measurement concepts and principles of geometry.
21	B	0008	Understand measurement concepts and principles of geometry.
22	D	0008	Understand measurement concepts and principles of geometry.
23	A	0008	Understand measurement concepts and principles of geometry.
24	A	0008	Understand measurement concepts and principles of geometry.
25	A	0008	Understand measurement concepts and principles of geometry.
26	C	0007	Understand number properties and number operations.
27	B	0010	Understand problem-solving principles and techniques.
28	B	0010	Understand problem-solving principles and techniques.
29	C	0010	Understand problem-solving principles and techniques.
30	C	0009	Understand statistical concepts and data analysis and interpretation.

Question	Answer	Objective	
31	A	0009	Understand statistical concepts and data analysis and interpretation.
32	B	0009	Understand statistical concepts and data analysis and interpretation.
33	C	0009	Understand statistical concepts and data analysis and interpretation.
34	C	0009	Understand statistical concepts and data analysis and interpretation.
35	D	0009	Understand statistical concepts and data analysis and interpretation.
36	C	0007	Understand number properties and number operations.
37	D	0007	Understand number properties and number operations.
38	A	0009	Understand statistical concepts and data analysis and interpretation.
39	B	0010	Understand problem-solving principles and techniques.
40	A	0010	Understand problem-solving principles and techniques.
41	B	0010	Understand problem-solving principles and techniques.
42	C	0010	Understand problem-solving principles and techniques.
43	A	0007	Understand number properties and number operations.
44	A	0007	Understand number properties and number operations.

Question	Answer	Objective	
45	**C**	0007	Understand number properties and number operations.
46	**A**	0007	Understand number properties and number operations.
47	**D**	0007	Understand number properties and number operations.
48	**A**	0007	Understand number properties and number operations.

Practice Test 1, Part 2 Progress Chart

0007 Understand Number Properties and Number Operations —/19

1	2	3	4	5	6	7	8	9	10

26	36	37	43	44	45	46	47	48

0008 Understand Measurement Concepts and Principles of Geometry —/11

15	16	17	18	19	20	21	22	23	24	25

0009 Understand Statistical Concepts and Data Analysis and Interpretation —/7

30	31	32	33	34	35	38

0010 Understand Problem-Solving Principles and Techniques —/11

11	12	13	14	27	28	29	39	40	41	42

Detailed Explanations for Practice Test 1, Part 2: Mathematics

1. **C**

   The traditional approach to multiplying simple fractions (those between 0 and 1) is to first multiply the numerators together and then multiply the denominators together to find the product. In this case, $\frac{2}{3} \times \frac{4}{5} = \frac{8}{15}$.

2. **D**

   When solving addition or subtraction problems with fractions, first compute the fractional part. In this case, add $\frac{3}{4}$ and $\frac{1}{2}$. To do this, you must find equivalent fractions with common denominators. The common denominator here is 4, so the fraction $\frac{3}{4}$ stays the same, and the fraction $\frac{1}{2}$ is changed to $\frac{2}{4}$. Adding the fractions together results in $\frac{5}{4}$, or $1\frac{1}{4}$. Add $1\frac{1}{4}$ to the whole numbers (2 + 1), arriving at the answer of $4\frac{1}{4}$.

3. **B**

   When subtracting mixed numbers, the first step is to subtract the fractions (in this case, $\frac{1}{2} - \frac{2}{3}$). Because the denominators are different, equivalent fractions with a common denominator must be obtained. The least common denominator is 6, so $\frac{1}{2}$ converts to $\frac{3}{6}$ (making the top number $7\frac{3}{6}$) and $\frac{2}{3}$ converts to $\frac{4}{6}$ (making the bottom number $3\frac{4}{6}$). It is impossible to subtract $\frac{4}{6}$ from $\frac{3}{6}$, so we must rename the top number by "borrowing" one whole from the 7 and adding $\frac{6}{6}$ to the fraction. This results in the problem now reading $6\frac{9}{6} - 3\frac{4}{6}$. We are able to easily subtract now, arriving at the answer of $3\frac{5}{6}$.

4. **D**

   When dividing fractions, the traditional algorithm involves inverting, or "flipping," the second fraction and multiplying. Therefore, the algorithm would read

$\frac{2}{3} \times \frac{5}{4}$. Multiply the numerators, and then multiply the denominators. The resulting fraction is $\frac{10}{12}$, which, in simplest form, is $\frac{5}{6}$.

5.   **A**

   To subtract a negative number, think first about subtracting a number, and what that would look like on a number line. If this problem read $-16 - 5$, we would move to the left on the number line (as we do when we subtract), and the answer would be -21 (which is answer choice C; thus you can eliminate that answer choice). If one subtracts a negative number, we must move to the right on the number line, because you are subtracting the opposite. Therefore, $-16 - (-5)$ may be thought of as $-16 + 5$. Therefore, the appropriate answer choice is A, -11.

6.   **B**

   The first step when dividing decimals is to make the divisor appear as a whole number by moving the decimal point to the right. In this problem, move the decimal point in the divisor two places to the right, to make the divisor read 5. Then, move the decimal point in the dividend two places to the right. The dividend now looks like 820. Move the decimal point straight up from the end of the 820 into the same spot in the quotient. Divide normally to reach the answer of 164.

7.   **D**

   To solve this problem, you must set up an equation. The easiest way to do so is to write the equation as it is read: $14 = 22\%n$ (with n being the unknown number). Rewrite the 22% as .22, and you have $14 = .22n$. Divide both sides by .22 to isolate the unknown number. The result is 63.63, which is approximately 64, thus answer D.

8.   **C**

   To solve this problem in scientific notation, simply multiply the first two digits inside each group of parentheses ($2 \times 6 = 12$). To multiply the 10s notations, simply add the exponents ($10^3 \times 10^4$, add the 3 and 4, which results in 10^7). Thus far, the solution reads: 12×10^7. In scientific notation, however, the initial factor must be greater than zero and less than ten. Therefore, we change the 12. $12 = 1.2 \times 10$. This gives us another power of ten, which changes the 10^7 to 10^8. The simplified answer to this problem, therefore, is 1.2×10^8.

9. **B**

    The order of operations is used to solve this problem. Multiplication comes before addition and subtraction, so the first step is to multiply 2×5, which equals 10. Then, add and subtract left to right $(3 + 10 - 4 = 9)$.

10. **D**

    This problem simply requires that you know how to find a missing number in an equation. To solve this problem, start with 1,806 and subtract 358 to find the missing number, which is 1,448.

11. **B**

    To find how much money Bob and Jana made together, you must first determine how much each made separately, then add those numbers together. Bob babysat for 4 hours and received $6 per hour, which is $24. Jana babysat for half as long as Bob – 2 hours – and received $7 per hour, which is $14. The total that the two made together was $38.

12. **A**

    First, find the number of people that a 0.5% increase in population illustrates. To find that amount, multiply the population by the increase $(2,460 \times 0.005)$, which equals 12.3. Add the increase (12.3) to the original population (2,460) to reach the answer of 2,472.3, which, when rounded to the nearest person (whole number), would give an approximate population of 2,472.

13. **C**

    One way to solve this problem is to draw a chart that shows the growth of each rose bush.

Week	1	2	3	4	5	6	7	8	9
Red 39 in.	$39\frac{1}{2}$	40	$40\frac{1}{2}$	41	$41\frac{1}{2}$	42	$42\frac{1}{2}$	43	$43\frac{1}{2}$
Yellow 36 $\frac{3}{4}$ in.	$37\frac{1}{2}$	$38\frac{1}{4}$	39	$39\frac{3}{4}$	$40\frac{1}{2}$	$41\frac{1}{4}$	42	$42\frac{3}{4}$	$43\frac{1}{2}$

Track the rate of the red rose bush by adding $\frac{1}{2}$ an inch for each week, and do the same for the yellow rose bush at the rate of $\frac{3}{4}$ of an inch per week. At the 9th week, both bushes are the same height: $43\frac{1}{2}$ inches.

14. **D**

   To solve this problem, consider the total amount of time illustrated in the problem, including the 15-minute break that Sarah took from 2:05–2:20. From 11:20 to 3:15 is 3 hours 55 minutes. Subtract the 15-minute break that Sarah took to arrive at the answer of 3 hours 40 minutes.

15. **A**

   To solve this problem, consider the following:

   1000 milligrams = 1 gram

   The problem is: 120 milligrams = ___ grams

   One way to do this problem is to set up and solve a ratio.

   $$\frac{120 \text{ milligrams}}{1000 \text{ milligrams}} = \frac{x \text{ grams}}{1 \text{ gram}}$$

   $120 = 1000x$ Then divide both sides by 1000.

   $$\frac{120}{1000} = \frac{1000x}{1000} \quad = 0.12 \text{ grams}$$

16. **D**

   To solve this problem, consider that 1km = 1000 m and 1 m = 100 cm.
   First, change 5.6 km to meters (5.6 × 1000 = 5600).
   Then, change 5,600 m to cm (5600 × 100 = 560,000).
   Thus, answer D.

17. **C**

   Since there are 12 inches in a foot, simply multiply 14 feet by 12 inches to reach the answer of 168 inches.

18. **B**

     To convert 4 feet 3 inches to inches only, first convert the 4 feet to inches (4×12 = 48 inches), and then add the extra 3 inches to arrive at the answer of 51 inches.

19. **A**

     The area of any rectangle is equal to the measure of its length times the measure of its width (or to say it differently, the measure of its base times the measure of its height). A right triangle can be seen as half of a rectangle (sliced diagonally). Answer A represents, in effect, a rectangle's area cut in half (i.e., divided by two).

20. **A**

     The formula used for finding the area of a triangle is $\frac{1}{2} \times$ base $\times$ height. In this case:

     $$\frac{1}{2} \times (8 \times 20)$$
     $$\frac{1}{2} \times (160) = 80 \text{ square inches}$$

21. **B**

     If a square has a perimeter of 20 centimeters, that means that the length of each side is 5 centimeters. To find the area of a square, multiply the length (5) by the width (5) to reach the answer of 25 square centimeters.

22. **D**

     To find the area of a circle, use the formula πr^2. In this problem, substitute 4 for r, and the result is: 16π. When you use 3.14 for pi and multiply that by 16, the answer is 50.24 square centimeters.

23. **A**

     To find the volume of a cylinder, use the formula $\pi r^2 \times h$. Substitute 3.14 for pi, 4 for r, and 8 for h.

     $3.14 \times 4^2 \times 8$ $3.14 \times 16 \times 8 = 401.92$ cubic inches

24. **A**

   If two triangles are similar, that means that they have the exact same shape (although not necessarily the same size). It also means that the corresponding angles of the two triangles have the same measure, and that corresponding sides are proportional.

   One way to find the solution to this problem is to set up a proportion with one corner being the unknown value (x), and then solve the proportion:

   $$\frac{12}{10} = \frac{15}{x}$$

   This can be read as "12 is to 10 as 15 is to x". The problem can be solved using cross-multiplication, then finding the unknown value.

   $$12x = 15x \times 10$$
   $$12x = 150$$
   $$x = 12.5$$

25. **A**

   There are two things one must know in order to answer the question. One is the meaning of the small square at the vertex of angle BXC. That symbol tells you that angle BXC is a right angle (which measures 90°). A straight line can be thought of as an angle that measures 180°. This is a straight angle.

   In the figure in problem 25, therefore, the sum of the angles DXC (42°) and BXC (90°) is 132°. That means that the remaining angle on the line must have a measure of 48° (180° − 132°).

26. **C**

   To find the average (mean) of a set of values, first add them together. In this case, the negative and positive integers should be added together separately. Those two sums are −12 and 5. (The 0 may be ignored, since it does not affect either sum.) Then −12 and 5 should be added together for a sum of −7.

   To complete the work, the sum of −7 must be divided by the number of values (7), giving −1.

27. **B**

   To find the average trial time for the sprinter, add all four values together, and then divide by the number of trials (4).

   $$11.95 + 12.25 + 12.4 + 13 = 49.6$$
   $$49.6 \text{ divided by } 4 = 12.4 \text{ seconds}$$

28. **B**

> To find the likelihood, set up a fraction that shows the number of desired outcomes (3 pennies with the date of 2003) over the total possibilities (15 pennies in all).

$$\frac{3}{15} = \frac{1}{5} \text{ or } 20\%$$

29 **C**

> To find the likelihood of drawing a white marble, set up a fraction that shows the number of desired outcomes (8 white marbles) over the total possibilities (24 marbles in all).

$$\frac{8}{24} = \frac{1}{3} \text{ or } 33\%.$$

30. **C**

> The difference in gross income and profits in the year 2005 was 2,897 (4,459 – 1,562), which is the largest difference of all the years shown.

31. **A**

> The somewhat steep straight line to the left shows that Mr. Cain worked at a steady rate for awhile. The completely flat lines in the middle shows that he stopped for a while. The line doesn't go up because no grass was cut then. Finally, the line continues upward (after his break) less steeply (and therefore more flatly), indicating that he was working at a slower rate.

32. **B**

> Because Ms. Patton's increases were consistent ($3,000 yearly), and because the directions tell you that only one statement is true, answer B must be correct. Consider:
>
> The range of Ms. Patton's earnings is $12,000 (the jump from $30,000 to $42,000), so answer A cannot be correct.
>
> Although Ms. Patton may have earned $45,000 in 2003, you don't know that, so answer C cannot be correct.
>
> Answer D gives the incorrect earnings average; it was $36,000, not $38,000.

33. **C**

Draw a line through the set of data points. Notice that low grade levels go with low hours of reading, and that high grade levels go with high hours of reading. Next, evaluate the truth of each possible answer. The graph shows that as the grade level goes up, the number of reading hours goes up.

34. **C**

The chart shows that Madison received less than half of the votes (this slice takes up less than half of the pie), so statement I cannot be true.

Washington and Monroe together received 55% of the votes, and everyone else voted for Madison, so Madison must have received 45% of the votes (all of the candidates' percentages must add up to 100%). Therefore, statement II is true.

Monroe received 30% of the 600 votes. 0.30 times 600 is 180, so statement III is true.

Madison received 45% of the vote, and 45% of 600 is 270, so statement IV is false.

35. **D**

D is the correct solution. We can see from the figure that as shoe size increases so does height, so there is a positive relationship which rules out (A) and (C). The problem with (B) is that neither variable causes a change in the other variable.

36. **C**

In this sequence, the pattern is "divided by 4" to reach the next number.

4096 divided by 4 is 1024
1024 divided by 4 is 256
256 divided by 4 is 64
64 divided by 4 is 16; thus answer C is correct.

37. **D**

In this sequence, the pattern is progressive. Each number is the result of subtraction by a larger number each time.

60 minus 3 = 57
57 minus 4 = 53
53 minus 5 = 48
48 minus 6 = 42; therefore, D is the correct answer.

38. **A**

    To convert a Celsius temperature to a Fahrenheit temperature, multiply the Celsius value by $\frac{9}{5}$, then add 32. Thus:

    $$\left(\frac{9}{5} \times -20\right) + 32 = \underline{\quad\quad} \text{ degrees Fahrenheit}$$

    $-36 + 32 = -4$ degrees Fahrenheit (therefore, answer A is correct).

39. **B**

    To find the height of Niagara Falls, multiply $\frac{2}{7}$ by the height of Bridal Veil Falls (189 meters).

    (2×189) divided by $7 = $ height of Niagara Falls
    378 divided by $7 = 54$ meters (answer B).

40. **A**

    To find the amount of tax, multiply the tax rate of 6.5% (.065 in decimal form) by $31.99, the cost of the bracelet. (.065 × $31.99 = 2.079, which rounds to $2.08.) Therefore, the total cost of the bracelet with tax is $34.07. If she paid with $35.00, subtracting $34.07 from that amount will give the change she should receive ($0.93, answer choice A).

41. **B**

    To determine the number of children in the entire sample of 415 that would watch TV for an hour or less, multiply 415 by the percentage in the survey who answered "one hour or less" (18.4%).

    $415 \times .184 = 76.36$

    Because we cannot have .36 of a person, round the answer to 76; thus answer B is correct.

42. **C**

    One way to solve this deductive reasoning problem is to draw a chart, and use the clues to "rule out" sports that are not favorites, or identify which sports are favorites. First, read through all of the clues to determine the possibilities for favorite sports and list them across the top of the chart. Then, list the names of the people identified. When you "rule out" a sport for each person, mark an X in the chart.

	Basketball	Soccer	Volleyball	Golf	Tennis
Sue			O	X	
Ron	X		X	X	
Bev	X	X	X	X	
Kim			X	X	
Lee			X	O	

Ron's favorite sport is not basketball. Put an X beside Ron's name under basketball.

Bev's favorite sport is not basketball or soccer, so put an X beside her name under those two sports.

Sue's favorite sport is volleyball. Put an O beside her name in volleyball to show that it is her favorite.

Because we know that volleyball is Sue's favorite, put an X under volleyball beside everyone else's name.

Kim doesn't like golf. Put an X beside Kim's name under golf.

Lee's favorite sport is the one that Kim does not like (golf), so put an O beside his name under golf, and an X beside everyone else's name under golf.

Looking beside Bev's name, all of the sports have an X except tennis. Therefore, tennis is her favorite sport (answer choice C).

43. **A**

First, simplify the expression. Combine like terms $[5x + (-3x)]$ and $[3 + (-8)]$.

$$5x - 3x = 2x \qquad 3 - 8 = -5$$

Therefore, the expression becomes: $2x - 5$

Substitute 3 for x, and the result is: $2(3) - 5$ or $6 - 5 = 1$ (answer A).

44. **A**

To solve this expression, substitute the given numbers for the variables in the expression, then use the order of operations to solve.

$$2x (z + 3y) = 2(3) (6 + 3(4))$$
$$= 6 (6 + 12)$$
$$= 6 (18)$$
$$= 108 \text{ (therefore, answer A is correct.)}$$

45. **C**

To solve this equation for q, first you must isolate the term that contains q. In this example, add 9 to both sides.

$$\frac{1}{4}q - 9 = 3$$

$$\frac{1}{4}q - 9 + 9 = 3 + 9$$

Combine like terms: $\frac{1}{4}q = 12$

Multiply both sides by 4 to eliminate the fraction. $(4)\frac{1}{4}q = 12\,(4)$

Therefore, $q = 48$ (answer choice C).

46. **A**

To solve this equation for x, first add 11 to each side, which gives $3x^2 = 12$.
Dividing both sides by 3 gives $x^2 = 4$.
Find the square roots of 4; 2 and –2.
The solutions can be checked by substituting them (one at a time) into the original question to see if they work. In this case, both 2 and –2 work.

47. **D**

To solve this inequality, treat it as a typical equation and solve it.

$2(x + 1) \geq 3x - 2$

First, use the distributive property to simplify the left side.

$2x + 2 \geq 3x - 2$

To isolate the variable terms, subtract $2x$ from each side.

$2x + 2 - 2x \geq 3x - 2 - 2x$

Combine like terms: $2 \geq x - 2$

Add 2 to both sides to isolate the variable completely: $2 + 2 \geq x$

The answer currently reads $4 \geq x$. We typically read the expression with the variable first, in which case, we must "flip" the sign. The answer, then, is $x \leq 4$.

48. **A**

You know that the correct equation must show three consecutive odd numbers being added to give 117. Odd numbers (just like even numbers) are each two apart from each other. Only the three values given in answer A are each two apart.

Because the numbers being sought are odd, one might be tempted to choose answer D. However, the second value in answer D ($x + 1$) is not two numbers apart from the first value (x); it is different by only one.

Practice Test 1
Part 3: Writing

GACE Basic Skills

1 _____	11 _____	22 _____	33 _____
2 _____	12 _____	23 _____	34 _____
3 _____	13 _____	24 _____	35 _____
4 _____	14 _____	25 _____	36 _____
5 _____	15 _____	26 _____	37 _____
6 _____	16 _____	27 _____	38 _____
7 _____	17 _____	28 _____	39 _____
8 _____	18 _____	29 _____	40 _____
9 _____	19 _____	30 _____	41 _____
10 _____	20 _____	31 _____	42 _____
	21 _____	32 _____	

PART 3:   **Writing**
             42 questions

Read the passage below; then answer the three questions that follow.

[1]Actually, the term "Native American" is incorrect. [2]Indians migrated to the North American continent from other areas, just earlier than Europeans did. [3]The ancestors of the Anasazi—Indians of the four-state area of Colorado, New Mexico, Utah, and Arizona—probably crossed from Asia into Alaska. [4]About 25,000 years ago, while the continental land bridge still existed. [5]This land bridge arched across the Bering Strait in the last Ice Age. [6]About 500 C.E. the ancestors of the Anasazi moved onto the Mesa Verde, a high plateau in the desert country of Colorado. [7]The Wetherills, five brothers who ranched in the area, are general given credit for the first exploration of the ruins in the 1870s and 1880s. [8]There were some 50,000 Anasazi thriving successfully in the four-corners area by the 1200s C.E. [9] At their zenith, 700 to 1300 C.E., the Anasazi had established widespread communities and built thousands of sophisticated structures—cliff dwellings, pueblos, and kivas. [10]They even engaged in trade with Indians in surrounding regions by exporting pottery and other goods.

1.   Which of the following number parts is a sentence fragment?

   A.   Part 1

   B.   Part 2

   C.   Part 4

   D.   Part 5

2.   Which of the following draws attention away from the main idea of the paragraph?

   A.   Part 3

   B.   Part 4

   C.   Part 7

   D.   Part 8

3. Which of the following changes is needed to make the passage conform to the conventions of Standard American English?

   A. Part 2: Change "earlier" to "more early."

   B. Part 3: Change "probably" to "more probably."

   C. Part 7: Change "general" to "generally."

   D. Part 8: Change "successfully" to "most successful."

Read the passage below; then answer the three questions that follow.

[1]Many events happened in both the South and the North to prevent African Americans from gaining civil rights. [2]Many whites did not want to associate with former slaves and were supportive of segregating the races. [3]The laws that were passed to keep the races segregated were known as Jim Crow laws which made it illegal for blacks to go to white public facilities like hospitals, libraries, schools and parks as well as private facilities like restaurants and churches. [4]The Jim Crow laws and other legal segregation are known as *de jure* segregation, meaning by law segregation another type of segregation is *de facto* segregation which is the segregation that occurs when people follow unwritten rules or customs that segregate the races. [5]When these laws were brought before the Supreme Court as a violation of the 14th Amendment, the Supreme Court ruled that the 14th Amendment had only prohibited states, not individuals or businesses, from discriminating against blacks.

[6]Booker T. Washington, who founded the Tuskegee Institute, believed that fighting discrimination should occur through economic advancement. [7]He believed that if African Americans learned skills through education, they would make themselves equal to whites economically and this would help them to become socially equal. [8]He argued that protesting against discrimination only increased white's hostility toward the blacks. [9]Even though there were few changes in the lives of many African Americans changes were coming. [10]Many African Americans sought to further the black cause by trying to get along with the white population.

4. Which of the following changes is needed to improve the unity and focus of the second paragraph?

   A. Reverse the order of Parts 7 and 8

   B. Delete Part 7

   C. Reverse the order of Parts 8 and 9

   D. Delete Part 10

5. Which of the following numbered parts of the passage is a run-on sentence?

   A. Part 3

   B. Part 4

   C. Part 5

   D. Part 7

6. Which of the following changes is needed to correct an error in punctuation?

   A. Part 1: Insert a comma after "North."

   B. Part 5: Insert a comma after "Court."

   C. Part 7: Insert a comma after "believed."

   D. Part 9: Insert a comma after "Americans."

Read the passage below; then answer the three questions that follow.

[1]Being an optimist or pessimist may have a weighty effect on your health, emotional state of mind, and longevity. [2]A thirty-year study of patients who were being treated at the Mayo Clinic provide insight into what it means to have a sunny disposition. [3]Researchers followed up with patients to whom they had given a personality test thirty years previously. [4]After thirty years, those patients who had reported being more optimistic had lived longer than expected, while the pessimists had a shorter-than-expected lifespan.

[5]Other research that promotes having a brighter outlook on life has found that people who described himself as being pessimistic have higher blood pressure and are more likely to have increased anxiety and depression. [6]An optimist can expect to recover more quickly after being sick and he or she is also less likely to get sick in the first place. [7]If you have a better outlook on life, you are likely to be in better physical and mental health, and possibly live longer.

7. Which of the following changes is needed to correct an error in subject/verb agreement?

    A. Part 2: Change "provide" to "provides."

    B. Part 3: Change "followed" to "follows."

    C. Part 6: Change "expect" to "expects."

    D. Part 7: Change "are" to "were."

8. Which of the following changes is needed to correct an error in noun/pronoun agreement?

    A. Part 3: Change "they" to "he or she."

    B. Part 5: Change "himself" to "themselves."

    C. Part 6: Change "he or she" to "they."

    D. Part 7: Change "you" to "him."

9. What is the thesis of this passage?

    A. After thirty years, those patients who had reported being more optimistic had lived longer than expected, while the pessimists had a shorter-than-expected lifespan.

    B. An optimist can expect to recover more quickly after being sick and he or she is also less likely to get sick in the first place.

    C. Researchers followed up with patients to whom they had given a personality test thirty years previously

    D. Being an optimist or pessimist may have a weighty effect on your health, emotional state of mind, and longevity.

Read the passage below; then answer the three questions that follow.

[1]Savannah, Georgia, founded in 1733, was the first colonial and state capital of Georgia. [2]It has long been recognized as one of the most beautiful and most walkable cities in America and has a large National Historical Landmark district that includes the 22 squares that were originally laid out by the British philanthropist James Oglethorpe. [3]He originally envisioned founding the colony of Georgia with colonists that had been imprisoned for their inability to pay their debts. [4]Oglethorpe had experienced the loss of a good friend, not just a good friend but his best friend, who had died in a debtors' prison. [5]Oglethorpe

wanted to create a colony that would give people a fresh start. [6]While this vision of shipping debtors on a large scale to Georgia was never realized, the city of Savannah continues to celebrate the altruism of James Oglethorpe and one of the most lavish squares contains a larger-than-life statue of him. [7]Most of the other squares have only a fountain at their center, but Chippewa Square (not Oglethorpe Square as one might expect) has a statue of General Oglethorpe that was sculpted by the same artist, Daniel Chester French, who created the seated Lincoln in Washington D.C. [8]It is often referred to as the most beautiful when compared to the Gordon monument in Wright Square.

10. Which of the following parts contains redundant phrasing?

    A. Part 2
    B. Part 4
    C. Part 6
    D. Part 7

11. Which of the following parts contains a nonstandard pronoun use?

    A. Part 2
    B. Part 3
    C. Part 6
    D. Part 7

12. Which of the following contains a nonstandard use of a comparative form?

    A. Part 1
    B. Part 2
    C. Part 6
    D. Part 8

Read the passage below; then answer the three questions that follow.

[1]The Lincoln Cent was first struck in 1909 to celebrate the 100th Anniversary of the birth of Abraham Lincoln. [2]The coin carried the motto "In God We Trust"—the first time it appeared on this denomination coin. [3]Though we might not think so at first glance, the lowly Cent is a fitting memorial for the great

man whose profile graces this most common coin of the realm, and a tolerable symbol for the nation whose commerce it serves.

[4]The obverse has the profile of Lincoln as he looked during the trying years of the Civil War. [5]Faced with the immense problems of a divided nation, the prevention of the split between North and South was difficult. [6]With the outbreak of hostilities at Fort Sumter. Lincoln was saddened to see his beloved country caught up in the senseless violence that is war. [7]Throughout America, war captured the attention of people: the woman who saved the lives of the wounded, the soldier waiting to go into battle, the bewildered child trying hard to understand the loss of a parent.

[8]Barely a month before the end of the war, Lincoln took the oath of office a secondly time as President. [9]With the war still raging, his inaugural address took on added meaning: [10]"With malice toward none, with charity for all, with firmness in the right as God gives us to see the right, let us strive on to finish the work we are in, to bind up the nations wounds, to care for him who shall have borne the battle and his widow and his orphan, to do all which may achieve and cherish a just and lasting peace among ourselves and with all nations."

13. Which of the following changes is needed in the third paragraph?

    A. Part 8: Change "end" to "climax."

    B. Part 8: Change "secondly" to "second."

    C. Part 9: Change "With" to "Of."

    D. Part 9: Change "on" to "in."

14. Which of the following changes is needed in the second paragraph?

    A. Part 4: Change "has" to "had."

    B. Part 5: Change "the prevention of the split between North and South was difficult" to "Lincoln found it difficult to prevent the split between North and South."

    C. Part 7: Change "waiting" to "waited."

    D. Part 7: Change "captured" to "captures."

15. Which of the following is a nonstandard sentence?

    A.   Part 2
    B.   Part 3
    C.   Part 6
    D.   Part 8

Read the passage below; then answer the three questions that follow.

[1]The Tuskegee Experiment's true nature had to be hidden from the subjects to ensure their cooperation. [2]The sharecroppers' grossly disadvantaged lot in life made them easy to manipulate. [3]Pleased at the prospect of free medical care—almost none of them had ever seen a doctor before—these unsophisticated and trusting men became the dupes in what has been identified as a "long-standing misuse of the therapeutic medical model".

[4]The study was meant to discover how syphilis affected African Americans as opposed to whites—the theory being that whites experienced more neurological complications from syphilis whereas African Americans were more susceptible to cardiovascular damage. [5]_____

_____. [6]Although scientists touted the study as one of great scientific merit, from the outset its actual benefits were unclear. [7]It took almost forty years before someone involved in the study took a hard and honest look at the end result, there was no interest in the study or its participants outside of a small group of doctors and civil right activists.

16. Which of the following sentences, if inserted as Part 5, would be most consistent with the writer's purpose and intended audience?

    A.   If the theory had been proven, much would have changed in
          the clinical treatment of syphilis.

    B.   How this knowledge would have changed the clinical treatment
          of syphilis is uncertain.

    C.   On the other hand, neurological complications were much
          more important to the scientists.

    D.   We will never know what the racist scientists of the 1920s
          were thinking when they devised this theory.

17. Which of the numbered parts should be revised to correct a nonstandard use of a comma?

    A. Part 2

    B. Part 4

    C. Part 6

    D. Part 7

18. Which of the following changes is needed in the first paragraph?

    A. Part 1: Change "Experiment's" to "Experiments"

    B. Part 3: Change "had" to "has."

    C. Part 2: Change "easy to manipulate" to "easily manipulated."

    D. Part 3: Move the period at the end inside the quotation mark.

Read the passage below; then answer the three questions that follow.

[1]The zoning regulations of Westside have long been a thorn in the side of local real estate developers. [2]The authors of those regulations apparently believed that their regulations would be appropriate in perpetuity, because they _____ to amend. [3]The result is a growing area of blight bounded on the north by Forrest Drive and on the east by Cascade Circle.

[4]The Westside's city council has a chance to bring the zoning practices into the twenty-first century. [5]The decisive votes will come from Council members Nelson and Crawford. [6]The votes of these two in particular will be of interest to their constituents, because the residents of their districts would stand to gain a great deal from rezoning. [7]The proposed changes would bring the Fifth District some much-needed commerce in the currently run-down Forrest Drive area and would help _____ the Fifth District's steady population loss. [8]Although each of these self-styled "progressives" have displayed reluctance to vote for anything that would spur development in the recent past, both have strong opposition in the upcoming election and would do well to consider how their votes on this issue will impact the results of that election.

19. Which of the following changes is needed in the previous passage?

    A. Part 1: Change "have" to "has."

    B. Part 4: Change "Westside's" to "Westside."

    C. Part 8: Change the comma after "past" to a semicolon.

    D. Part 8: Change "how" to "that."

20. Which of the numbered sentences should be revised to correct an error in verb form?

    A. Part 3

    B. Part 5

    C. Part 6

    D. Part 8

21. Which of the following phrases, if inserted into the blank in Part 2, would make sense and would be free of errors?

    A. made the regulations very easy

    B. ensured that the provisions would be difficult

    C. made them almost impossible

    D. said the zoning ordinances would be hard

Read the passage below; then answer the three questions that follow.

[1]Water is a most unusual substance because it exists on the surface of the Earth in it's three physical states: ice, water, and water vapor. [2]There are other substances that exist in a solid and liquid and gaseous state at temperatures normally found at the Earth's surface, but there are fewer substances that occur in all three states.

[3]Water is odorless, tasteless, and colorless. [4]It is the only substance known to exist in a natural state as a solid, liquid, or gas on the surface of the Earth. [5]It is a universal solvent. [6]Water does not corrode, rust, burn, or separate into its components easily. [7]It is chemically indestructible. [8]It can corrode almost any metal and erode the most solid rock. [9]A unique property of water is that, when frozen in its solid state, it expands and floats on water. [10]Water has a freezing

point of 0°C and a boiling point of 100°C. [11]Water has the capacity to absorb great quantities of heat with relatively little increase in temperature. [12]When distilled, water is a poor conductor of electricity but when salt is added, it is a good conductor of electricity.

22. The writer's main purpose in this passage is to

    A.   explain the taste of water.

    B.   examine the effects of water on solids.

    C.   define the properties of water.

    D.   describe the three physical states of all liquids.

23. Which of the following changes is needed in the passage above?

    A.   Part 1: Change "it's" to "its."

    B.   Part 2: Change "exist" to "exists."

    C.   Part 6: Change "its" to "it's."

    D.   Part 9: Change "its" to "it's."

24. Which of the following changes is needed in Part 2?

    A.   There are other substances that exist in a solid, liquid, and gaseous state at temperatures normally found at the Earth's surface, but there are fewer substances that occur in all three states.

    B.   There are other substances that exist in a solid and liquid or gaseous state at temperatures normally found at the Earth's surface, but there are fewer substances that occur in all three states.

    C.   There are other substances that exist in a solid or liquid or gaseous state at temperatures normally found at the Earth's surface, but there are fewer substances that occur in all three states.

    D.   There are other substances that exist in a solid, liquid, and gaseous state at temperatures normally found at the Earth's surface, but there are fewer substances that occur in all three states.

Read the passage below; then answer the three questions that follow.

[1]A submarine was first used as a military weapon during the American Revolutionary War. [2]The *Turtle*, a one-man submersible designed by an American named David Bushnell and hand-operated by a screw propeller, attempted to sink a British warship in New York Harbor. [3]The plan was to attach a charge of gunpowder to the ship's bottom with screws and explode it with a time fuse. [4]After repeated failures to force the screws through the copper sheathing of the H.M.S. *Eagle*, the submarine was giving up and withdrew, exploding its powder a short distance from the *Eagle*. [5]Although the attack was unsuccessful, it caused the British to move their blockading ships from the harbor to the outer bay.

[6]On February 17, 1864, a Confederate craft, a hand-propelled submersible carrying a crew of eight men, sank a Federal corvette that was blockading Charleston Harbor. [7]The crew hadn't no hope of coming close enough to the corvette to fire upon it with a cannon, so the submarine was used to stealthily approach the ship. [8]The hit was accomplished by a torpedo suspended ahead of the Confederate *Hunley* as she rammed the union frigate *Housatonic*, and is the first recorded instance of a submarine sinking a warship.

25. Which of the following is a nonstandard sentence?

    A. Part 3
    B. Part 5
    C. Part 7
    D. Part 8

26. Which of the following contains nonstandard capitalization?

    A. Part 1
    B. Part 5
    C. Part 6
    D. Part 8

27. Which of the following changes is needed for Part 4?

    A. Change "force" to "forcing."

    B. Change "was giving up" to "gave up."

    C. Change "withdrew" to "withdraw."

    D. Change "exploding" to "exploded."

Read the passage below; then answer the three questions that follow.

¹The dismissal of Dr. Dennis Griffin has brought many of the students and faculty together to fight for this beloved professor. ²It does not promote a feeling of academic freedom to know that a tenured professor can be run out of his post because he disagrees with the Board of Regents. ³True, his was the only negative vote on the retirement fund issue promoted by the university system. ⁴However, since when has a dissenting opinion been the prompt for persecution of faculty members on this campus? ⁵_____. ⁶English professors, especially, have traditionally had the reputation of fighting courageously for out-of-the-box thinking and innovative approaches to problem solving. ⁷They have also historically been the school's champion against injustice.

⁸There cannot be an issue closer to the basis of America's founding principles than this one because the foundation of America is based on the freedom of speech. ⁹The students of this university need to know whose to blame for the loss of Dr. Griffin. ¹⁰He is a stimulating speaker, an engaging person, and one of the finest teachers. ¹¹Where will this issue come to a halt? ¹²Will other tenured professors now be more intimidated and hesitate to express those views not consistent with the general consensus of opinion? ¹³Will students receive a quality education from a university that infringes on freedom of speech?

28. Which of the following requires revision for redundancy?

    A. Part 3

    B. Part 6

    C. Part 8

    D. Part 12

29. Which of the following, if added between sentences 4 and 6, best supports the writer's purpose and audience?

    A. We should allow teachers to express their own opinions regardless of what we ourselves think.

    B. This university has always prided itself on instructors who are rather maverick in their thinking.

    C. Don't you think this is a pitiful way to treat a fine instructor?

    D. One must acknowledge that university professors, as a whole, should support the opinions of fellow faculty members.

30. Which one of the following changes is needed?

    A. Part 8: Change "closer" to "closest."

    B. Part 9: Change "whose" to "who's."

    C. Part 10: Change "finest" to "finer."

    D. Part 11: Change "Where" to "When."

Read the passage below; then answer the three questions that follow.

[1]Madison County's business and professional community along with the Price College faculty and staff donated a record $1.4 million to the 35th annual Scholarship Fund Drive. [2]The total marks the 10th straight year the one-day fundraising drive has topped $1 million in contributions to Price College. [3]The scholarship fund drive helps meet the scholarship commitments of Price College that are not met by state funding. [4]Proceeds from the program go to support both academic and athletic scholarship programs. [5]While the local businesses have often been recognized for their support of the College, the Scholarship Fund Drive demonstrates what a giving community this is, especially in its maintenance of those scholarships available to students within Madison County. [6]Several new endowments were created to be used specific for students who graduate from Madison County public and private high schools. [7]The Eleanor A. Harper Scholarship was established in memory of the former principle of Madison High School and a Price College graduate. [8]This annual scholarship is available to those students who graduate from Madison High School and wish to pursue a degree in education. [9]The legacy of generosity by the members of this community is part and parcel of what makes this such a great place to live and raise a family.

31. Which of the following changes is needed?

    A.   Part 5: Change "its" to "it's."

    B.   Part 6: Change "specific" to "specifically."

    C.   Part 8: Change "available" to "availability."

    D.   Part 9: Change "generosity" to "generous."

32. Which of these is the best way to rewrite Part 7?

    A.   The Eleanor A. Harper Scholarship was established in memory of the former principal of Madison High School and a former Price College graduate.

    B.   The Eleanor A. Harper Scholarship was established in memory of the former principal of Madison High School who was also a Price College graduate.

    C.   The Eleanor A. Harper Scholarship was established in memory of the former principal of Madison High School and a graduate of Price College.

    D.   The Eleanor A. Harper Scholarship was established in memory of the former principal of Madison High School, a Price College graduate.

33. Which of the following parts contains a distracting detail that impairs the development of the main idea of this passage?

    A.   Part 2

    B.   Part 4

    C.   Part 8

    D.   Part 9

Read the passage below; then answer the three questions that follow.

[1]About 3,000 years ago in the Zhou dynasty, the Chinese government began to establish specialized institutions to train blind music officials who were appointed to record history and it was common to find blind scholars, story-tellers and musicians in ancient China. [2]The famous Confucian classic 'Book of Rites' advocated that the government should be responsible for the care and well-being of those who were disabled and sick. [3]A few Chinese scholars claimed that the humanistic attitude and treatment to people with disabilities

under the influence of Confucian philosophy in ancient China were about 10 centuries earlier than the advocacy of liberty and humanity initiated during the Renaissance in the West. [4]Despite the fact that discrimination, alienation, and stigma of people with disabilities characterized the early history of China most of them survived with the support of family, government, and the society at large. [5]A social attitude of sympathy towards people with disabilities had been carefully nurtured, and it was so deeply rooted in Chinese society that we cannot ignore its strong influence today.

[6]Nevertheless, people with disabilities were kept at the bottom of the hierarchical feudal pyramid under this philosophy and a culture of sympathy instead of education was adopted to respond to the needs of those with disabilities in China. [7]Special education institutions began to be established by the American and European missionaries in China after 1840. [8]When Chairman Mao founded the People's Republic of China in 1949, 42 special schools were serving more than 2,000 students with blindness and deafness. [9]The open reform policy under Deng Xiaoping's leadership in the 1980s resulted in tremendous social and political changes as well as economic growth. [10]This encouraged more governmental attention to the rights of people with disabilities. [11]However, the enrollment rate of students with disabilities has since become a nationwide quality index of school district performance.

34. Which of the following contains nonstandard comma use?

    A.   Part 1
    B.   Part 2
    C.   Part 4
    D.   Part 5

35. Which of the following changes needs to be made?

    A.   Part 3: Change "to" to "of."
    B.   Part 5: Change "sympathy" to "sympathetic."
    C.   Part 8: Change "were" to "are."
    D.   Part 10: Change "to" to "for."

36. Which of the following contains an error in transitional phrasing?

    A. Part 5
    B. Part 6
    C. Part 8
    D. Part 11

Read the passage below; then answer the three questions that follow.

[1]Students who are placed in residential programs for behavior or emotional problems or who are adjudicated into detention centers historically have not experienced success in school. [2]These students usually do not have a consistent record of school attendance; their absenteeism can be for more than an entire school year, as they often have been moved from different placements or institutions. [3]Residential treatment provides the longest period of secondary school attendance for many of the students. [4]_____ [5]Students who are incarcerated have not experienced classroom involvement or positive teacher interaction prior to their detainment; this may be the only time they have ever been in a setting where they feel that the teacher recognizes them. [6]For some of them, their incarceration or admission to a residential treatment facility afford them opportunities to participate in appropriate relationships with teachers.

[7]Transitioning back to public schools, where they have not had success should be addressed by the school to which they are returning as well as the facility from which they are leaving. [8]This reintegration is essential in providing students with opportunities for success and a full measure of participation in the educational community; the students' success can be a measure of society's willingness to work with at-risk students.

[9]Academic achievement is related not only to delinquency; but also to recidivism. [10]The ability for students to quickly reintegrate into a public school promotes continued academic effort and better relationships within the school setting. [11]It may be possible in fact, to reduce recidivism by providing necessary skills for academic achievement such as self-advocacy and self-determination, two skills used in developing transition plans for students.

37. Which of the following, if added between sentences 3 and 5, best supports the writer's purpose and audience?

    A.   As such, it provides an opportune setting for many of these students to experience some type of academic success both within the content area coursework and in their relationships with educators.

    B.   No one knows how long these students have been absent.

    C.   But, it isn't the answer to poor judgment by the student.

    D.   Residential treatment first came to the forefront of treatment facilities with the onset of drug treatment facilities in the 1960s.

38. Which of the following contains nonstandard semicolon use?

    A.   Part 2

    B.   Part 5

    C.   Part 8

    D.   Part 9

39. Which of the following changes needs to be made in the first paragraph?

    A.   Part 1: Change "who" to "whom."

    B.   Part 3: Change "provides" to "provide."

    C.   Part 5: Change "feel" to "feels."

    D.   Part 6: Change "afford" to "affords."

Read the passage below; then answer the three questions that follow.

¹The situation for men has changed as a result of women's massive entry into the workforce for the better. ²Men who would have felt unrelenting pressure to remain with one firm and climb the career ladder are often freed up by a second income to change careers in midlife. ³They enjoy greatest intimacy and involvement with their children.

⁴The benefits for business are also readily apparent. ⁵No senior manager in the country would deny that the huge generation of women who entered management a decade ago has functioned superbly, often outperforming men.

[6]Yet the prevailing message from the media on the subject of women and business is one filled with pessimism. [7]We hear about women leaving their employers in the lurch when they go on maternity leave. [8]Or we hear the flip side, that women are overly committed to their careers and neglectful of their families. [9]And, in fact, it is true that problems arising from women's new work force role do exist, side by side with the benefits.

[10]The problems hurt business as well as individuals and their families, affordable quality childcare, for one example is still a distant dream. [11]Some women are distracted at work, and men who would have felt secure about their children when their wives were home are also anxious and distracted. [12]Distraction also impedes the productivity of some high-achieving women with the birth of their first child and causes some to depart with the birth of their second.

40. Which of the following sentences displays a nonstandard placement of a modifying phrase?

    A. Part 1
    B. Part 2
    C. Part 5
    D. Part 11

41. Which of the following sentences displays a nonstandard use of a comparative form?

    A. Part 2
    B. Part 3
    C. Part 7
    D. Part 9

42. Which of the following sentences is a nonstandard sentence?

    A. Part 8
    B. Part 9
    C. Part 10
    D. Part 12

Constructed-Response Assignment Directions

For the constructed-response assignment, you are asked to prepare a written response and record it on the pages that you are given in your Written Response Booklet.

Be sure to read the assignment carefully and plan your response before you start to write. You may use any blank space provided in the test booklet following the question to outline your ideas or simply to jot down notes. **However, when you take the GACE Basic Skills, you must write your final version on the pages that the test administrators provide in the test booklet.**

Test scorers use the following criteria to evaluate your constructed-response submission:

- Appropriateness of your response in that you address the topic directly and use language that would be appropriate for the specified occasion, audience, and purpose

- Your focus and organization in sticking to your topic and providing a logical flow to your reasoning

- The support you give to your thesis in the examples you provide

- Your use of correct grammar, sentence structure, and word usage

- Your use of conventions, which include spelling, punctuation, and capitalization

Constructed-Response Question

Writing Assignment

Many scholars note the decline in the use of research resources that are only available in print form. With the onset of the availability of many resources such as journal articles, encyclopedias, and other sources such as public records and almanacs online, the use of libraries by individuals who are seeking information has also declined.

In an essay written to an English instructor, argue whether you feel the trend of accessing research resources online versus physically visiting a library is commendable or contemptible. Reflect on modern research techniques and the effects of a strictly online environment on the culture of academic investigation. Discuss the advantages and/or disadvantages of researching a topic that excludes or minimizes the need to physically search for resources. Finally, draw upon your own exposure to and attitude toward online resources and print copy resources, respectively.

ANSWER KEY – WRITING PRACTICE TEST 1

Question	Answer	Objective	
1	C	0013	Recognize effective sentences.
2	C	0011	Recognize unity, focus, and development in writing.
3	C	0014	Recognize Standard American English usage.
4	D	0011	Recognize unity, focus, and development in writing.
5	B	0013	Recognize effective sentences.
6	D	0014	Recognize Standard American English usage.
7	A	0014	Recognize Standard American English usage.
8	B	0013	Recognize effective sentences.
9	D	0011	Recognize unity, focus, and development in writing.
10	B	0013	Recognize effective sentences.
11	B	0014	Recognize Standard American English usage.
12	D	0014	Recognize Standard American English usage.
13	B	0013	Recognize effective sentences.
14	B	0014	Recognize Standard American English usage.
15	C	0014	Recognize Standard American English usage.
16	B	0011	Recognize unity, focus, and development in writing.
17	D	0014	Recognize Standard American English usage.
18	D	0014	Recognize Standard American English usage.
19	B	0013	Recognize effective sentences.
20	D	0013	Recognize effective sentences.

Question	Answer	Objective	
21	B	0012	Recognize effective organization in writing.
22	C	0011	Recognize unity, focus, and development in writing.
23	A	0014	Recognize Standard American English usage.
24	B	0011	Recognize unity, focus, and development in writing.
25	C	0013	Recognize effective sentences.
26	D	0014	Recognize Standard American English usage.
27	B	0013	Recognize effective sentences.
28	C	0013	Recognize effective sentences.
29	B	0011	Recognize unity, focus, and development in writing.
30	B	0013	Recognize effective sentences.
31	B	0014	Recognize Standard American English usage.
32	B	0011	Recognize unity, focus, and development in writing.
33	D	0011	Recognize unity, focus, and development in writing.
34	C	0014	Recognize Standard American English usage.
35	A	0013	Recognize effective sentences.
36	D	0012	Recognize effective organization in writing.
37	A	0011	Recognize unity, focus, and development in writing.
38	D	0014	Recognize Standard American English usage.
39	D	0013	Recognize effective sentences.
40	A	0014	Recognize Standard American English usage.
41	B	0014	Recognize Standard American English usage.
42	C	0013	Recognize effective sentences.

Practice Test 1, Part 3 Progress Chart

0011   Recognize Unity, Focus, and Development in Writing   ——/10

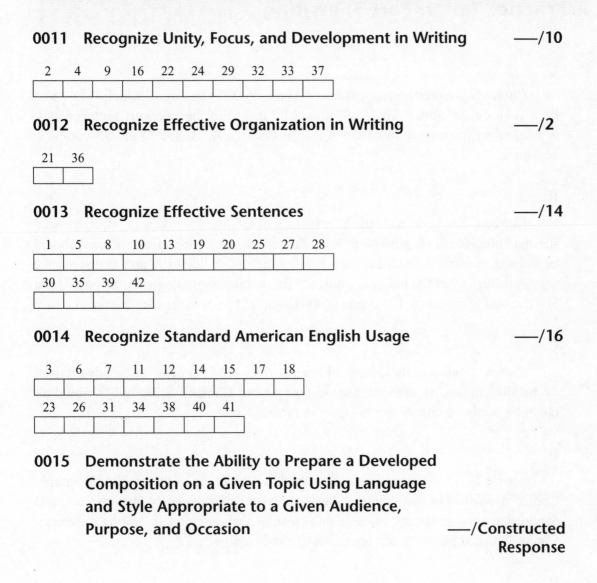

2	4	9	16	22	24	29	32	33	37

0012   Recognize Effective Organization in Writing   ——/2

21	36

0013   Recognize Effective Sentences   ——/14

1	5	8	10	13	19	20	25	27	28

30	35	39	42

0014   Recognize Standard American English Usage   ——/16

3	6	7	11	12	14	15	17	18

23	26	31	34	38	40	41

0015   Demonstrate the Ability to Prepare a Developed Composition on a Given Topic Using Language and Style Appropriate to a Given Audience, Purpose, and Occasion   ——/Constructed Response

193

Detailed Explanations for
Practice Test 1, Part 3: Writing

1. **C**

    Choice C is a prepositional phrase, "About 25,000 years ago," which is followed by a subordinate clause. This part should be linked to the previous sentence as it is integral to the migration of the Anasazi. Choices A, B, and D are all complete sentences.

2. **C**

    Choice C has to do with the later history of the Mesa Verde area, after the Anasazi had abandoned it. Since this is so far removed chronologically, Part 7 should be deleted or further developed in a third paragraph. Choices A and B discuss the very early history of the Indians. Choice D follows the chronological time order from 500 C.E. and leads into a discussion of the height of the Anasazi civilization.

3. **C**

    Choice C indicates the change of the incorrect word "general" to an adverb form "generally" to modify the verb phrase "are given." Choices A, B, and D would all change a correct comparison phrase to an incorrect one.

4. **D**

    Choice D is a sentence that does not add to the focus of the second paragraph. Choice A would not continue the thesis statement introduced in Part 6. Choice B would remove a necessary piece of information that supports the thesis statement. Choice C would place the sentences out of a coherent order.

5. **B**

    Choice B has two distinct sentences contained in a single sentence. A period should be placed between "segregation" and "another." Choices A, C, and D are all single ideas represented in single sentences.

6. **D**

    Choice D contains a subordinate phrase that occurs at the beginning of the sentence and should be offset with a comma. Any comma added to the suggested places in Choices A, B, and C would create a comma splice.

7. **A**

    Choice A will change the verb to "provide," which will make it agree with the subject of the sentence "study," which is singular. Choice B would make the verb an incorrect tense. Choice C would make the verb plural, which would create an error with the singular subject "optimist." Choice D would make the verb an incorrect tense.

8. **B**

    Choice C changes the pronoun to a plural one, making it agree with the noun "people." Choices A, C, and D are all correct noun/pronoun agreement.

9. **D**

    The thesis in this passage occurs at the beginning and is restated again at the end. Choices A, B, and C are supporting details for the thesis.

10. **B**

    The sentence contains a restatement of "good friend" as "best friend" and is unnecessary. No redundancy occurs in Choices A, C, and D.

11. **B**

    Part 3 contains the indirect pronoun "that" when referring to the noun "colonists." Standard American English requires the use of the pronoun "who" when referring to people. Choices A, C, and D contain standard pronoun use.

12. **D**

    Choice D contains a comparison of only two subjects, the Oglethorpe statue and the Gordon monument, but the superlative case "most beautiful" is used rather than the correct comparative form "more beautiful." Choice A does not contain a comparative form. Choice C uses the superlative forms "most beautiful" and "most walkable" to compare Savannah to all other cities in America. Choice C uses the superlative form "most lavish" to compare Chippewa Square with all the other squares.

13. **B**

    The adjective form "second" not the adverbial form "secondly" is appropriate here, since it modifies a noun, not a verb.

14. **B**

The opening verb phrase is a dangling modifier. "Prevention" is not "faced with" anything; Lincoln is. All the other choices are standard American English sentences.

15. **C**

"With the outbreak . . . " is a prepositional phrase that is stopped with a period. It has no subject and is not a standard American English sentence. All the rest are correct.

16. **B**

Part 6 begins with "Although"—used for mentioning the scientists' public statements—and refers to the "hazy" benefits derived from the study. Thus, the sentence has to deal with speculation about the "uncertain" benefits. Choice D fits in the paragraph's development fairly well, but it is not the best answer because the pejorative word "racist" would not generally be used to characterize someone.

17. **D**

Part 7 contains a comma splice. The sentence has two independent clauses, and they are not joined by a coordinating conjunction. They, therefore, must be separated by a semicolon, not a comma.

18. **D**

By convention in Standard American English, periods and commas are always placed inside of quotation marks except in certain technical copy.

19. **B**

The presence of "the" before "Westside's" means that the reference is *the* council, not to a council belonging to Westside. The other choices are all correct, and changing them would make them nonstandard.

20. **D**

The subject of the first clause is "each" which is singular, so the verb should be "has."

21. **B**

    Choice A is wrong because it makes no sense within the sentence; the zoning regulations cannot be easy to change. Choice C makes no sense, its use of "them" is ambiguous—does it refer to the authors or the regulations? Choice D is wrong because, if the authors *said* the regulations would be hard to change, the word *apparently* earlier in the sentence would make no sense. Thus, Choice B is the best answer.

22. **C**

    The writer's didactic summary of water's properties is the only perspective found in the passage. Choice A refers to only one property of water and Choice B is the subject of a single paragraph. An in-depth discussion of the physical states of liquids is not offered within the passage.

23. **A**

    The contraction "it's" is used to replace "it is" and is not the possessive form of "it." Choice B would change the number of the verb to singular, and the subject "substances" is plural. Choices C and D would change the correct possessive form "its" to the incorrect contraction "it's."

24. **B**

    The writer is stating that it is possible for substances to occur in two states: a solid and either a liquid or gas. Choice A infers that substances occur in all three states. Choice C infers that substances are found in only one state. Choice D infers that a single state can have all three properties.

25. **C**

    Part 7 contains the double negative "hadn't no." It should read either "the crew had no hope…" or "the crew hadn't any hope…" Choices A, B, and D are all standard sentences.

26. **D**

    "Union" should be capitalized because it refers to a part of the United States during the Civil War. You will note that earlier in the same sentence the word "Confederate" is capitalized.

27. **B**

It is necessary to change the verb phrase so it is parallel with the verb "withdrew." Choices A, C, and D would each change the tense of the sentence.

28. **C**

Choice C unnecessarily repeats the words "basis," "based," "founding," and "foundation." These forms need not be repeated and the sentence should be condensed. Choices A, B, and D are all well-worded sentences.

29. **B**

Choice B fits between sentence 4 and sentence 6. Sentence 4 mentions the topic of dissenting opinion, and sentence 6 elaborates by stating the position that English professors have always been outspoken. This idea is continued in sentence 7. Choice A changes the voice to plural first-person "we," which is out of place in this passage. Choice C is too casual. Choice D directly contradicts the thesis of the letter.

30. **B**

Choice B contains an inappropriate use of words. The contraction for "who is" should be used to make the sentence correct. The possessive "whose" is not correct in this context. Choice A correctly uses the comparative degree. Choice C correctly uses the superlative degree. Choice D does not make a needed change.

31. **B**

An adverb form is needed to modify the verb phrase "to be used." The word "specific" in its current form serves as an adjective. Choice A correctly uses the possessive form of "its." Choice C would change the adjective "available" which is describing the noun "scholarship," to an incorrect noun form "availability." Choice D would change the noun "generosity" to the incorrect adjective form "generous."

32. **B**

Choice B is a revision that makes clear that the scholarship was named for a woman who was both a principal and a graduate. Choice A does not provide clarity on whether the scholarship was named for one or two people. Choice C only changes the order of the second noun phrase. Choice D could be used, but is still somewhat unclear about the person's role.

33. **D**

    Choice D is not congruent with the focus of the passage. While there is some mention of the generosity of the community, this doesn't promote the idea that it is a great place to raise a family. Choices A, B, and C all provide details that are related to the thesis of the passage.

34. **C**

    Part 4 begins with a insubordinate clause, "Despite the fact that discrimination, alienation, and stigma of people with disabilities characterized the early history of China" and should be offset by a comma. Choices A, B, and D all contain standard comma use.

35. **A**

    The preposition "to" is incorrect because the sentence is referring to "treatment" and "attitudes" of one person. Choice B would change the noun form "sympathy" to the incorrect adjective form "sympathetic." Choice C would incorrectly change tense. Choice D would create an error in direction of the government's attention.

36. **D**

    The transitional word "However" should be used to compare and contrast different viewpoints. The transition that is needed is cause and effect because the cause is the increased attention by the government and the effect is the use of enrollment rate as a way to determine school district performance. Choice A does not contain transitional phrasing. Choice B uses the transitional word "Nevertheless" to point out a comparison between the sympathetic attitude and the continued poor lot of people with disabilities. Choice C does not contain a transition word.

37. **A**

    Choice A contains the transition phrase "As such" which is referring to residential treatment and it further supports Part 5 which mentions both academic success and relationships with teachers. Choice B is a detail that is unnecessary and may not be true. Choice C draws the focus away from the characteristics of residential treatment and onto the student. Choice D could be expanded in another paragraph, but does not lend itself to further focus on the topic.

38. **D**

Semicolons are used to separate main clauses that can stand alone as sentences. The subordinate clause "but also to recidivism" cannot stand alone as a sentence and should be offset by a comma, not a semicolon. Choices A, B, and C all contain semicolons that are separating main clauses.

39. **D**

Choice D changes the plural verb "affords" to a correct singular verb "afford" so that it will agree with the singular subject "incarceration or admission." Choice A correctly uses the pronoun form. Choice B correctly uses the singular verb form. Choice C correctly uses the plural verb form.

40. **A**

It is not the workforce that is "for the better," but the situation for men. This is also supported by the rest of the evidence offered in the paragraph. The other sentences have their modifying phrases directly related to the idea they qualify.

41. **B**

The writer is comparing the situation before and after the appearance of women in management. That's only two things—therefore, the comparative form, not the superlative, is correct: greater. Choices A, C, and D are all incorrect responses: they have no comparative adjectives, just adverbs used as qualifiers, e.g., "overly." These are used in a standard way.

42. **C**

Part 10 is a run-on sentence, incorrectly punctuated with a comma after "families" instead of a period or a semicolon (i.e., it's a comma splice). The rest of the choices are all standard sentences.

Sample Response for Constructed-Response Question

Writing Sample with a Score of 4

The ability to search for resources for research papers at any time of the day or night makes the online environment very appealing. Not having to be restricted by library hours or reserving computer time in the labs means that an individual can complete assignments that require research whenever he or she feels like it. Being able to search for appropriate supporting documentation whether in one's pajamas or dressed for work is a very liberating idea and also provides the opportunity to more quickly locate needed citations through a variety of helpful search engines.

Unfortunately, much can be lost through this ease-of-use research modality. Libraries themselves in many ways promote a sense of academic integrity that cannot be experienced by simply searching for a topic online. When unsure of a topic or thesis, roaming through the stacks of journals contained within a library's research section often provide inspiration that cannot be found with the electronic version of a journal. Many times the topic selection and all supporting details can be located within a relatively short period of time if the existing catalogs are used. The librarians are real people who are familiar with the available resources and can point the would-be researcher in the right direction. This human touch can often provide clarification on topic selection as well as provide insight into resources that the researcher might not have considered.

Research in many ways is meant to be excavated, discovered, and illuminated through the skill of the researcher, not masticated, reconstituted and regurgitated through the wonders of modern technology. A research topic that allows the researcher to use only resources available online reduces input from other sources that may support or refute whatever the topic is that has been selected.

While this essay does not support the abandonment of the use of the internet to search for supporting documentation, it is more important to search all possible resources rather than just those available online.

Considering this practice of using online sources exclusively for research purposes brings to mind the question of whether libraries may eventually be abandoned. The peculiar experience afforded by going to a library to study or to conduct research cannot be replaced by sitting in front of a computer. The ease of skimming through a wide range of printed resources versus reading from a computer screen means that the individual can quickly decide if the resource is viable or not and move on without having to click one's way back to a list. Unfortunately, the library and librarian may indeed be a thing of the past. With the onset of strictly online coursework and degrees, more and more journals may be transposed to online availability and the days of searching through the stacks of journals in the library for a particular issue may be over.

Features of the Writing Sample Scoring 4

Appropriateness—The essay addressed the topic of whether it was better to use online sources exclusively or if going to the library to do a thorough search of all sources was more appropriate. While the topic paragraph did promote the idea that there were advantages to using online resources, the remainder of the essay was focused on how going to the library to find print sources added to the total research experience.

Focus and Organization—The essay followed the prompts as given and the opinion of the writer, that the sources found in print were important, was the evident focus of the essay. The organization went from refuting the advantages of using online sources to the less tangible advantages of studying and researching in a library.

Support—The writer provides a strong argument that all possible resources should be investigated and utilized, and not just those that may be found online. The writer also puts forth the point that by searching through the connections available in printed text, the researcher strengthens his or her own researching techniques, something that cannot be done as easily by using search engines.

Grammar, Sentence Structure, and Usage—The sentences contain appropriate grammar and are standardized and vary in form with the use of different phrases to begin sentences ("While this essay . . . ," "With the onset . . . ") to add interest. The use of vivid imagery (working in pajamas, roaming through journal stacks) also adds to the readability of the essay. The comparison of researching using the printed word as a discovery as compared to researching using the computer and simply eating is easy to follow.

Conventions—Spelling and punctuation are mostly standard throughout the essay. There are some lengthy sentences throughout the essay, but for the most part all sentences and transitions can be easily followed.

Writing Sample with a Score of 2 or 1

It is obvious to nearly everyone that nobody uses the library to do research papers any more and that most people preefer to just search for the topic online. The time it takes to gather up paper and pencil and drive to the library is a waist of time and most people end up just searching for stuff on the computer when they get to the library. Almost everything you need can be found through online sources and those journals that aren't online don't have to be used.

Using the research online makes it easier and quicker to do assignments. Having to find information in journals and magazines can be hard to do if you don't know how to use the card catalog and who wants to ask the librarian? Not me. It makes more sense to use the computer to find the research that is out there and put that in your paper. Using online resources helps the writer use your time more efficiently and finish more quicker. Most topics have already been completely researched, so the technique of doing research is to find what has already been done and paraphrase it. There is plenty of research out there to support whatever topic you want to write about, so going to the library to try and find more just doesn't make any sense to me.

Using online sources esclusively from here on out to write about whatever topic is assigned is the way of the future and soon everything will be online so there's no real need to figure out how to use the library and the Dewey decimal system and all that other stuff anyway. There's no reason to ever bother to go to the library to write a research paper again.

Features of the Writing Sample Scoring 2 or 1

Appropriateness—The writer uses only one argument, that everything necessary to write a research paper is online. This argument fails to properly embrace the topic, which is the advantages and disadvantages of the process of online research versus using the printed text. The language used is also not appropriate for the audience, an English instructor, as it is too informal. There are also examples of colloquialisms ("from here on out," "all that stuff") that are not appropriate for a formal paper.

Focus and Organization—The thesis statement is that all resources to complete research are easily found online, but there is no clarity about what that means or how that comes about. The paragraphs and sentences within the paragraphs do restate this single thesis, but the thesis itself is unclear and unfounded.

Support—There is no reasoned support or specific examples given to develop the thesis. The support that is given, that the existing information about any given topic can be taken and paraphrased and so there is no need for any input from the researcher, is nonsensical and doesn't portray a mature attitude toward the process of conducting research.

Grammar, Sentence Structure, and Usage—Sentence 5 in the second paragraph has an incorrect use of comparison ("more quicker" instead of "more quickly") and Sentence 3, which answers the question at the end of Sentence 2, is a fragment. The first sentence of the third paragraph is a run-on sentence even with the use of "and." There are several instances of switching from point of view (Sentence 5 switches from the third person "the writer" to second person "your.") and the use of first and second persons throughout the essays adds to the informal tone.

Conventions—Spelling is generally badly attempted. This appears to be an obvious lack of care on the part of the test-taker. Samples of misspelling would be: "preefer" for "prefer;" "resourses" for "resources;" "waist" for "waste;" "efficieny" for "efficiently;" "esclusively" for "exclusively."

Practice Test 2
Part 1: Reading

GACE Basic Skills

1 _____	11 _____	22 _____	33 _____
2 _____	12 _____	23 _____	34 _____
3 _____	13 _____	24 _____	35 _____
4 _____	14 _____	25 _____	36 _____
5 _____	15 _____	26 _____	37 _____
6 _____	16 _____	27 _____	38 _____
7 _____	17 _____	28 _____	39 _____
8 _____	18 _____	29 _____	40 _____
9 _____	19 _____	30 _____	41 _____
10 _____	20 _____	31 _____	42 _____
	21 _____	32 _____	

Part 1:   **Reading**
                             42 questions

Read the passage below; then answer the three questions that follow.

In view of the current emphasis on literature-based reading instruction, a greater understanding by teachers of variance in cultural, language, and story components should assist in narrowing the gap between reader and text and improve reading comprehension. Classroom teachers should begin with students' meaning and intentions about stories before moving students to the commonalities of story meaning based on common background and culture. With teacher guidance, students should develop a fuller understanding of how complex narratives are when they are writing stories as well as when they are reading stories.

1. Which of the following is the intended audience for the passage?

     A.   Teachers using literature-based curriculum

     B.   Professors teaching a literature course

     C.   Parents concerned about their child's comprehension of books

     D.   Teacher educators teaching reading methods course

2. Which of the following is the most complete and accurate definition of the term <u>variance</u> as used in the passage?

     A.   change

     B.   fluctuations

     C.   diversity

     D.   deviation

3. The passage supports a concept of meaning primarily residing in

    A. culture, language, and story components.
    B. comprehension.
    C. students' stories only.
    D. students and narratives.

Read the passage below; then answer the four questions that follow.

As noted by Favat in 1977, the study of children's stories has been an ongoing concern of linguists, anthropologists, and psychologists. The past decade has witnessed a surge of interest in children's stories from researchers in these and other disciplines. The use of narratives for reading and reading instruction has been commonly accepted by the educational community. The notion that narrative is highly structured and that children's sense of narrative structure is more highly developed than expository structure has been proposed by some researchers.

Early studies of children's stories followed two approaches for story analysis: The analysis of story content or the analysis of story structure. Story content analysis has centered primarily on examining motivational and psychodynamic aspects of story characters as noted in the works of Erikson and Pitcher and Prelinger in 1963 and Ames in 1966. These studies have noted that themes or topics predominate and the themes change with age.

Early research on story structure focused on formal models of structure, such as story grammar and story schemata. These models specified basic story elements and formed sets of rules similar to sentences grammar for ordering the elements.

The importance or centrality of narrative in a child's development of communicative ability has been proposed by Halliday (1976) and Hymes (1975). Thus, the importance of narrative for language communicative ability and for reading and reading instruction has been well documented. However, the question still remains about how these literacy abilities interest and lead to conventional reading.

4.   This passage is most probably directed at which of the following audiences?

   A.   reading educators

   B.   linguists

   C.   psychologists

   D.   reading researchers

5.   According to the passage, future research should address

   A.   how story structure and story schema interact with
        comprehension.

   B.   how children's use and understanding of narrative interacts and
        leads to conventional reading.

   C.   how story content interacts with story comprehension.

   D.   how narrative text structure differs from expository text
        structure.

6.   The major distinction between story content and story structure is that

   A.   story content focuses on motivational aspects whereas story
        structure focuses on rules similar to sentence grammar.

   B.   story content focuses on psychodynamic aspects whereas story
        structure focuses on formal structural models.

   C.   story content and story structure essentially refer to the same
        concepts.

   D.   story content focuses primarily on characters whereas story
        structure focuses on story grammar and schemata.

7.   Which of the following is the most complete and accurate definition of the term
     <u>surge</u> as used in the first paragraph?

   A.   a heavy swell

   B.   a sudden rise

   C.   a sudden increase

   D.   a sudden rush

Read the passage below; then answer the four questions that follow.

Throughout its history, the American school system has often been the target of demands that it change to meet the social priorities of the times. This theme has been traced to the following significant occurrences in education: Benjamin Franklin's advocacy in 1749 for a more useful type of education; Horace Mann's zealous proposals in the 1830s espousing the tax supported public school; John Dewey's early twentieth century attack on traditional schools for not developing the child effectively for his or her role in society; the post-Sputnik pressure for academic rigor; the prolific criticism and accountability pressures of the 1970s; and the ensuing disillusionment and continued criticism of school through the last decade of the twentieth century. Indeed, the waves of criticism about American education have reflected currents of social dissatisfaction for any given period of this country's history.

As dynamics of change in the social order result in demands for change in the American educational system, so in turn insistence has developed for revision of teacher education (witness the more recent Holmes report [1986]). Historically, the education of American teachers has reflected evolving attitudes about public education. With slight modifications, the teachers' education pattern established following the demise of the normal school during the early 1900s has persisted in most teacher preparation programs. The pattern has been one requiring certain academic and professional (educational) courses often resulting in teachers prone to teach as they had been taught.

8.   The author of this passage would probably agree with which of the following statements?

   A.   Social dissatisfaction should drive change in the American school systems.

   B.   Schools were eliminated.

   C.   Critics of American education reflect vested interests.

   D.   Teachers' teaching methods tend to reflect what they have learned in their academic and professional courses.

9.   The evolving attitudes about public schools are

    A.   stated.

    B.   unstated.

    C.   alluded.

    D.   unwarranted.

10.   One possible sequence of significant occurrences in education noted in the passage is

    A.   Mann's tax-supported public school, post-Sputnik pressures for academic rigor, and the Holmes' report.

    B.   Franklin's more useful type of education, Dewey's educating children for their role in society, and Mann's tax supported public schools.

    C.   Franklin's more useful type of education, the Holmes' report, and accountability pressures of the 1970s.

    D.   Mann's tax-supported public schools, accountability pressures of the 1970s, and the post-Sputnik pressures for academic rigor.

11.   Which of the following statements most obviously implies dissatisfaction with the preparation of teachers in the United States?

    A.   Demands for change in the American education system led to the insistence for revision of teacher education programs.

    B.   The pattern of teacher education requires certain academic and professional education courses.

    C.   The education of U.S. teachers has reflected evolving attitudes about public education.

    D.   Teacher education has changed very little since the decline of the normal school.

Read the passage below; then answer the four questions that follow.

Hawk on a Freshly Plowed Field

My Lord of the Field, proudly perched on the sod,
You eye with disdain
And mutter with wings
As steadily each furrow I tractor-plod.
"Intruder!" You glare, firmly standing your ground,
Proclaim this fief yours
By Nature so willed—
Yet bound to the air on my very next round.
You hover and soar, skimming close by the earth,
Distract me from work
To brood there with you
Of changes that Man wrought your land—for his worth.
In medieval days, lords were god over all:
Their word was the law.
Yet here is this hawk
A ruler displaced—Man and Season forestall.
My Lord of the Field, from sight you have flown.
For purpose untold,
When brave, you return
And perch once again, still liege-lord—but Alone.

Jacqueline K. Hultquist (1952)

12. Which of the following is the most complete and accurate definition of the term
   liege-lord as used in the passage?

   A.   monarch

   B.   king

   C.   sovereign

   D.   master

13. Which of the following best describes the author's attitude toward the hawk?

    A. Romantic

    B. Pensive

    C. Intimidating

    D. Fearful

14. Which of the following groups of words about the hawk carry human qualities?

    A. Mutter, brood, and ruler

    B. Brave, disdain, and perch

    C. Brave, brood, and distract

    D. Mutter, disdain, and skimming

15. Which of the following is the most complete and accurate definition of the term <u>medieval</u> as used in the passage?

    A. antiquated

    B. feudal

    C. old

    D. antediluvian

Read the passage below; then answer the three questions that follow.

Representatives of the world's seven richest and most industrialized nations held a three-day economic summit in London on July 14–16, 1991. On the second day of the summit, Mikhail Gorbachev, of the Soviet Union, who appealed for help, was offered support by the seven leaders for his economic reforms and his "new thinking" regarding political reforms. However, because the allies were split on giving a big aid package to Gorbachev, the seven leaders decided to provide help in the form of technical assistance in fields such as banking and energy, rather than in hard cash.

16. Which of the following statements bests synthesizes what the passage is about?

    A. A seven-nation economic summit was held in London in July 1991.

    B. Mikhail Gorbachev appealed for help and the seven leaders agreed to support his economic reforms.

    C. At a three-day economic summit held in London in July 1991, leaders of the world's seven richest and most industrialized nations agreed to provide technical assistance to Gorbachev.

    D. Representatives of the world's seven most industrialized nations, at a summit conference in London, were split on giving Gorbachev assistance in the form of hard cash.

17. The passage implies that

    A. under the leadership of Gorbachev, the Soviet Union was faced with a financial crisis.

    B. Gorbachev's "new thinking" on democratic reforms needed support from the seven nations meeting in London.

    C. the seven leaders meeting in London were split on giving Gorbachev economic and political support.

    D. with the support of political and economic reforms along with provisions for technical assistance from the seven nations that met in London, the Soviet Union, under the leadership of Gorbachev, would be able to achieve political and economic stability.

18. The passage suggests that technical assistance would be provided to the Soviet Union

    A. only in the fields of banking and energy.

    B. in the fields of banking and energy and possibly other fields.

    C. by the U.S. in the fields of banking and energy.

    D. by all seven nations—U.S., Great Britain, France, Germany, Italy, Canada, and Japan.

Read the passage below; then answer the three questions that follow.

A follow-up survey of the 2000 census showed an estimated undercount of 5.2 million people nationwide. This "undercount" was greatest in California, where approximately 1.1 million people were not recorded. This estimated undercount was based on a post-census survey of 171,390 households nation-wide. Failure to achieve an accurate count would affect federal funding and political representation. If the higher numbers were used, California would gain eight congressional seats instead of seven and about $1 billion in federal funds. In July 2001, however, the Commerce Secretary decided to stick to the original figures of the 2000 census.

19. Which of the following statements gives the main idea of the passage you just read?

   A. California would have gained an additional congressional seat and more federal money if the 1.1 million people undercounted in the census were included.

   B. An undercount in the census, if not considered, would be a disadvantage to any state.

   C. A post-census survey would be necessary to get to a more accurate population figure for the states.

   D. California suffered the most due to the 1.1 million undercount in the 2000 census.

20. If the 1.1 million undercount was considered for California,

   A. it would settle any political dispute arising from the undercount.

   B. it would give California eight congressional seats and one billion dollars in federal funds.

   C. it would discourage the practice of a post-census survey.

   D. it would reverse the decision made by the Commerce Secretary.

21. What would it mean for California if the original figures of the 2000 census were to remain the same?

    A. No additional federal funding would be given.

    B. There would be no additional political representation.

    C. The amount of federal funding and number of congressional seats would remain the same.

    D. The results of the follow-up survey of the 2000 census would be meaningless.

Read the passage below; then answer the four questions that follow.

A toxic spill took place on the upper Sacramento River in California when a slow-moving Southern Pacific train derailed north of the town of Dunsmuir. A tank car containing 19,500 gallons of pesticide broke open and spilled into the river. This pesticide is used to kill soil pests. Since the spill, thousands of trout and other fish were poisoned along a 45-mile stretch of a river. In addition, 190 people were treated at a local hospital for respiratory and related illnesses. Residents along the river were warned to stay away from the tainted water. Once this water reached Lake Shasta, a source of water for millions of Californians, samples were taken to assess the quality of the water.

22. Which of the following statements conveys the message in the passage?

    A. Pesticides intended to kill pests can be dangerous to all living things.

    B. Water uncontaminated by pesticides is safe to drink.

    C. Take every precaution not to come in contact with pesticide-infected water.

    D. Pesticides that killed thousands of trout and other fish would not necessarily kill human beings.

23. The Southern Pacific train that derailed was

    A.   a passenger train.

    B.   a freight train.

    C.   a freight and passenger train.

    D.   a special train.

24. The most serious problem that could have come about as a result of the toxic spill was

    A.   possible movement of residents in Dunsmuir to another place of residence.

    B.   the negative effects on those whose livelihood depended on the fishing industry.

    C.   when the tainted water reached Lake Shasta, which is a source of water supply for millions of Californians.

    D.   the uncertain length of time it would take to make the tainted water safe and healthy again.

25. This unfortunate incident of a toxic spill resulting from a train derailment implies

    A.   that there is the need for more environmental protection.

    B.   that other means for transporting pesticides need to be considered.

    C.   that there should be an investigation as to the cause of the train derailment and that effective measures to prevent its occurrence again should be applied.

    D.   that there should be research on how to expedite making infected water safe and healthy again.

Read the passage below; then answer the three questions that follow.

Labor Day, a national holiday observed in the United States, is really a day we should remember to give thanks to the labor unions. In the days before the unions became effective, a holiday meant a day off, but also the loss of a day's pay to working people. It was not until World War II that unions succeeded, through negotiations with the federal government, in making paid holidays a common practice.

26. The main idea in the passage you just read is

    A.   the role labor unions played in employer-employee relations.

    B.   that Labor Day as a national holiday in the U.S.

    C.   the role labor unions played in effecting paid holidays.

    D.   the dispute between granting paid and unpaid holidays.

27. The passage implies that before World War II

    A.   a holiday gave working people a chance to rest from work.

    B.   Labor Day meant losing a day's pay.

    C.   a holiday was a day to make up for upon returning to work.

    D.   labor unions were ineffective.

28. As a national holiday, Labor Day should really be a day to remember and be thankful for

    A.   working people.

    B.   paid holidays.

    C.   labor unions.

    D.   a free day.

Read the passage below; then answer the three questions that follow.

Ash from Mt. Pinatubo in the Philippines has been found to contain gold and other precious metals. However, officials warned against any hopes of a new "gold rush." They found gold content of only 20 parts per billion, which is far below commercial levels. Other metals found were chromium, copper, and lithium.

29. The passage indicates

   A. the possibility of existing gold mines beneath Mt. Pinatubo.

   B. the need for further exploration of what else lies beneath the volcano.

   C. that other active volcanoes might be worth exploring as possible gold resources.

   D. that the gold content of the ash from Mt. Pinatubo does not warrant a commercial level.

30. Which of the following makes a good title for the passage you just read?

   A. A New Gold Rush

   B. Ash Content from Mt. Pinatubo

   C. A Philippine Discovery

   D. Precious Metals

31. What might be a possible research project resulting from the ash contents finding of Mt. Pinatubo?

   A. Research on the ash content from the eruption of Mt. Fujiyama in Japan

   B. Potential market value of the gold and other metal contents in the volcanic ash from Mt. Pinatubo

   C. Further excavation into possible gold underneath Mt. Pinatubo

   D. Research on what lies underneath active volcanoes

Read the passage below; then answer the four questions that follow.

Lead poisoning is considered by health authorities to be the most common and devastating environmental disease of young children. According to studies made, it affects 15% to 20% of urban children and from 50% to 75% of inner-city, poor children. As a result of a legal settlement, all of California's medical-eligible children, ages one through five, will now be routinely screened annually for lead poisoning. Experts estimate that more than 50,000 cases will be detected in California because of the newly mandated tests. This will halt at an early stage a disease that leads to learning disabilities and life-threatening disorders.

32. Lead poisoning among young children, if not detected early, can lead to

    A. physical disabilities.
    B. mental disabilities.
    C. learning disabilities.
    D. death.

33. The mandate to screen all young children for lead poisoning is required of

    A. all young children in California.
    B. all children with learning disabilities.
    C. all medical-eligible children, ages one through five, in California.
    D. all school-age children in California.

34. According to findings, more cases of lead poisoning are found among

    A. urban children.
    B. inner-city, poor children.
    C. immigrant children.
    D. children in rural areas.

35. The implication of this mandate in California regarding lead poisoning is that

    A.   non-eligible children will not be screened.

    B.   children older than five years will not be screened.

    C.   middle-class children will not be screened.

    D.   thousands of young children in California will remain at risk
         for lead poisoning.

Read the passage below; then answer the three questions that follow.

The U.S. Postal Service issued a 50-cent stamp in Anchorage, Alaska, on October 12, 1991, to commemorate the 500th anniversary of the arrival of the Italian explorer Christopher Columbus in the New World. The stamp series showed the pre-Columbian voyages of discovery. The stamp depicts how America may have appeared to Asians crossing the Bering Strait.

36. Which of the following makes an appropriate title for the passage?

    A.   The Discovery of the Americas

    B.   The 500th Anniversary of the Discovery of America

    C.   The Significance of the Bering Strait

    D.   A New Commemorative U.S. Postal Stamp

37. The passage implies that

    A.   historical facts need to be verified.

    B.   Christopher Columbus was not the first to arrive in the New
         World.

    C.   Native Americans came from Asia.

    D.   history books need to be rewritten.

38. Which of the following would you consider as the most historically significant?

A. Asians crossed over the Bering Strait to the New World before Columbus came.

B. It has been 500 years since Christopher Columbus arrived in the New World.

C. A tribute to Christopher Columbus was held on October 12, 1991.

D. There were other voyages undertaken before Christopher Columbus'.

Read the passage below; then answer the four questions that follow.

Assignment: Research for a White Paper Proposing U.S. Foreign Policy

Imagine you are in charge (or assigned to) a foreign policy desk in the U.S. Department of State. First, select one of the following regions (descriptors are merely suggestions):

Western Europe—A Changing Alliance
Eastern Europe—Out from Behind the Iron Curtain
The Middle East—Still an Enigma
Africa—Rising Expectations in the Postwar Continent
South and Southeast Asia—Unrest in Far Away Places
The Far East—Alienation and Alliance
The Western Hemisphere—Neighbors; Pro and Con

After selecting one of the regions above, conduct research and prepare a White Paper for the area that will indicate:

1. a General Policy Statement toward the nations of that region;

2. a statement as to how World War II set the stage for that policy;

3. a summary of the major events since 1945 in that region which have affected U.S. foreign policy; and

4. a list of suggested problems and/or possibilities for near-future interactions of that region and the U.S.

39. In order to complete this assignment, it is necessary to

    A.   select a region and use the descriptor given with that region before conducting research.

    B.   select a region and conduct research to prepare the White Paper.

    C.   conduct research and choose a region in the world of your choice before writing the White Paper.

    D.   interview someone familiar with the history of the region before conducting research.

40. Which of the following is the most complete and accurate definition of the term *enigma* as used in the passage?

    A.   Riddle

    B.   Puzzle

    C.   Secret

    D.   Mystery

41. Which of the following is the most appropriate secondary school audience for the assignment?

    A.   Students in a World Geography class

    B.   Students in a World History class

    C.   Students in an Economics class

    D.   Students in an American Government class

42. Which of the following statements is not part of the directions provided?

    A.   The White Paper should include a General Policy Statement toward the nations of the region selected.

    B.   The White Paper should include one of the seven regions that are listed.

    C.   If the Middle East is chosen, the descriptor "Still an Enigma" must be used.

    D.   The White Paper must indicate a statement as to how World War II set the stage for the policy.

ANSWER KEY – READING PRACTICE TEST 2

Question	Answer	Objective	
1	A	0002	Identify a writer's purpose and point of view.
2	C	0006	Determine the meaning of words and phrases.
3	D	0004	Use critical reasoning skills to evaluate written material.
4	D	0002	Identify a writer's purpose and point of view.
5	B	0004	Use critical reasoning skills to evaluate written material.
6	B	0003	Analyze the relationship among ideas in written material.
7	C	0006	Determine the meaning of words and phrases.
8	D	0002	Identify a writer's purpose and point of view.
9	B	0004	Use critical reasoning skills to evaluate written material.
10	A	0003	Analyze the relationship among ideas in written material.
11	D	0004	Use critical reasoning skills to evaluate written material.
12	D	0006	Determine the meaning of words and phrases.
13	B	0002	Identify a writer's purpose and point of view.
14	A	0006	Determine the meaning of words and phrases.
15	B	0006	Determine the meaning of words and phrases.
16	C	0001	Understand the main idea and supporting details in written material.
17	D	0003	Analyze the relationship among ideas in written material.
18	B	0004	Use critical reasoning skills to evaluate written material.

Question	Answer	Objective	
19	A	**0001**	Understand the main idea and supporting details in written material.
20	B	**0001**	Understand the main idea and supporting details in written material.
21	C	**0004**	Use critical reasoning skills to evaluate written material.
22	C	**0001**	Understand the main idea and supporting details in written material.
23	B	**0004**	Use critical reasoning skills to evaluate written material.
24	C	**0003**	Analyze the relationship among ideas in written material.
25	C	**0003**	Analyze the relationship among ideas in written material.
26	C	**0001**	Understand the main idea and supporting details in written material.
27	B	**0003**	Analyze the relationship among ideas in written material.
28	C	**0004**	Use critical reasoning skills to evaluate written material.
29	D	**0004**	Use critical reasoning skills to evaluate written material.
30	B	**0001**	Understand the main idea and supporting details in written material.
31	B	**0004**	Use critical reasoning skills to evaluate written material.
32	D	**0003**	Analyze the relationship among ideas in written material.
33	C	**0004**	Use critical reasoning skills to evaluate written material.
34	B	**0004**	Use critical reasoning skills to evaluate written material.

Question	Answer	Objective	
35	D	0003	Analyze the relationship among ideas in written material.
36	D	0001	Understand the main idea and supporting details in written material.
37	B	0003	Analyze the relationship among ideas in written material.
38	A	0004	Use critical reasoning skills to evaluate written material.
39	B	0005	Use reading strategies to comprehend written materials.
40	B	0006	Determine the meaning of words and phrases.
41	D	0002	Identify a writer's purpose and point of view.
42	C	0005	Use reading strategies to comprehend written materials.

Practice Test 2, Part 1 Progress Chart

**0001 Understand the Main Idea and Supporting
Details in Written Material**   —/7

16	19	20	22	26	30	36

0002 Identify a Writer's Purpose and Point of View   —/5

1	4	8	13	41

**0003 Analyze the Relationship Among Ideas
in Written Material**   —/9

6	10	17	24	25	27	32	35	37

**0004 Use Critical Reasoning Skills to Evaluate
Written Material**   —/13

3	5	9	11	18	21	23	28	29

31	33	34	38

**0005 Use Reading Strategies to Comprehend
Written Materials**   —/2

39	42

0006 Determine the Meaning of Words and Phrases   —/6

2	7	12	14	15	40

Detailed Explanations for
Practice Test 2, Part 1: Reading

1. **A**

    Although audiences in choices B, C, and D may benefit from the information provided in the passage, the passage explicitly states that a greater understanding of the information in the passage should assist teachers—choice A.

2. **C**

    Each of the choices is a definition of variance. However, for this passage, choice C is the most appropriate.

3. **D**

    Although meaning is found in the components of each choice, the passage states that we should begin with students' meaning before moving to the commonalities of story meaning—choice D.

4. **D**

    As the passage presents information by various researchers on children's stories, the passage ends with an unanswered question that still needs to be addressed by reading researchers as provided in choice D.

5. **B**

    Although more information may be needed about story content and story structure as indicated in choices A, C, and D, the main question that remains to be answered is choice B.

6. **B**

    Each choice provides partially correct information about story content and story structure; choice B provides the most complete response.

7. **C**

    Each choice is a possible definition. However, choice C is most appropriate as there was an increased interest by researchers in these and other areas even though it has been an ongoing concern of some researchers.

8. **D**

    Choice B is not supported by the passage. Choices A and C go beyond the passage. The last sentence states, "The pattern … resulting in teachers prone to teach as they had been taught"—thus choice D.

9. **B**

    The other choices, A, C, and D, are not supported by the passage. Although the passage mentions that teacher education has reflected evolving attitudes about education, the attitudes are not spelled out—choice B.

10. **A**

    Only choice A has the correct sequence; the other sequences are incorrect.

11. **D**

    Choices A, B, and C are statements about education in general, teacher education, and teachers. Choice D's statement that teacher education has changed very little implies that this lack of change could be a source of dissatisfaction.

12. **D**

    Choices A, B, and C suggest rights either by heredity or supreme authority. The hyphenated term *liege-lord* connotes both entitled rights and power to command respect. Thus choice D, "master" (one who assumes authority and property rights through ability and power to control), best represents the hawk.

13. **B**

    Choices C and D are not supported by the passage. Choice A represents a possible conclusion, but choice B suggests real thought about the hawk.

14. **A**

    Each of the other choices contains a term that does not refer to human qualities. The other qualities may refer to the hawk, e.g., *perch*, or to the author of the passage, e.g., disdain.

15. **B**

    Choice D is incorrect because of definition. Choices A and C are possible definitions, but *feudal* most clearly denotes an association to the Middle Ages.

16. **C**

The question asks for the best synthesis of the passage and C is the best and most complete answer. Choices A, B, and D are not as complete. For example, A left out the duration of the conference, B left out both the duration of the conference and the number of the nations represented at the summit, and D left out the number of nations represented and support for Gorbachev's "new thinking."

17. **D**

Of the choices provided, D gives the most logical and sound implication of the passage. A falls short of the capabilities of Gorbachev's leadership; in B the "new thinking" referred to already had the support of the seven leaders at the summit; and C is a rather sweeping, unfair statement.

18. **B**

The mention of banking and energy does not rule out technical assistance in other fields, hence, B is the correct answer. Choice A limited the assistance to only the fields of banking and energy; in C the statement is only partly true—the U.S. is not alone in providing support; and in D technical assistance could likewise come from other nations outside of the seven.

19. **A**

The question asks for the main idea in the passage and A gives the best and complete main idea. Choices B and C are generalizations derived from the passage and D, while it is true and specific to the passage, is stated in the negative.

20. **B**

B gives the most specific consequence for California. The other choices, while all plausible or possible answers, do not get to the root of the issue specific to California.

21. **C**

Based on the passage read, the answer to this question is C—two things are mentioned that could affect California and these are federal funding and the number of congressional seats. While A and B are correct, they are incomplete. Choice D is a consequential generalization that is correct but lacks the preciseness of C.

22. **C**

    The question asks for the "message" conveyed in the passage. Choice C is the correct answer, as it gives a warning. In choice A, pesticides cannot necessarily be dangerous to all living things—some are good for the protection of plants, for example; in B, water can be contaminated by something other than pesticides; and the statement in choice D may be true, but it is certainly not the best answer.

23. **B**

    The train is definitely a freight train; hence, B is the correct answer. In A, if it were a passenger train, hundreds would have been killed; in C, according to the clues, the choices here don't apply; and in D, the answer used "special train" but could have appropriately used "freight train" instead.

24. **C**

    The question here asks for the most "serious problem" that could have come about; so, of all the choices, C provides the most serious problem resulting from the pesticide spill for Californians. Choices A, B, and D are not life-threatening; C is.

25. **C**

    C is the most logical and straightforward answer. C prioritizes which action should be taken first, and is therefore the correct answer. While the choices in A, B, and D are sound answers, they don't list the most urgent thing to do.

26. **C**

    The correct answer here is C because this choice synthesizes the key or main idea in the passage. The other choices, while partly true, don't give the main idea.

27. **B**

    Before World War II, during the depression years, one can easily presume that people were more practical or money minded; hence, Labor Day, as celebrated then, could mean the loss of a day's pay for working people. Thus, B is the correct answer. While choices A, C, and D are also possible answers, they don't get to the root of the issue.

28. **C**

    Explicitly given in the passage is C, the correct answer. Choices A, B, and D, while they may all be true and correct, are not what is precisely given in the passage.

29. **D**

   The gold content found in the volcanic ash from Mt. Pinatubo could easily stir or trigger a "gold rush." However, people are warned that the gold content found is not at a "commercial level." Hence, D is the correct answer. The other choices provided are all mere speculations.

30. **B**

   Choice B is the most appropriate answer—it also synthesizes the content of the reading passage; hence, it is the correct answer. Choice A is incorrect. Choices C and D are somewhat applicable as titles but do not really synthesize the main idea of the passage as choice B.

31. **B**

   If priorities have to be established to determine the most immediate research needed on the ash content from Mt. Pinatubo, choice B will have to be the most logical choice because there is already some data with which to work. Other research possibilities such as those in choices A, C, and D would have to come later.

32. **D**

   All the choices in this question are possible answers; however, since the question asks what lead poisoning, if not detected early, "can lead to," it calls for the ultimate consequence. Hence, D is the correct answer inasmuch as the passage states "life-threatening disorders" as among the possible consequences.

33. **C**

   The correct answer to this question is choice C—it gives the complete and precise category. Other choices are incomplete—A left out the age group and the medical eligibility; B is narrowed down and all-inclusive of "children with learning disabilities;" and choice D is incorrect.

34. **B**

   As indicated by figures in the passage, the correct answer is B. Other choices A, C, and D are obviously incorrect. This is an example of a question in which the incorrect choices are not possible answers. The correct answer is derived from the figures provided in the passage.

35. **D**

   The implications provided in choices A through D are correct. However, each of the implications for A through C is narrowed down to only one specific category of children—not any one is inclusive of all that needs to be addressed. Hence, D is the best answer because it addresses the thousands who will not be screened, which include those in choices A through C.

36. **D**

   A title is supposed to synthesize the main idea and D does. Choice A leaves out the main idea of a commemorative stamp; choice B is incorrect because it implies Columbus discovered the Americas; choice C is not the main idea of the passage.

37. **B**

   The underlying fact behind the passage is heavily implied; therefore, B is the correct answer. Choice A, while true, is a generalized implication, not addressing the specific issue; choice C is debatable; choice D, like A, is also a generalized implication.

38. **A**

   Of the choices given, A is the most historically significant, and, therefore, the correct answer. Choice B is significant but leaves out the fact that Columbus was not the first to arrive in the New World, the main point in the passage; choice C is a mere commemoration day; and choice D is not specific enough as an historically significant fact.

39. **B**

   B is the most appropriate choice. A is incorrect because the descriptors are only suggestions. Likewise, C is incorrect because the list of regions is given. There are no directions that state someone must be interviewed; hence, D is also not a correct answer.

40. **B**

   Although each definition appears appropriate, choices A, C, and D assume that a solution is known, or had been known at one time, and could be solved. Choice B suggests a situation that is intricate enough to perplex the mind. Choice B is the most appropriate for this passage, as one definition of *enigma* is "an inexplicable situation."

41. **D**

    Although choices A, B, and C may touch on such a topic, the roles and functions of governmental offices and departments are generally addressed in an American Government class. Thus, choice D is correct.

42. **C**

    C is not part of the directions. "Still an Enigma" is suggested, but not required. The other choices, A, B, and D are part of the directions.

Practice Test 2
Part 2: Mathematics

GACE Basic Skills

ANSWER SHEET
PRACTICE TEST 2, PART 2: MATHEMATICS

1 _____
2 _____
3 _____
4 _____
5 _____
6 _____
7 _____
8 _____
9 _____
10 _____
11 _____
12 _____

13 _____
14 _____
15 _____
16 _____
17 _____
18 _____
19 _____
20 _____
21 _____
22 _____
23 _____
24 _____

25 _____
26 _____
27 _____
28 _____
29 _____
30 _____
31 _____
32 _____
33 _____
34 _____
35 _____
36 _____

37 _____
38 _____
39 _____
40 _____
41 _____
42 _____
43 _____
44 _____
45 _____
46 _____
47 _____
48 _____

DEFINITIONS AND FORMULAS

Measurement

U.S. Standard Metric

Distance
1 inch = 2.54 centimeters
12 inches = 1 foot
3 feet = 1 yard
5280 feet = 1 mile
1 centimeter = 10 millimeters
1 meter = 100 centimeters
1 kilometer = 1000 meters

Volume (liquid)
1 quart = 32 ounces
1 quart ≈ 0.95 liters
1 gallon = 4 quarts
1 liter = 1000 milliliters
1 cubic centimeter = 1 milliliter

Mass
1 pound = 16 ounces
1 ton = 2000 pounds
2.2 pounds ≈ 1 kilogram
1 gram = 1000 milligrams
1 kilogram = 1000 grams

Time
1 minute = 60 seconds
1 hour = 60 minutes
1 day = 24 hours
1 year = 365 days
1 year = 52 weeks

Definitions
=	equal to
>	greater than
<	less than
≥	greater than or equal to
≤	less than or equal to
π	≈ 3.14
$\angle$	angle
$m\angle$	measure of angle
∟	right angle
$\overline{AB}$	line segment
AB	length of line segment AB
$\angle ABC$	angle with vertex B formed by rays BA and BC

Formulas

Square
Area = s^2
Perimeter = $4s$

Rectangle
Area = bw
Perimeter = $2b + 2w$

Triangle
Area = $\frac{1}{2}bh$
Sum of the interior angles = 180°

Right triangle
Pythagorean formula: $c^2 = a^2 + b^2$

Circle
Area = πr^2
Circumference = $2\pi r$
Diameter = $2r$

Right cylinder
Surface area = $2\pi rh + 2\pi r^2$
Volume = $\pi r^2 h$

Cube
Surface area = $6s^2$
Volume = s^3

Rectangular solid
Surface area = $2bw + 2bh + 2wh$
Volume = bwh

PART 2:   **Mathematics**
48 questions

1. Multiply $\frac{2}{5}$ by $\frac{3}{4}$. Show your answer in simplified (reduced) form.

    A. $\frac{5}{9}$

    B. $\frac{6}{20}$

    C. $\frac{5}{20}$

    D. $\frac{3}{10}$

2. Add $3\frac{2}{3}$ and $1\frac{1}{2}$. Show your answer in simplified (reduced) form.

    A. $5\frac{1}{6}$

    B. $4\frac{2}{5}$

    C. $4\frac{3}{5}$

    D. $4\frac{7}{6}$

3. Subtract $1\frac{2}{5}$ from $6\frac{1}{3}$.

    A. $4\frac{5}{15}$

    B. $5\frac{5}{15}$

C. $4\frac{14}{15}$

D. $4\frac{1}{3}$

4. Divide 6 by $\frac{3}{5}$.

A. $\frac{2}{5}$

B. $\frac{3}{5}$

C. 10

D. $3\frac{3}{5}$

5. Perform the indicated operation.

$$(-25) - 7$$

A. −32

B. 32

C. −18

D. 18

6. Multiply 1.35 by 0.06.

A. 0.81

B. 0.081

C. 8.1

D. 0.0081

7. What percentage of 120 is 36?

A. 24%

B. 30%

C. 36%

D. 40%

8. Simplify to a single term in scientific notation.

$$(3 \times 10^4) \times (7 \times 10^5)$$

   A. 21×10^{20}
   B. 21×10^9
   C. 2.1×10^9
   D. 2.1×10^{10}

9. Simplify: $7 \times 2 + \dfrac{4}{4}$

   A. 10
   B. 14
   C. 15
   D. 21

10. Select the number that is missing in the problem below.

$$348 + \underline{\hspace{1.5cm}} = 1{,}961$$

   A. 1613
   B. 1623
   C. 1627
   D. 2309

11. Williams Clothing Store sold sweaters for $70 at the beginning of September. In October, the price of the sweaters was raised by 10%. In December, the sweaters were placed on sale for 25% off. What was the price of the sweaters in December?

   A. $59.50
   B. $57.75
   C. $55.00
   D. $52.50

12. Three pounds of peanuts cost $4.65. What would five pounds cost (at the same price per pound)?

   A. $5.45

   B. $6.20

   C. $7.75

   D. $9.30

13. At 11:00 A.M., the temperature was 86° in San Francisco and was decreasing at a rate of 4 degrees per hour. At the same time, the temperature was 56° in Saint Louis and was increasing at the rate of 2 degrees per hour. At what time (San Francisco time) will the temperatures be the same?

   A. 3:00 P.M.

   B. 4:00 P.M.

   C. 5:00 P.M.

   D. The temperatures don't reach the same point on that day.

14. Steven began working on a project at 8:00 A.M. He worked until 12:30 P.M. Steven is paid $9.50 per hour for his work. How much did he make working on this project?

   A. $36.00

   B. $38.00

   C. $42.75

   D. $47.50

15. Convert: 123 ml = _____ liters

   A. 0.0123 l

   B. 0.123 l

   C. 1.23 l

   D. 12.3 l

16. Convert: 45.6 m = _____ centimeters

   A. 456 cm

   B. 4,560 cm

   C. 45,600 cm

   D. 456,000 cm

17. Convert: 64 fluid ounces = _____ pints

    A.   4

    B.   8

    C.   12

    D.   16

18. Convert: 12000 pounds = _____ tons

    A.   2

    B.   3

    C.   4

    D.   6

19. What is the area of a triangle that has a base length of 12 cm and a height of 6 cm?

    A.   72 square centimeters

    B.   36 square centimeters

    C.   18 square centimeters

    D.   60 square centimeters

20. What is the length of the base of a triangle with height 18 cm and an area measure of 252 square centimeters?

    A.   14 cm

    B.   20 cm

    C.   24 cm

    D.   28 cm

21. A rectangle is 5 inches wide. The area of the rectangle is 30 square inches. What is the perimeter of the rectangle?

    A.   30 inches

    B.   22 inches

    C.   20 inches

    D.   There is not enough information given to determine the perimeter.

22. Use the figure below to answer the question.

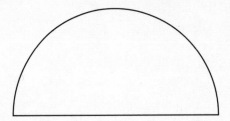

Which formula can be used to find the area of the figure? (Assume the curve is *half* of a circle.)

A. $A = \pi r$

B. $A = 2\pi r^2$

C. $A = \pi r^2$

D. $A = \dfrac{\pi r^2}{2}$

23. What is the approximate volume of the following cylinder?

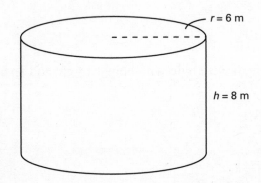

A. 904 cm^3

B. 301 cm^3

C. 151 cm^3

D. 452 cm^3

24. Use the Pythagorean theorem to answer this question: Which answer comes closest to the actual length of side *x* in the triangle below?

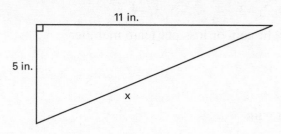

A.   14 in.

B.   12 in.

C.   11 in.

D.   13 in.

25. Use the figures to answer the question that follows.

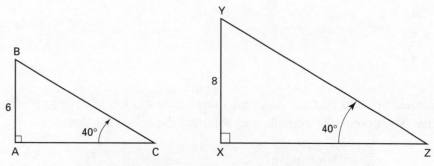

Which of the following statements about the two triangles are true?

    I.   The triangles are similar.
    II.   The triangles are congruent.
    III.   The measures of angles ABC and XYZ are the same.
    IV.   The lengths of sides BC and YZ are the same.

A.   I and III only

B.   I and IV only

C.   II and III only

D.   II and IV only

26. Mr. Johnson coaches the school's wrestling team. During the month of January, the 10 members of the team recorded the following weight gains and losses (in pounds):

    $$-3, -5, 0, 2, -2, -4, -2, -5, 3, -4$$

    What was the average weight gain or loss per team member?

    A. Gain of 2 pounds

    B. Gain of 1 pound

    C. There was no loss or gain

    D. Loss of 2 pounds

27. At a neighborhood pond, you measure the pH level of the water each day for 10 days. The measurements were:

    $$7.1, 6.9, 6.7, 6.5, 6.3, 6.9, 6.8, 6.5, 6.3, 6.1$$

    What is the median pH level of the water?

    A. 6.6

    B. 6.4

    C. 6.5

    D. 6.2

28. Olivia took a poll to find out how many days each week that college students exercise. She asked 300 students and obtained the following data.

Number of Exercise Days	Number of Respondents
0	18
1	34
2	48
3	65
4	84
5	35
6	13
7	3

If Olivia asked another student how many days each week he or she exercises, what is the probability that the answer will be four or more days?

A.   25%

B.   35%

C.   45%

D.   50%

29.   Erica's change purse has 28 quarters, 13 dimes, 21 nickels, and 18 pennies. When she picked up her purse, a single coin fell out. What is the likelihood that the coin was a quarter?

A.   30%

B.   35%

C.   28%

D.   40%

30.   Use the table below to answer the question that follows.

Minutes Spent in Instruction

	Monday	Tuesday	Wednesday	Thursday	Friday
Reading	45	50	50	45	30
Math	35	50	40	45	25
Science	30	25	35	20	25
Social Studies	20	30	25	40	40

Which of the following is true?

A.   The largest variation in time spent teaching is in math.

B.   Exactly twice as much time is spent in teaching reading as in teaching social studies.

C.   The greatest increase in time spent teaching occurred from Tuesday to Wednesday in science.

D.   The greatest decrease in time spent teaching occurred from Thursday to Friday in reading.

31. The following graph shows the distribution of test scores in Ms. Alvarez's class.

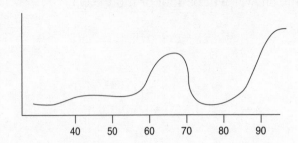

Which of the following statements do you know to be true?

    I.   The majority of students scored higher than 60.
    II.   The test was a fair measure of ability.
    III. The mean score is probably higher than the median.
    IV. The test divided the class into distinct groups.

A.   I and II only

B.   I and IV only

C.   I, III, and IV only

D.   IV only

32. According to the graph below, which one of the following statements is true?

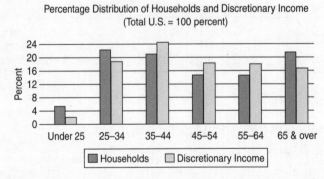

A.   Middle-age households tend to have greater discretionary income.

B.   The youngest have the most discretionary income.

C.   The oldest have the most discretionary income.

D.   The older one gets, the less discretionary income one has.

33. According to the graph, the profit for Kay's Computers in 2006 was what percent increase over the profit in 2003?

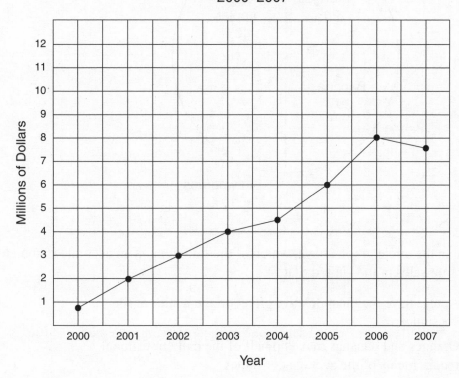

Profit for Kay's Computers
2000–2007

A.   50%

B.   100%

C.   150%

D.   200%

34.

Fruit Sales in the United States

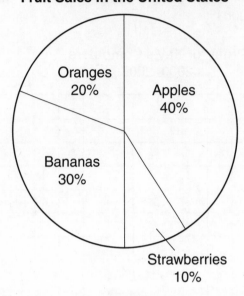

Based on the circle graph above, which of the following is an accurate statement about fruit sales in the United States?

A.   Apples have the most positive effect on the health of the consumer.

B.   Oranges and bananas make up half of the daily nutritional requirements of the average consumer.

C.   More apples are sold than any other fruit.

D.   Without the sales of oranges, the fruit industry would not be profitable.

35. The members of the Striders walking team participated in a 5K Fun Run. The scatter plot below represents the relationship between the age of the participants and their race completion times. Which statement best describes this relationship?

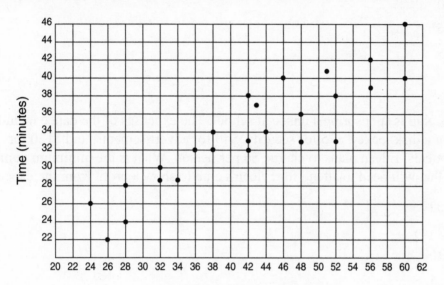

Age of Participants (years)

A. There appears to be no relationship between the participants' age and race completion time.

B. There appears to be a negative relationship between age and race completion time.

C. There appears to be a positive relationship between age and race completion time.

D. There is no way to accurately describe the relationship between the two variables using the diagram given.

36. What is the next number in this sequence?

1, 5, 2, 6, _____

A. 3

B. 4

C. 7

D. 8

37. What is the next number in this sequence?

$$100, 81, 64, 49, \underline{\hspace{1cm}}$$

A. 40

B. 36

C. 25

D. 20

38. Eileen's club is sponsoring a dance at school. The expenses of the dance include $600 for a disk jockey, $75 for security, $40 for advertisements, and $120 for refreshments. Eileen plans to charge $6 per person. What is the minimum number of people that will need to attend for Eileen's club to show a profit from the dance?

A. 100

B. 125

C. 140

D. 155

39. Kay bought $1\frac{3}{4}$ pounds of apples, $2\frac{1}{2}$ pounds of bananas, and $3\frac{2}{5}$ pounds of oranges. How much fruit did she buy in all?

A. $6\frac{1}{2}$ pounds

B. $6\frac{6}{11}$ pounds

C. $7\frac{1}{10}$ pounds

D. $7\frac{13}{20}$ pounds

40. Jared obtained a loan in the amount of $1200 from a local bank. At the end of a year, he will pay back all of the loan, plus interest, at the rate of 9.25%. How much will he owe at the end of a year?

A. $1209.25

B. $1292.50

C. $1311.00

D. $1320.00

41. Michael works for a newpaper that has 60,000 subscriptions: 31,500 for the morning paper, 10,000 for the evening paper, and 18,500 for the Sunday paper. About what percentage of the subscriptions are for the morning paper?

    A. 50%

    B. 53%

    C. 60%

    D. 62%

42. There are 6 people who attend a meeting. Everyone shakes hands with all of the other attendees. How many handshakes is that in all?

    A. 36

    B. 30

    C. 15

    D. 384

43. Evaluate the expression when $n = 4$.

    $$\frac{1}{4}\,(n \times 8)$$

    A. 2

    B. 8

    C. 14

    D. 16

44. Evaluate the following expression using the following values: $x = 3$, $y = 4$, and $z = 6$.

    $$4y(x + y + z + 3)$$

    A. 128

    B. 200

    C. 256

    D. 272

45. Simplify: $(-2b^5)(6a^2)(2a)$

    A. $24a^2b^5$

    B. $-25a^2b^5$

    C. $-24a^3b^5$

    D. $6a^3b^5$

46. Find the sum of $3c^2 + 12c - 4$ and $6c^2 + 11c - 7$.

    A. $9c^2 - c + 11$

    B. $9c^2 + 23c + 3$

    C. $9c^2 + 23c - 11$

    D. $3c^2 + 23c - 11$

47. Solve the following inequality:

    $$13n + 6 \leq 97$$

    A. $n \geq 7$

    B. $n \leq 7$

    C. $n \geq 6$

    D. $n \leq 5$

48. Amelia, Jackie, Carla, and Kim are in a leadership club at State University. One is majoring in education, one is majoring in English, one is majoring in business, and one is majoring in theater. Amelia and Jackie have an 8:00 class with the education major. Carla and Kim commute with the theater major. Jackie eats lunch with the theater major.

    Who is majoring in theater?

    A.   Amelia

    B.   Carla

    C.   Kim

    D.   It is impossible to determine the theater major with the information provided.

ANSWER KEY – MATHEMATICS PRACTICE TEST 2

Question	Answer	Objective	
1	D	0007	Understand number properties and number operations.
2	A	0007	Understand number properties and number operations.
3	C	0007	Understand number properties and number operations.
4	C	0007	Understand number properties and number operations.
5	A	0007	Understand number properties and number operations.
6	B	0007	Understand number properties and number operations.
7	B	0007	Understand number properties and number operations.
8	D	0007	Understand number properties and number operations.
9	C	0007	Understand number properties and number operations.
10	A	0007	Understand number properties and number operations.
11	B	0010	Understand problem-solving principles and techniques.
12	C	0010	Understand problem-solving principles and techniques.
13	B	0010	Understand problem-solving principles and techniques.
14	C	0010	Understand problem-solving principles and techniques.

Question	Answer	Objective	
15	B	0008	Understand measurement concepts and principles of geometry.
16	B	0008	Understand measurement concepts and principles of geometry.
17	A	0008	Understand measurement concepts and principles of geometry.
18	D	0008	Understand measurement concepts and principles of geometry.
19	B	0008	Understand measurement concepts and principles of geometry.
20	D	0008	Understand measurement concepts and principles of geometry.
21	B	0008	Understand measurement concepts and principles of geometry.
22	D	0008	Understand measurement concepts and principles of geometry.
23	A	0008	Understand measurement concepts and principles of geometry.
24	B	0008	Understand measurement concepts and principles of geometry.
25	A	0008	Understand measurement concepts and principles of geometry.
26	D	0010	Understand problem-solving principles and techniques.
27	A	0009	Understand statistical concepts and data analysis and interpretation.
28	C	0009	Understand statistical concepts and data analysis and interpretation.

Question	Answer	Objective	
29	B	0009	Understand statistical concepts and data analysis and interpretation.
30	A	0009	Understand statistical concepts and data analysis and interpretation.
31	B	0009	Understand statistical concepts and data analysis and interpretation.
32	A	0009	Understand statistical concepts and data analysis and interpretation.
33	B	0009	Understand statistical concepts and data analysis and interpretation.
34	C	0009	Understand statistical concepts and data analysis and interpretation.
35	C	0009	Understand statistical concepts and data analysis and interpretation.
36	A	0007	Understand number properties and number operations.
37	B	0007	Understand number properties and number operations.
38	C	0010	Understand problem-solving principles and techniques.
39	D	0010	Understand problem-solving principles and techniques.
40	C	0010	Understand problem-solving principles and techniques.
41	B	0010	Understand problem-solving principles and techniques.
42	C	0010	Understand problem-solving principles and techniques.

Question	Answer	Objective	
43	**B**	0007	Understand number properties and number operations.
44	**C**	0007	Understand number properties and number operations.
45	**C**	0007	Understand number properties and number operations.
46	**C**	0007	Understand number properties and number operations.
47	**B**	0007	Understand number properties and number operations.
48	**A**	0010	Understand problem-solving principles and techniques.

Practice Test 2, Part 2 Progress Chart

**0007   Understand Number Properties and Number
Operations**   —/17

1	2	3	4	5	6	7	8	9	10

36	37	43	44	45	46	47

**0008   Understand Measurement Concepts and
Principles of Geometry**   —/11

15	16	17	18	19	20	21	22	23	24	25

**0009   Understand Statistical Concepts and Data
Analysis and Interpretation**   —/9

27	28	29	30	31	32	33	34	35

**0010   Understand Problem-Solving Principles
and Techniques**   —/11

11	12	13	14	26	38	39	40	41	42	48

Detailed Explanations for
Practice Test 2, Part 2: Mathematics

1. **D**

   The traditional approach to multiplying simple fractions (those between 0 and 1) is to first multiply the numerators together and then multiply the denominators together to find the product. In this case, $\frac{2}{5} \times \frac{3}{4} = \frac{6}{20}$. Written in simplified form, $\frac{6}{20} = \frac{3}{10}$.

2. **A**

   To add mixed numbers, first address the fractions. To add $\frac{2}{3}$ and $\frac{1}{2}$, find a common denominator, which in this case is 6. Equivalent fractions for $\frac{2}{3}$ and $\frac{1}{2}$ with the denominator of 6 are $\frac{4}{6}$ and $\frac{3}{6}$, respectively. Add the two fractions together to reach $\frac{7}{6}$. Simplified, $\frac{7}{6}$ equals $1\frac{1}{6}$. Add the one to the other whole numbers (therefore, 1 + 3 + 1) to reach 5. The final, simplified answer is $5\frac{1}{6}$, answer A.

3. **C**

   When subtracting mixed numbers, the first step is to subtract the fractions (in this case, $\frac{1}{3} - \frac{2}{5}$). Because the denominators are different, equivalent fractions with a common denominator must be obtained. The least common denominator of these fractions is 15, so $\frac{1}{3}$ converts to $\frac{5}{15}$ (making the top number $\frac{6}{15}$) and $\frac{2}{5}$ converts to $\frac{6}{15}$ (making the bottom number $1\frac{6}{15}$). It is impossible to subtract $\frac{6}{15}$ from $\frac{5}{15}$, so we must rename the top number by "borrowing" one whole from the 6, and adding $\frac{15}{15}$ to the fraction. This results in the problem now reading $5\frac{20}{15} - 1\frac{6}{15}$. We are able to easily subtract now, arriving at the answer of $4\frac{14}{15}$.

4. **C**

When dividing fractions, the traditional algorithm involves inverting, or "flipping," the second fraction and multiplying. Therefore, the algorithm would read $6 \times \dfrac{5}{3}$. It is easier to think of 6 as $\dfrac{6}{1}$, so that you may multiply the numerators (6 × 5) and then the denominators (1 × 3). The answer, therefore, is $\dfrac{30}{3}$, which, when simplified, is 10.

5. **A**

To subtract a negative number, think first about what subtraction looks like on a number line. When we subtract on a number line, we move to the left. Beginning at –25 and moving left (in the negative direction) 7 results in the answer of –32.

6. **B**

When multiplying decimals, set up the problem vertically, aligned on the right, then multiply regularly.

$$
\begin{array}{r}
1.35 \\
\times\,.06 \\
\hline
810 \\
+0000 \\
\hline
.0810
\end{array}
$$

Count the number of digits to the right of the decimal in the original problem (in this case, 4 digits are to the right). Beginning at the far right of the answer, move the decimal point so that there will be 4 digits to the right of the decimal, making the answer .0810, which is equal to 0.081 (answer choice B).

7. **B**

To solve this problem, you must set up an equation. The easiest way to do so is to write the equation as it is read: What percentage $\left(\dfrac{n}{100}\right)$ of 120 (× 120) is 36 (=36)?

$$\frac{x}{100} \times 120 = 36$$

Multiply both sides by 100 to eliminate the fraction: $100\left(\dfrac{n}{100}\right) \times 120 = 36 \times 100$

Simplify: $n \times 120 = 3600$

$120n = 3600$

Divide both sides by 120: $n = 30$

Therefore, 30% of 120 = 36, answer B.

8. **D**

To solve this problem in scientific notation, simply multiply the first two digits inside each group of parentheses (3 × 7 = 21). To multiply the 10's notations, simply add the exponents ($10^4 \times 10^5 = 10^9$). Thus far, the solution reads: 21×10^9. However, in scientific notation, the initial factor must be greater than zero and less than ten. Therefore, we change the 21 to 2.1, and increase the power of ten in the second factor by one. 21 changes to 2.1 and 10^9 changes to 10^{10}. The simplified answer to this problem, therefore, is 2.1×10^{10}.

9. **C**

The order of operations is used to solve this problem. Multiplication comes before addition, so the first step is to multiply 7 × 2, which equals 14. Then add $\dfrac{4}{4}$ (or 1), which brings the answer to 15.

10. **A**

This problem simply requires that you understand that to find a missing number in an addition sentence, you simply subtract the smaller from the larger of the two given numbers. In this case, 1,961 − 348 equals 1,613.

11. **B**

First, find the cost of the sweaters when the price was increased by 10% ($70.00 × 0.10 = $7.00 increase). Therefore, after the price increase, sweaters cost $77.00. Then, to find the sale price, first find the amount that 25% off would be by multiplying $77.00 by 0.25, which is $19.25. Subtract $19.25 from $77.00, which equals $57.75, answer B.

12. **C**

　　To solve this problem, first find the cost of 1 pound of peanuts. The problem says that 3 pounds of peanuts cost $4.65. Therefore, to find the cost of one pound, divide $4.65 by 3, which equals $1.55 per pound. To find the cost of five pounds, then, multiply $1.55 × 5, which equals $7.75.

13. **B**

　　The easiest way to solve this problem is to make a chart showing the temperature changes by the hour. The first row shows the hourly temperature change for San Francisco (a decrease of 4° per hour) and the second row shows the hourly temperature change for St. Louis (an increase of 2° per hour). The temperatures are the same at 4:00 P.M., thus answer B.

City	11:00 A.M.	12:00 noon	1:00 P.M.	2:00 P.M.	3:00 P.M.	4:00 P.M.
San Francisco	86°	82°	78°	74°	70°	66°
St. Louis	56°	58°	60°	62°	64°	66°

14. **C**

　　To solve this problem, first determine the number of hours that Steven worked, which is $4\frac{1}{2}$ (or 4.5). Then, multiply his time (4.5) by his rate of pay per hour ($9.50) to find that for this project, he earned $42.75.

15. **B**

　　To solve this problem, consider that:　1 liter = 1000 milliliters.

　　The easiest way to solve this problem is to think in terms of a ratio:

$$\frac{123 \text{ milliliters}}{1000 \text{ milliliters}} = \frac{n \text{ liters}}{1}$$

　Cross multiply to set up the equation:　$123 = 1000n$

$$\frac{123}{1000} = \frac{1000n}{1000}$$　Divide both sides by 1000.

$n = 0.123$

16. **B**

   Because there are 100 centimeters in 1 meter, simply multiply 100 by the number of meters given (in this case, 45.6) to obtain the answer of 4,560 cm.

17. **A**

   In capacity conversions, 1 pint equals 16 ounces. To find how many pints are in 64 ounces, divide 64 ounces by the number of ounces in a pint (16), which results in the answer of 4 pints.

18. **D**

   In weight conversions, 1 ton equals 2000 pounds. Therefore, to find how many tons equal 12,000 pounds, divide 12,000 pounds by the number of pounds in a ton (2000) to obtain the answer of 6 tons.

19. **B**

   The formula used for finding the area of a triangle is $\frac{1}{2} \times$ base $\times$ height. In this case:

   $$\frac{1}{2} \times (12 \times 6)$$

   $$\frac{1}{2} \times 72 = 36$$

   Note that area is always reported in square units.

20. **D**

   To solve this problem, recall the formula used for finding the area of a triangle $\left(\frac{1}{2} \times \text{base} \times \text{height} \right)$. In the given problem, the base (b) is unknown.

   Substitute the numbers that you know. $\qquad \frac{1}{2}(b \times 18) = 252$

   Multiply both sides by 2 to eliminate the fraction. $\qquad (2)\frac{1}{2}(b \times 18) = 252\,(2)$

   $$b \times 18 = 504$$

   Divide both sides by 18 to determine the base (b). $\qquad b = 28$

21. **B**

    To find the perimeter of any figure, you must know the length of each side. In this case, the width of the rectangle is given (5 inches). To find the perimeter, we must find the length. The area of the rectangle is 30 square inches.

Set up an equation using the area formula.	A = length × width
In this case:	30 = length × 5
Divide both sides by 5.	6 = length

    Now we know the dimensions of the rectangle. Two sides are length, and two sides are width; therefore, $6 + 6 + 5 + 5 = 22$ inches, answer B.

22. **D**

    The formula for finding the area of any circle is pi (3.14) times the length of the radius times itself. In thise case, you need to take half of pi $\times r^2$; hence, the answer D.

23. **A**

    The formula for finding the volume of a cylinder is: $V = \text{pi } (r^2) \times h$.

    This means that the volume is equal to pi (about 3.14) times the measure of the radius squared times the height of the cylinder. In this case, that is:

    $$3.14 \times 6^2 \times 8 \quad \text{or} \quad 3.14 \times 36 \times 8$$

    or about 904. (Note that the final answer is given in cubic centimeters.)

24. **B**

    Use the Pythagorean theorem to compute the length of any side of any right triangle, as long as you know the lengths of the other two sides. Here is the theorem:

    For any right triangle with side lengths of a, b, and c, and where the length of the hypotenuse (the longest side, and the one opposite the right angle) equals $a^2 + b^2 = c^2$.

    Substituting the given values for a and b for problem 24:

    $$11^2 + 5^2 = c^2$$

    or

    $$121 + 25 = c^2$$

    or

    $$146 = c^2$$

    To complete the work, take the square root of 146, which is approximately 12.

25. **A**

> If you know the measure of two angles of any triangle, you can calculate the measure of the third angle. (The sum of the three angles is always 180°.) So the measure of the third angle in both of the triangles is 50°, and statement III is correct.
>
> If two triangles have the same degree measures (as established above), then they are similar triangles (which means they have the same shape). Statement I is therefore correct.
>
> Triangles are congruent only if they are exactly the same shape and size. One triangle is larger than the other, so statement II is false.
>
> Because the second triangle is larger than the first, and they are the same shape, there is no way that sides BC and YZ could be the same length. Therefore, statement IV is false.

26. **D**

> To find the average (mean) of a set of values, first add them together. In this case, the negative and positive integers should be added together separately. Those two sums are −25 and 5. (The 0 may be ignored, since it does not affect either sum.) Then −25 and 5 should be added together for a sum of −20.
>
> To complete the work, the sum of −20 must be divided by the number of values (10), giving −2, or a weight *loss* of 2 pounds.

27. **A**

> To find the median of a set of data, list the values from smallest to largest. In this case, the list would be:
>
> 6.1, 6.3, 6.3, 6.5, 6.5, 6.7, 6.8, 6.9, 6.9, 7.1
>
> The two middle values are 6.5 and 6.7. To find the median, take the average of those two values; hence, the answer is 6.6.

28. **C**

> To solve this problem, you must find the total number of students who responded "4 days or more," which is 135 of the 300. To find the percentage, divide 135 by 300, which equals .45 or 45%. If another student is asked, there is a 45% chance that he or she will answer 4 days or more.

29. **B**

> To solve this problem, find the total number of coins in Erica's purse, which is 80. The percentage of quarters in her purse is 28/80 or .35. Therefore, if one coin falls from her purse, the likelihood it will be a quarter is 35%.

30. **A**

> Consider statement A: The range (which is the amount of variation in a data set) of time spent teaching mathematics is from 25 minutes on Friday to 50 minutes on Tuesday, which is a range of 25 minutes. The range of time spent for reading instruction is 20 minutes, for science instruction is 15 minutes, and for social studies instruction is 20 minutes. Therefore, statement A is true.

> Statement B says that twice as much time is spent teaching reading as social studies. The total time for teaching reading is 220 minutes, and the total time for social studies instruction is 155 minutes, which is not exactly half of 220. Therefore, statement B is false.

> Statement C says that the greatest increase in time spent teaching occurred from Tuesday to Wednesday in science. That increase in time was 10 minutes, which is less than the increase in math instruction between Monday and Tuesday. Therefore, statement C is false.

> Statement D says that the greatest decrease in time spent teaching occurred from Thursday to Friday in reading. This decrease was 15 minutes, while the decrease in math instruction on those days was 20 minutes. Therefore, statement D is false.

31. **B**

> Just from looking at the graph, it is clear that most of the space under the curve is past the 60 mark on the x-axis. Answer D is eliminated because it doesn't include statement I.

> Statement II can't be answered by what the graph shows. It appears possible that certain questions were too hard for many in the class and that there weren't enough questions to differentiate B students from C students, but perhaps the class performed exactly as it should have, given the students' ability and Ms. Alvarez's teaching. The distribution can give a teacher many clues about the test, the students, and herself, but by itself it tells us nothing about the fairness of the test. Thus, answer A can be eliminated.

> Statement III is also false; in left-skewed distributions such as this one, the median is higher than the mean. This is true because the mean is lowered by the lowest scores while the median is relatively unaffected by them.

> Statement IV is true; one fairly large group has scored in the high 80s and 90s and another discernible group in the low to mid-60s, whereas a few students fall outside these two groups. Thus, the answer has to be B.

32. **A**

Graph reading and interpretation is the primary focus of this question. Choice B is obviously wrong because the bar representing the discretionary income of the youngest households ("Under 25") is the shortest bar on the chart, indicating that this group has the least discretionary income. Choices C and D are also incorrect. The oldest group has less discretionary income than those between 25 and 65, but more than those under 25.

33. **B**

This graph shows that the profit in 2003 was $4 million and the profit in 2006 was $8 million. Because the profit in 2006 is exactly double the profit of 2003, that shows that the company made 100% additional profit, therefore, answer B.

34. **C**

The title of the graph indicates that the graph shows fruit sales. Therefore, any question that is not specifically about fruit sales may be eliminated. Both A and B are about health and nutrition, so they may be eliminated. We do not know how the sales of oranges affect profits, so we can eliminate D. We can see that the largest section (40%) of the circle graph represents apples, so C is the correct answer.

35. **C**

From the graph, we can see that as age increases, so does the race completion time. Therefore, there is a positive relationship, which rules out A and B. The problem with D is that any scatter plot shows either a positive relationship, a negative relationship, or no relationship. No relationship between the variables is still an accurate way to describe variables in a scatter plot graph. Therefore, the correct answer is C.

36. **A**

In this sequence, the pattern is plus 4, minus 3. ($1 + 4 = 5$; $5 - 3 = 2$; $2 + 4 = 6$) So, the next part of the pattern is minus 3; therefore, $6 - 3 = 3$.

37. **B**

In this sequence, the pattern is perfect squares, decreasing. The first number is 100 or 10^2, the second number is 81 or 9^2, the third number is 64 or 8^2, the fourth number is 49 or 7^2. Following this pattern, the next number would be 6^2, or 36.

38. **C**

    To solve this problem, first find the total amount of expenses ($600 + 75 + 40 + 120), which equals $835. If each person is going to pay $6 to enter the dance, divide $835 by $6 to determine how many people need to attend for the club to make that amount.

    $$\$835 \div \$6 = 139.1666$$

    Rounded up, this means that 140 people must attend the dance for Eileen's club to make a profit. ($140 \times \$6 = \$840$, which would be a profit of $5.)

39. **D**

    To find out how many total pounds were purchased, add all of the values together. When adding mixed numbers, address the fractions first. In this problem, you must find a common denominator for $\frac{3}{4}$, $\frac{1}{2}$, and $\frac{2}{5}$. The least common denominator of those fractions is 20.

    Change the given fractions to equivalent fractions with a denominator of 20. $\quad \frac{3}{4} = \frac{15}{20} \quad \frac{1}{2} = \frac{10}{20} \quad \frac{2}{5} = \frac{8}{20}$

    Add the fractions together. $\quad \frac{15}{20} + \frac{10}{20} + \frac{8}{20} = \frac{33}{20}$

    $\frac{33}{20}$ changes to the mixed number $1\frac{13}{20}$.

    Add the 1 from the mixed number to the other whole number in the problem (1, 2, and 3) to reach the whole number of 7. Combine that with the fraction to obtain the answer of $7\frac{13}{20}$.

40. **C**

To find the amount of interest that will be due with Jared's loan, multiply the amount of the loan ($1200) by the amount of interest (it is easiest if you change the 9.25% to a decimal – 0.0925).

$$\$1200 \times 0.0925 = \$111$$

Add the amount of interest ($111) to the principal amount of the loan ($1200) to get the total amount due of $1311.

41. **B**

To find the percentage of subscriptions that are for the morning paper, make a fraction that shows the number of morning paper subscriptions over the total subscriptions:

$\dfrac{31,500}{60,000}$ Divide 31,500 by 60,000 = 0.525, which is 52.5%. The closest answer to this number is answer B, 53%.

42. **C**

The easiest way to solve this problem is to develop a chart or a diagram. In chart form, the problem looks like this:

Shakes hands with	Person 1	Person 2	Person 3	Person 4	Person 5	Person 6
Person 1	Can't shake with himself	X	X	X	X	X
Person 2	Already shaken with person 1	Can't shake with himself	X	X	X	X
Person 3	Already shaken with person 1	Already shaken with person 2	Can't shake with himself	X	X	X
Person 4	Already shaken with person 1	Already shaken with person 2	Already shaken with person 3	Can't shake with himself	X	X
Person 5	Already shaken with person 1	Already shaken with person 2	Already shaken with person 3	Already shaken with person 4	Can't shake with himself	X
Person 6	Already shaken hands with everyone else.					

Count the X's to show 15 total handshakes.

43. **B**

To solve this problem, apply the order of operations and substitute 4 for n.

$$\frac{1}{4}(4 \times 8) = \frac{1}{4}(32) = 8$$

44. **C**

To solve this problem, apply the order of operations and substitute the given values.

$$4(4)\,(3+4+6+3) = 16\,(16)$$
$$= 256$$

Therefore, answer C is correct.

45. **C**

$$(-2b^5)(6a^2)(2a)$$

To simplify this expression, first multiply the whole numbers ($-2 \times 6 \times 2$) to get -24. Then combine like terms ($a^2 \times a = a^3$). There is only one b term (b^5). Put the constant and variables together, which results in the answer $-24a^3b^5$.

46. **C**

To add $3c^2 + 12c - 4$ and $6c^2 + 11c - 7$, simply combine the two expressions into one, keeping the signs as they are. Note: if you were subtracting the second expression, you would need to change the signs for each variable and constant.

Therefore: $3c^2 + 12c - 4 + 6c^2 + 11c - 7$

Combine like terms: $3c^2 + 6c^2 = 9c^2$
$$12c + 11c = 23c$$
$$-4 + (-7) = -11$$

Put the expressions together to get the answer of $9c^2 + 23c - 11$.

47. **B**

To solve this inequality, treat it like a regular algebraic equation and solve for n.

$$13n + 6 \leq 97$$

Subtract 6 from both sides: $13n + 6 - 6 \leq 97 - 6$
Simplify: $13n \leq 91$

Divide both sides by 13 to isolate the variable: $\dfrac{13n}{13} \leq \dfrac{91}{13}$

$$n \leq 7$$

48. **A**

To solve this problem, make a chart showing all the possibilities.

	Education Major	English Major	Business Major	Theater Major
Amelia	X			
Jackie	X			X
Carla				X
Kim				X

Using the clues, put an X in each column when a person can be eliminated from consideration for that particular major. First, Amelia and Jackie have an 8:00 class with the education major. Therefore, put an X under education major for Amelia and Jackie. Second, Carla and Kim commute with the theater major. So, put an X under theater major for Carla and Kim. Finally, Jackie eats lunch with the theater major, so she cannot be majoring in theater; therefore, put an X beside her name under theater major, leaving Amelia as the only possible theater major.

Practice Test 2
Part 3: Writing

GACE Basic Skills

1 _____   11 _____   22 _____   33 _____

2 _____   12 _____   23 _____   34 _____

3 _____   13 _____   24 _____   35 _____

4 _____   14 _____   25 _____   36 _____

5 _____   15 _____   26 _____   37 _____

6 _____   16 _____   27 _____   38 _____

7 _____   17 _____   28 _____   39 _____

8 _____   18 _____   29 _____   40 _____

9 _____   19 _____   30 _____   41 _____

10 _____   20 _____   31 _____   42 _____

            21 _____   32 _____

PART 3:   **Writing**
                     42 questions

Read the passage below; then answer the three questions that follow.

[1]The campaign against smoking has intensified in the last forty years, with special focus now on stopping young people from ever starting to smoke. [2]Since research has linked smoking to cancer, heart disease, and emphysema, it is somewhat mystifying as to why anyone would want to smoke in the first place. [3]Many groups, including the American Cancer Society, have worked to raise awareness of the dangers of smoking cigarettes. [4]Because of the efforts of groups like this, the Surgeon General placed the following warning on cigarette packaging: "The Surgeon General has determined that cigarette smoking is dangerous to your health." [5]The Surgeon General is appointed by the President.

[6]Even with the well-documented links between smoking and disease, people continue to smoke. [7]_____[8]While more people may not be starting to smoke, it is concerning that them who do smoke may, in fact, be smoking more.

[9]There is a growing body of research that links smoke from cigarettes to cancer in individuals who do not smoke themselves. [10]This threat from second-hand smoke has led to bans against smoking in most federal and state buildings and requirements that restaurants and other businesses set aside nonsmoking areas. [11]Some smokers do claim that this is a form of discrimination, but it is hard to argue that one person's right to smoke is more important than the health of others who may come in contact with secondhand smoke.

1.   Which of the following, if added between sentences 6 and 8, best supports the writer's purpose and audience?

   A.   There is some information that indicates that the daily consumption of cigarettes is on the increase.

   B.   These people who smoke are just killing themselves.

   C.   Maybe some people are unconcerned with the research and enjoy smoking.

   D.   It is hard to quit smoking cigarettes.

2. Which of the following contains nonstandard pronoun use?

    A. Part 2
    B. Part 4
    C. Part 8
    D. Part 11

3. Which of the following number parts draws attention away from the main idea of the first paragraph of the passage?

    A. Part 1
    B. Part 2
    C. Part 4
    D. Part 5

Read the passage below; then answer the three questions that follow.

[1]The influx of immigrants that America had been experiencing slowed during the conflicts with France and England, but the flow increased between 1815 and 1837, when an economic downturn sharply reduced their numbers. [2]Thus, the overall rise in population during these years was due more to incoming foreigners than to a natural, domestically derived increase. [3]Most of the newcomers were from Britain, Germany, and Southern Ireland.[4] The Germans usually fared best. [5]Since they brought more money and more skills. [6]Discrimination was common in the job market, primarily directed against the Catholics. [7]"Irish Need Not Apply" signs were common. [8]However, the persistent labor shortage prevented the natives from totally excluding the foreign elements. [9]These newcomers huddled in ethnic neighborhoods in the cities, or those who could moved on westward to try their hand at farming.

[10]The rapid growth in urban areas was not matched by the growth of services. [11]Clean water, removing the trash, housing, and public transportation all lagged behind the growing need for these services. [12]Bad water and poor sanitation produced poor health, and epidemics of typhoid fever, typhus, and cholera were common. [13]Police and fire protection were usually inadequate and the development of professional forces was resisted because of the cost.

4. Which of the following is a sentence fragment?

   A. Part 2

   B. Part 5

   C. Part 8

   D. Part 12

5. Which of the following changes is needed in Part 11?

   A. Change "clean water" to "cleaning the water."

   B. Change "removing the trash" to "trash removal."

   C. Change "housing" to "providing housing."

   D. Change "public transportation" to "busing."

6. Which of the following contains an error in capitalization?

   A. Part 3

   B. Part 4

   C. Part 6

   D. Part 7

Read the passage below; then answer the three questions that follow.

[1]Language not only expresses an individual's ideology, it also sets perimeters while it persuades and influences the discourse in the community that hears and interprets its meaning. [2]Therefore, the language of failure should not be present in the learning environment because it will have a prohibitive impact on the students' desire to learn as well as a negative influence on the students' self-esteem. [3]Failure can be defined as a lack of success. [4]When students do not immediately succeed, we award a failing grade to those students. [5]As educators we might well ask ourselves if this is the type of doctrine who we want to permeate our classrooms.

⁶One must remain aware that individuals acquire knowledge at indepen-dent rates of speed and everyone learns at a particular pace that is unique unto himself or herself. ⁷Certainly no one would suggest that one infant "failed" the art of learning to walk because she acquired the skill two months behind her infant peer. ⁸Would anyone suggest that infant number one failed walking? ⁹What would a mentor project to either toddler were he to suggest that a slower acquisition of walking skills implied failure? ¹⁰Sometimes we as educators feel the need to suggest Student A failed due to the slower procurement of abstract concepts it is essential to shift the learning focus from failure to success.

7. Which of the following requires revision for redundancy?

    A. Part 2
    B. Part 4
    C. Part 6
    D. Part 8

8. Which of the following changes is needed?

    A. Part 1: Change "individual's" to "individuals'"
    B. Part 4: Change "students" to "student's"
    C. Part 5: Change "who" to "that"
    D. Part 7: Change "no one" to "anyone."

9. Which of the following numbered parts of the passage is a run-on sentence?

    A. Part 1
    B. Part 5
    C. Part 6
    D. Part 10

Read the passage below; then answer the three questions that follow.

[1]Vitamins were once thought to be a cure all for a wide range of illnesses and symptoms. [2]It was also believed that vitamins could provide preventative powers if taken prior to high-risk exposure. [3]Now findings by long-term trials indicate that vitamin C, vitamin E, and selenium supplements do not reduce the risk of being diagnosed with lung or pancreatic cancer as once believed. [4]Other research has found no connection between over-the-counter vitamins and minerals and reducing risk of stroke or cardiovascular disease.

[5]It might be a better plan to forego a regimen of vitamins and minerals and focus instead on eating a healthy diet. [6]All necessary vitamins can be ingested by making healthy choices for meals and snacks. [7] _____ [8]Probably the best advice to follow when choosing foods to meet suggested vitamin requirements is to follow the food pyramid. [9]And choose wisely.

10. Which of the following sentences, if inserted as Part 7, would best fit the writer's organizational pattern in the second paragraph of the passage?

    A. A healthy diet involves one that is high in unprocessed fruits and vegetables and low in foods that contain sugars and fats.

    B. Until there is more support for taking vitamins, just eat right.

    C. While there is conflicting reports about the advantages of over-the-counter vitamins and minerals, everyone knows about vegetables.

    D. You could be on the safe side and eat healthy and take vitamins.

11. Which of the following changes needs to be made?

    A. Part 1: Change "wide" to "wider."
    B. Part 3: Change "being diagnosed" to "diagnosis."
    C. Part 4: Change "reducing" to "reduced."
    D. Part 8: Change "best" to "better."

12. Which of the numbered sentences is a nonstandard sentence?

    A.   Part 3

    B.   Part 4

    C.   Part 8

    D.   Part 9

Read the passage below; then answer the three questions that follow.

[1]Hillary Rodham Clinton, born in Park Ridge, Illinois, grew up in a relatively affluent family, the youngest daughter of a textile magnate. [2]She was a student leader in high school and campaigned for presidential candidate Barry Goldwater in 1964 as the chair of the local Young Republicans chapter. [3]The political upheaval and unrest of the 1960s, as evidenced by the assignation of John F. Kennedy, Martin Luther King, Jr., and Robert Kennedy, led Clinton to change her political activism. [4]During her college career at Wellesley College, she campaigned for the Democratic anti-war candidate Eugene McCarthy.

[5]It was at Yale attending law school that Hillary Rodham Clinton first became interested in family law and children's issues. [6]It was also while at Yale that she first met her future husband, Bill Clinton. [7]The two followed separate paths after graduation from Yale, while Hillary continuing her focus on children by working on the Children's Defense Fund. [8]She moved to Arkansas to teach at the University of Arkansas Law School in 1974, in what has been referred to as the more important turning point of her career. [9]It is during this period that she began her courtship with Bill Clinton, who she married in 1975. [10]By marrying Bill Clinton, a political power couple was created.

[11]In 2001 Hillary Rodham Clinton became the first first lady elected to public office. [12]She successfully ran for office as the junior senator from New York but was unsuccessful in her bid for president in 2008. [13]She was nominated by President-Elect Barack Obama as secretary of state, a position that requires Senate confirmation, which she received.

13. Which of the following changes needs to be made in the second paragraph?

    A. Part 5: Change "became" to "becomes."

    B. Part 6: Change "first" to "then."

    C. Part 7: Change "while" to "with."

    D. Part 9: Change "who" to "whom."

14. Which of the following displays a nonstandard use of a comparative form?

    A. Part 1

    B. Part 8

    C. Part 10

    D. Part 12

15. Which of the following sentences displays a nonstandard use of a modifying phrase?

    A. Part 10

    B. Part 11

    C. Part 12

    D. Part 13

Read the passage below; then answer the three questions that follow.

[1]If you ever visit the outside market in Charleston, South Carolina, be sure to visit one of the many booths where women can be witnessed weaving sweetgrass baskets, much as she did in the antebellum period. [2]These baskets and the art of making them represents one of the oldest remaining authentic African-American crafts left in this country. [3]The baskets were originally woven by slaves brought to the Charleston area from the West Indies. [4]The slaves were first brought to South Carolina to work on the rice plantations; the baskets were used in the harvesting of rice, a process known as "winnowing." [5]The baskets had other uses and were also used as containers for bread, cornmeal, and sewing materials.

⁶The baskets are woven from a type of grass called "sweetgrass" (*Muhlenbergia filipes*) so called because of its fragrance, which reminds me of sweet hay. ⁷The grasses are indigenous to the area around Charleston; they can be found in the marsh and coastal areas. ⁸Modern-day basket weavers still harvest these grasses; though private development of the coast has reduced the area in which the grasses can be found. ⁹Because the baskets are made from marsh grasses, they are impervious to water and can be washed without any harm being done to the basket. ¹⁰The baskets illustrate the long-standing usefulness of an item that has been tested over time; the baskets are still used on small rice farms to harvest rice.

16. Which of the following sentences displays a nonstandard use of a semicolon?

   A. Part 4

   B. Part 7

   C. Part 8

   D. Part 10

17. Which of the numbered sentences should be revised to correct an error in noun/pronoun agreement?

   A. Part 1

   B. Part 2

   C. Part 7

   D. Part 9

18. Which of the following is the best way to rewrite Part 6?

   A. The baskets are woven from a type of grass called "sweetgrass" (*Muhlenbergia filipies*) so called because of its fragrance, which reminds us all of sweet hay.

   B. The baskets are woven from a type of grass called "sweetgrass" (*Muhlenbergia filipies*) so called because of its fragrance, which is a reminder of sweet hay.

   C. ⁶The baskets are woven from a type of grass called "sweetgrass" (*Muhlenbergia filipies*) so called because of its fragrance which is reminiscent of sweet hay.

D.   Reminding me of sweet hay, the baskets are woven from a type of grass called "sweetgrass" (*Muhlenbergia filipies*) so called because of its fragrance.

Read the passage below; then answer the three questions that follow.

¹The domestication of dogs marks the first domestication of any wild animal and probably occurred sometime between 20,000 and 15,000 years ago. ²During the Mesolithic era, early man began using dogs for hunting and when livestock was domesticated approximately 7000 to 9000 years ago, there is an indication that dogs were used in herding. ³The skeletal remains of dogs reveal that by the bronze age, the following five types of domestic dogs were in existence: pointers, shepherds, mastiffs, greyhounds, and wolf-types. ⁴There is evidence that the Romans had bred guard dogs sometime around the 4th century B.C.E., and Aristotle listed known breeds of dogs as early as 350 B.C.E.

⁵As the Roman Empire spread across Europe, so did the breeds of dogs the Romans had developed. ⁶As the Romans took their dogs throughout Europe, other breeds arose as a result of cross-breeding the Roman breeds with the existing dogs found on the continent of Europe. ⁷Most of these dog breeds were advanced to provide assistance to their owners when hunting, but the rise of dogs for other purposes such as companionship was evident by the 4th century.

⁸After the fall of the Roman Empire, the struggle for survival became more important to the population than breeding dogs. ⁹What eventually saved the dog-breeding craft was the dog's useful in the hunt and assisting his human counterpart in locating food.

19.   Which of the following methods of organization does the writer use in the passage?

A.   Order of importance

B.   Explain a process

C.   Cause and effect

D.   Spatial relationships

20. Which of the following changes is needed for Part 9?

    A. Change "eventually" to "eventual."

    B. Change "saved" to "saves."

    C. Change "useful" to "usefulness."

    D. Change "assisting" to "assists."

21. Which of the following contains nonstandard capitalization?

    A. Part 2

    B. Part 3

    C. Part 5

    D. Part 8

Read the passage below; then answer the three questions that follow.

[1]No one wants to anticipate the trouble and stress that accompanies a flat tire, but a little forethought and preplanning can make the tire change less troublesome. [2]_____, be sure that all of the necessary tools and essentials are found in the trunk of the car so that the process of changing the tire can begin. [3]These essentials include the spare tire, the car jack, and tire iron.

[4]To begin changing the tire, the car should be parked, with the parking brake engaged, on the most level ground that is feasible. [5]If on a busy highway, it is often suggested that you open the hood to indicate that the car is in some type of disrepair. [6]Retrieve the tools and spare and remove the hubcap if necessary. [7]Loosen the lug nuts, which hold the tire in place, before elevating the car with the jack. [8]Before jacking the car up, be sure to check the owner's manual for the specific placement of the jack. [9]Jack the car up a little higher than the flat tire to have enough room to replace it with the full tire. [10]Remove the lug nuts and replace the flat tire with the new tire, making sure the valve on the tire is facing out. [11]Replace the lug nuts. [12]Tighten them in the opposite direction than they were removed. [13]Slowly lower the jack, remove it, and tighten the lug nuts again when the car is completely on the ground. [14]Now replace the hubcap and feel secure that you have correctly changed your flat tire.

22. Which of the following methods of organization does the writer use in the passage?

    A. Order of importance

    B. Explain a process

    C. Cause and effect

    D. Spatial relationships

23. Which of the following changes is needed to correct an error in sentence structure?

    A. Combine Parts 4 and 5 into a single sentence.

    B. Divide Part 10 into two sentences.

    C. Combine Parts 11 and 12 into a single sentence.

    D. Divide Part 13 into two sentences.

24. Which of the following transition words, if inserted into the blank in Part 2, would provide a more effective sequence of ideas?

    A. Next

    B. Then

    C. First

    D. Finally

Read the passage below; then answer the three questions that follow.

[1]There is a common misconception that the vice-president of the United States lives in separate quarters contained within the White House. [2]Many would be surprised to find out that the vice-president did not have a designated residence in Washington, D.C., until 1974. [3]Prior to 1974, the vice-president either lived in hotels or bought a home for himself and his family. [4]The vice-president's family were often moved from location to location during his tenure in office.

[5]In 1974, congress designated a house on the grounds of the U.S. Naval Observatory as the official residence of the vice-president. [6]The house was originally built in 1893 for the Superintendent of the Observatory and is built in the Victorian style of "Queen Anne" country home. [7]It was not designed for the vice-president as his residence. [8]The three-story residence has twelve rooms and six bathrooms, and covers 9,150 square feet.

[9]Gerald Ford was the first vice-president eligible to take up residence in the "Admiral's House," so called because the chief officer of the Naval Observatory lived there beginning in 1929. [10]The resignation of Richard Nixon preempted Ford's move to the newly renovated residence. [11]The next eligible vice-president was Nelson Rockefeller, who already maintained a home in Washington, D.C., and therefore used the residence mainly for entertaining. [12]The first full-time resident of the home was Walter Mondale, Jimmy Carter's vice-president, in 1976. [13]Since that time, all vice-presidents and their families have maintained the former "Admiral's House" as their home during their tenure.

25. Which of the following changes is needed to make the passage conform to the conventions of Standard American English?

   A. Part 3: Change "lived" to "lives."

   B. Part 4: Change "were" to "was."

   C. Part 8: Change "has" to "had."

   D. Part 9: Change "was" to "is"

26. Which of the following draws attention away from the main idea of the passage?

   A. Part 2

   B. Part 3

   C. Part 5

   D. Part 6

27. Which of the following sentences contains nonstandard capitalization?

   A. Part 2

   B. Part 5

   C. Part 9

   D. Part 12

Read the passage below; then answer the three questions that follow.

[1]The carousel, or merry-go-round, is a contraption that we remember as part of our elementary school days on the playground. [2]Riding the rotating platform with its six metal bars provided a common recess experience. [3]What a surprise to discover that the lowly merry-go-round was actually first developed as a tool to aid soldiers in the art of war! [4]The carousel was originally developed to provide practice for the cavalry.

[5]The original design was used by Turkish and arab horsemen as a military exercise meant to provide practice for combat done on the backs of horses. [6]The earliest known pictures of carousels depict baskets large enough for one man suspended from an innermost pole. [7]The baskets would be propelled around the pole and the warrior would attempt to joust stationary opponents or spear rings that were suspended from a rope. [8]The Europeans first observed this training exercise during the Crusades and brought the carousel (from the Spanish word *carosella*, meaning "little war") back to the royalty and nobility, where the humble carousel enjoyed elevated status as a form of entertainment.

[9]With its newfound popularity, carousels were created with elaborate horses and animals, though the game of ring tilt, where the riders attempt to grab golden rings, remained an integral part of the carousel riding event. [10]These types of carousels are what many people remember from city parks or county fairs. [11]It is interesting that what was first designed as a tool to aid warriors ended up as a beloved amusement ride and an integral part of urban culture.

28. What is the thesis statement of the passage?

    A. The earliest known pictures of carousels depict baskets large enough for one man suspended from an innermost pole.

    B. The carousel was originally developed to provide practice for the cavalry.

    C. These types of carousels are what many people remember from city parks or county fairs.

    D. The carousel, or merry-go-round, is a contraption that we remember as part of our elementary school days on the playground.

29. Which of the following contains nonstandard capitalization?

    A.   Part 4

    B.   Part 5

    C.   Part 8

    D.   Part 11

30. Which of the following changes is needed for Part 9?

    A.   Change "were created" to "create."

    B.   Change "though" to "although."

    C.   Change "attempt" to "attempted."

    D.   Change "remained" to "remains."

Read the passage below; then answer the three questions that follow.

[1]The health of students and their families depends not only on individual and family decisions, but on the factors involving the wider society. [2]One of these factors is advertising which often encourages children to make unhealthy decisions. [3]Students as young as kindergarten and first grade can learn how to recognize advertisements (e.g., for candy or sugar-laden cereal) that might lead him or her to unhealthy behavior. [4]By third of fourth grade, they should be able to demonstrate that they are able to make health-related decisions regarding advertisements in various media.

[5]In addition, any studies of the physical environment—in science, social studies, or other subjects—should be related to health whenever possible. [6]Examples include the effects of pollution on health, occupational-related disease, and the differences in healthcare options available to people in different parts of the world and in different economic circumstances.

[7]Differentiation between communicable and noncommunicable disease can be taught at the youngest grade levels.[8]_____
[9]Older children should be able to explain the transmission and prevention of communicable disease, and all children should learn which diseases cannot be transmitted through casual contact.

31. Which of the following, if inserted as Part 8, best supports the writer's purpose and audience?

    A. Very young children should learn to wash their hands frequently, for instance.

    B. Another aspect of physical education concerns awareness and avoidance of the health risks that are present in our everyday lives.

    C. Unfortunately, because of the presence of peer pressure and lack of parental control, the effect of education is sometimes not enough.

    D. It can be difficult to stress the importance of good hygiene.

32. Which of the following parts contains a nonstandard pronoun use?

    A. Part 1
    B. Part 2
    C. Part 3
    D. Part 4

33. Which of the following changes is needed to correct an error in punctuation?

    A. Part 1: Insert a comma after "individual."
    B. Part 2: Insert a comma after "advertising."
    C. Part 6: Insert a comma after "include."
    D. Part 9: Insert a comma after "prevention."

Read the passage below; then answer the three questions that follow.

[1]Folk dances are cultural dances that have remained quite stable for a long period of time. [2]The music has remained constant and the movements have changed little over the years. [3]It is also valuable to learn folk dances from other cultures. [4]Folk dances usually reflect the national traditions of various cultures they evoke pride in people's traditions and culture by keeping alive the dances of their ancestors. [5]Folk dances are usually about the group, not the specific dancer or couple. [6]Folk dance is a solid connection to the past and a vehicle for "belonging." [7]When one dances a folk dance, you belong to the group that

has danced that dance throughout the ages. [8]For some cultures that are being absorbed into western society and swallowed by global culture, such as the Inuit of northern Canada, languages are gradually lost, traditional crafts are lost and ancient religion is lost, but the folk dances are the last to go. [9]People cling to their dances as the last remnant of a shared past. [10]People dance their own culture's folk dance to understand who they are and where they came from.

34. Which of the following changes is needed to improve the unity and focus of the essay?

    A.   Reverse the order of Parts 8 and 9.

    B.   Delete Part 3.

    C.   Reverse the order of Parts 7 and 8.

    D.   Delete Part 4.

35. Which of the following numbered parts of the passage is an unnecessary shift in point of view?

    A.   Part 4

    B.   Part 5

    C.   Part 7

    D.   Part 10

36. Which of the following numbered parts is a run-on sentence?

    A.   Part 2

    B.   Part 4

    C.   Part 5

    D.   Part 7

Read the passage below; then answer the three questions that follow.

[1]The beloved Vulcan statue located in Vulcan Park located atop Red Mountain in Birmingham Alabama has been completely renovated and returned to its rightful spot. [2]The statue was removed from its pedestal in 1999 and recast and restored by Robinson Iron and Steel of Alexander City, Alabama. [3]It was a long and arduous process that took a total of four years, but the City of Birmingham is glad of his return.

[4]The statue was originally cast in 1904 as an entry to the 1905 World's Fair in St. Louis, Missouri. [5]It was commissioned by the city to promote Birmingham and the state of Alabama to the world and the god Vulcan was chosen to advertise the city's industrial might in the iron and steel business. [6]The sculptor, Giuseppe Moretti, cast the 56-foot iron statue in 21 pieces and then each piece was shipped to St. Louis for assembly. [7]The sculpture continues to reign as the largest iron structure in the world. [8]The statue of Vulcan was awarded the Grand Prize at the 1905 World's Fair.

[9]The years between Vulcan's return to Birmingham and 1999 were not kind to the statue, and a nonprofit organization was formed to return the symbol of Birmingham's steel industry to its former glory. [10]Funds were raised to not only refurbish the statue but to create a Vulcan Park where the Greek god could revel in his uniqueness. [11]It is to the park he returned in 2003, after a cost of $14 million, and the homecoming was celebrated on the 100th anniversary of the original dedication of the statue. [12]Vulcan now stands atop Red Mountain, a symbol of an industrial age that has since passed.

37. The writer's main purpose in writing this passage is to

    A. explain how iron statues are made.

    B. examine the cost of refurbishing landmarks.

    C. define the importance of maintaining landmarks.

    D. describe the statue and its restoration.

38. Which of the following changes is needed to correct an error in punctuation?

    A. Part 1: Insert a comma after "Birmingham" and after "Alabama."

    B. Part 2: Insert a comma after "Steel."

    C. Part 6: Insert a comma after "St. Louis."

    D. Part 10: Insert a comma after "Vulcan Park."

39. Which of the following changes is needed to improve the unity and focus of the second paragraph?

    A.   Reverse the order of Parts 4 and 5.

    B.   Delete Part 6.

    C.   Reverse the order of Parts 7 and 8.

    D.   Delete Part 8.

Read the passage below; then answer the three questions that follow.

[1]There is a continuing controversy about the existence of global warming, but if one chooses to look at the causes of global warming, it is easiest to assume that global warming does exist. [2]There are both natural and man-made causes of global warming, and it is important to examine both of these to get the total picture of the problem at hand. [3]Some causes of global warming can be eliminated, and some cannot.

[4]The natural causes of global warming include the release of methane gas from arctic tundra and wetlands. [5]The methane gas is a powerful greenhouse gas and serves to contain heat within the earth's atmosphere. [6]Another natural cause of global warming is the cyclical nature of climate change. [7]Every 40,000 years, the earth experiences a climate change, and this could be what is occurring now.

[8]There is little debate regarding whether human beings have added to the causes of global warming. [9]It is evident that the burning of fossil fuels has also created the release of increased amounts of CO_2 into the atmosphere, which is another greenhouse gas. [10]Human beings also promote the release of more methane gas into the atmosphere by the rise of population, creating a rise in food production. [11]Increased population also adds to the CO_2 problem because more people mean the exhalation of more of that gas also.

[12]Some of these causes can be reversed. [13]It is possible to reduce the amount of greenhouse gases emitted by using reusable energy and using fossil fuels more efficiently. [14]Planting more trees will also help by reducing CO_2 and increasing the oxygen in the atmosphere. [15]In short, those of us living on the planet need to reduce emission of fossil fuels and take better care of our environment.

40. Which of the following contains a nonstandard use of a comparative form?

    A. Part 1
    B. Part 2
    C. Part 11
    D. Part 15

41. Which of the following methods of organization does the writer use in the passage?

    A. Chronological order
    B. Spatial relationships
    C. Explain a process
    D. Cause and effect

42. What is the thesis statement of the passage?

    A. There is a continuing controversy about the existence of global warming, but if one chooses to look at the causes of global warming, it is easiest to assume that global warming does exist.

    B. Some causes of global warming can be eliminated, and some cannot.

    C. The natural causes of global warming include the release of methane gas from arctic tundra and wetlands.

    D. There is little debate regarding whether human beings have added to the causes of global warming.

Constructed-Response Assignment Directions

For the constructed-response assignment, you are asked to prepare a written response and record it on the pages that you are given in your Written Response Booklet.

Be sure to read the assignment carefully and plan your response before you start to write. You may use any blank space provided in the test booklet following the question to outline your ideas or simply to jot down notes. **However, when you take the GACE Basic Skills Test, you must write your final version on the pages that the test administrators provide in the test booklet.**

Test scorers use the following criteria to evaluate your constructed-response submission:

- Appropriateness of your response in that you address the topic directly and use language that would be appropriate for the specified occasion, audience and, purpose

- Your focus and organization in sticking to your topic and providing a logical flow to your reasoning

- The support you give to your thesis in the examples you provide

- Your use of correct grammar, sentence structure, and word usage

- Your use of conventions, which include spelling, punctuation, and capitalization

Constructed-Response Question

Writing Assignment

Of all general reference materials, a dictionary is the one probably used most often. If a dictionary is used to merely check the meaning or spelling of words, it is not being utilized to its full value. Write an essay to be read by a college instructor, in which you describe additional uses for the dictionary beyond that of finding word meanings. Identify which usage you think is the most important and provide support for this, using specific examples.

ANSWER KEY – WRITING PRACTICE TEST 2

Question	Answer	Objective	
1	A	0011	Recognize unity, focus, and development in writing.
2	C	0014	Recognize Standard American English usage.
3	D	0011	Recognize unity, focus, and development in writing.
4	B	0013	Recognize effective sentences.
5	B	0013	Recognize effective sentences.
6	A	0014	Recognize Standard American English usage.
7	C	0013	Recognize effective sentences.
8	C	0014	Recognize Standard American English usage.
9	D	0014	Recognize Standard American English usage.
10	A	0012	Recognize effective organization in writing.
11	C	0013	Recognize effective sentences.
12	D	0013	Recognize effective sentences.
13	C	0012	Recognize effective organization in writing.
14	B	0014	Recognize Standard American English usage.
15	A	0013	Recognize effective sentences.
16	C	0014	Recognize Standard American English usage.
17	A	0014	Recognize Standard American English usage.
18	C	0011	Recognize unity, focus, and development in writing.
19	B	0011	Recognize unity, focus, and development in writing.
20	C	0014	Recognize Standard American English usage.

Question	Answer	Objective	
21	B	0014	Recognize Standard American English usage.
22	B	0011	Recognize unity, focus, and development in writing.
23	C	0013	Recognize effective sentences.
24	C	0012	Recognize effective organization in writing.
25	B	0013	Recognize effective sentences.
26	D	0013	Recognize effective sentences.
27	B	0014	Recognize Standard American English usage.
28	B	0012	Recognize effective organization in writing.
29	B	0014	Recognize Standard American English usage.
30	C	0014	Recognize Standard American English usage.
31	A	0012	Recognize effective organization in writing.
32	C	0013	Recognize effective sentences.
33	B	0014	Recognize Standard American English usage.
34	B	0011	Recognize unity, focus, and development in writing.
35	C	0013	Recognize effective sentences.
36	B	0013	Recognize effective sentences.
37	D	0011	Recognize unity, focus, and development in writing.
38	A	0014	Recognize Standard American English usage.
39	C	0012	Recognize effective organization in writing.
40	A	0013	Recognize effective sentences.
41	D	0012	Recognize effective organization in writing.
42	B	0011	Recognize unity, focus, and development in writing.

Practice Test 2, Part 3 Progress Chart

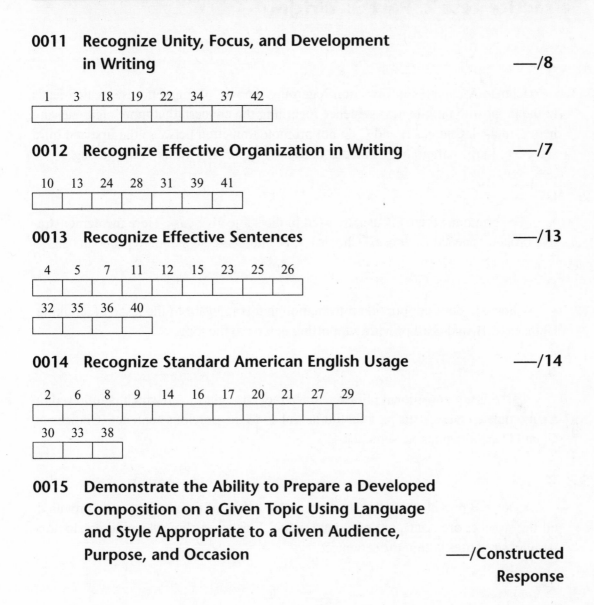

0011 Recognize Unity, Focus, and Development in Writing ——/8

1	3	18	19	22	34	37	42

0012 Recognize Effective Organization in Writing ——/7

10	13	24	28	31	39	41

0013 Recognize Effective Sentences ——/13

4	5	7	11	12	15	23	25	26

32	35	36	40

0014 Recognize Standard American English Usage ——/14

2	6	8	9	14	16	17	20	21	27	29

30	33	38

0015 Demonstrate the Ability to Prepare a Developed Composition on a Given Topic Using Language and Style Appropriate to a Given Audience, Purpose, and Occasion ——/Constructed Response

Detailed Explanations for
Practice Test 2, Part 3: Writing

1. **A**

   Choice A contains information regarding the rise of cigarette use, which leads to the proposition in the next sentence regarding the concern that more cigarettes are being smoked. Choices B and C do not promote transition between the first and third sentences in the paragraph. Choice D does not support the thesis of the passage.

2. **C**

   The pronoun "them" is usually used in the subjective case. Here the demonstrative pronoun needed is "those." Choices A, B, and D are all standard pronoun use.

3. **D**

   Choice D does not provide information that is relevant to the issue of smoking. Choices A, B, and C all provide supporting details to the topic.

4. **B**

   Part 5 is a prepositional phrase, "Since they brought . . . ," which is followed by a subordinate clause. This part should be linked to the previous sentence. Choices A, C, and D are all complete sentences.

5. **B**

   Choice B provides parallel structure in the listing of the services to be provided: all the services are nouns or compound nouns. The other choices would create non-parallel structures within the sentence.

6. **A**

   The direction or area of a country is only capitalized if it is a geographical name of the area (i.e., South Carolina, Southern Hemisphere) or a compass point (the Southeast), but not if it is a nonspecific direction or region (southern Ireland).

7. **C**

   The sentence contains the words "rates of speed" and "particular pace" which have the same meaning, as well as "acquire knowledge" and "learns" which are also repetitive. No redundancy occurs in Choices A, B, and D.

8.   **C**

The pronoun "who" is used to refer to people and the use of the demonstrative pronoun "that" is confusing in its reference. Choice A would change a correct possessive form to an incorrect plural form. Choice C would change the correct plural form to an incorrect possessive form, and Choice D would change the indefinite pronouns in such a way that the sentence would be nonsensical.

9.   **D**

Part 10 is two sentences that should be separated by a period between "concepts" and "it" to make two independent sentences. The rest of the choices are all standard sentence structure.

10. **A**

Choice A provides information that is needed for the transition from the idea that vitamins can be found by choosing the correct diet and following the food pyramid. Choice B is too informal for the tone of the passage. Choice C assumes information that may not be correct. Choice D demonstrates change of person and does not provide a sensible transition to Part 8.

11. **C**

Choice C provides agreement in parallel structures of the noun phrase "over-the-counter vitamins and minerals" and "reduced risk." Choices A and D would create an incorrect comparative structure. Choice B would change the existing verb phrase to a noun, which would be nonstandard sentence structure.

12. **D**

Choice D is a sentence fragment with no connection to the preceding sentence. All other choices are complete sentences.

13. **C**

Choice C changes the prepositions so that the sentence transitions from the additional service that Clinton acquired. Choice A creates a change of tense midsentence. Choice B changes transitions so that the information in the sentence is incorrect. Choice D would make the pronoun form incorrect.

14. **B**

    Choice B contains the comparison of more than two subjects: that is, moving to Arkansas and every other "turning point," but the incorrect comparative case "more important" is used rather than the correct superlative form "most important." Choices A and C do not contain a comparative form. Choice D uses the correct positive form "unsuccessful."

15. **A**

    The opening verb phrase is a dangling modifier. It is unclear who is marrying Bill Clinton or who is creating a power couple. A correct revision would include "A political power couple was created with the marriage of Hillary Rodham to Bill Clinton." All the other choices are Standard American English sentences.

16. **C**

    Semicolons are used to separate main clauses that can stand alone as sentences. The subordinate clause "though private development of the coast…" cannot stand alone as a sentence and should be offset by a comma, not a semicolon. Choices A, B, and D all contain semicolons that are separating main clauses.

17. **A**

    Choice A should be revised so that the singular pronoun "she" is changed to agree with the plural noun "women." Choices B, C, and D are all correct noun/pronoun agreement and require no revision.

18. **C**

    The revision in Choice C retains the existing third person point of view. Choices A and D change the point of view to first person, and Choice B has incorrect word choice of the noun "reminder" instead of the more appropriate adjective "reminiscent."

19. **B**

    The writer organizes the passage from the beginning of the domestication of dogs through the fall of the Roman Empire, which is chronological. Choice A suggests that some part of the breeding of dogs was more important, which is not stated in the passage. Choice C would describe perhaps how the domestication of dogs came about, but this is not stated in the passage. Choice D would be correct if the original area in which dogs were bred was described.

20. **C**

    Choice C changes the incorrect adjective form "useful" to the correct noun form "usefulness." Choice A would change the correct adverb form to the incorrect adjective form. Choices B and D would create incorrect changes of tense in the sentence.

21. **B**

    Part 3 contains the capitalization error "bronze age." Historical events, eras, and calendar items are all capitalized in Standard American English.

22. **B**

    The passage is organized to explain how to change a tire. Choice A is incorrect because there is no singular important event that occurs in changing a tire. Choice C is incorrect, as no mention is made of the cause of the flat tire. Though there are some descriptions ordered spatially, Choice D is incorrect because the passage itself is not organized this way.

23. **C**

    The very brief Part 11 should be combined with Part 12 with the addition of the conjunction "and." Choice A would create too many ideas within a single sentence. Choices B and D would create incomplete sentences.

24. **C**

    Choice C offers the transition word "First" that should be used to emphasize the first event to occur. Choices A and B provide transitions that would promote the following steps, not the initial step. Choice D is a transition word for the last step in the process.

25. **B**

    The noun "family" is a group noun used as a single entity, so the singular verb "was" is correct. Choices A, C, and D are incorrect changes in tense.

26. **D**

    Choice D is redundant and it has already been stated that the residence was built for another purpose. Choice A would remove a supporting statement of the thesis. Choice B provides information that is further explained in the following sentence. Choice C substantiates the original idea that the home was built for another purpose and gives specific details about the home.

27. **B**

Part 5 contains the word "congress," which should be capitalized as an institution.

28. **B**

The focus of the passage is on the origin of the carousel. Choice A provides interesting support for how the carousel was originally designed, but no supporting information is provided. Choices C and D provide personal insight into carousels and the shared experience, but are not the focus of the history of the carousel.

29. **B**

Part 5 contains the word "arab," which should be capitalized as an ethnic or national group or language.

30. **C**

Choice C makes the sentence consistent in past verb tense. Choices A and D provide incorrect verb tense. Choice B would do nothing to change the logic of the sentence and is unnecessary.

31. **A**

Part 7 states that information should be provided to children "at the youngest grade levels" and this statement is supported by the information in Choice A. Choice B does not provide support for the information in the paragraph. Choice C could be a paragraph unto itself, but does not provide transition between Parts 7 and 9. Choice D is important, but does not support the information that follows.

32. **C**

Part 3 contains a plural noun "students" with incorrect objective personal singular pronouns "him" and "her." The other choices are all correct noun/pronoun agreement.

33. **B**

Choice B inserts a comma to set off the participial phrase "which often encourages . . . " Any comma added to the suggested places in Choices A, C, and D would create a comma splice.

34. **B**

Choice B has to do with cultural awareness of others outside the culture, not of those within. This is far removed from the focus of the paragraph. Part 3 should be deleted or further developed in a second paragraph. Choices A and C would put the ideas out of sequence. Choice D would remove the thesis statement from the paragraph.

35. **C**

Part 7 changes from third person "one" to second person "you" within the sentence. The other choices maintain third person point of view.

36. **B**

Choice B has two distinct sentences contained in a single sentence. A period should be placed between "cultures" and "they." Choices A, C, and D are all single ideas represented in single sentences.

37. **D**

The writer's description of the statue and its restoration is the only perspective found in the passage. Choice A is not mentioned in the passage, and Choice B is the subject of a single sentence. An in-depth discussion of the importance of maintaining landmarks is not offered within the passage.

38. **A**

A comma is placed between a city and state. All other choices would create a comma splice.

39. **C**

Part 8, which describes the award given at the World's Fair, should be closer to supporting elements about that event. Part 7 is a good concluding sentence for that paragraph and should occur last. Choice A would place information out of sequence. Choices B and D would remove necessary information that gives unity to the passage.

40. **A**

Choice A contains a comparison of only two subjects, to examine or not examine the causes of global warming, but the superlative case "easiest" is used rather than the correct comparative form "easier." Choice B does not contain a comparative form. Choice C uses the correct comparative adjective "more" modifying the noun "people." Choice D contains the correct comparative adjective "better" modifying the noun "care."

41. **D**

The writer organizes the paragraphs to illustrate the causes of global warming. Choice A would suggest that the passage had been organized to illustrate the history of global warming, which it is not. Choice B is incorrect because there is no description regarding the environment of global warming other than the atmosphere. Choice C is incorrect because even though the passage does offer examples of greenhouse gases and how it is produced, the process itself is not the focus of the passage, but rather the effect that greenhouse gases have on global warming.

42. **B**

The thesis in this passage is stated in Part 2 and repeated in Part 3. Choices A, C, and D are all supporting elements for the thesis statement.

Sample Response for Constructed-Response Question

Writing Sample with a Score of 4

Dictionaries contain a wealth of information about words and can be used for many different purposes besides finding words' meanings. One of the best dictionaries to use when conducting research is an unabridged dictionary because of the exhaustive listing of words found and the other useful tools about the words. An unabridged dictionary will provide much more information about words than simply the word meaning. Unabridged dictionaries can be used to determine the syllables of words, the pronunciation of words, the spelling of the plural or inflected form of the word, and their etymology.

One important use of an unabridged dictionary is to determine the syllabication of a word. When writing, it is important to correctly break words at the end of lines by dividing the word into the correct syllables. The dictionary will illustrate these syllables by using dots, spaces, or slashes where the word may be divided into syllables. Using a dictionary to check the correct syllabication will ensure that mistakes are avoided in written work.

Another important use of the unabridged dictionary is the pronunciation guide which accompanies the entry word. While sometimes the dictionary is used to provide a guide to spelling, the dictionary also provides a guide to how to say the particular word. The pronunciation guide uses symbols to indicate the syllabus that gets the most stress, and other symbols to indicate particular sounds. Using a dictionary to check the pronunciation of a word can help in pronouncing the word correctly and may help an individual recognize a word with which they are unfamiliar.

Perhaps the least appreciated use of the unabridged dictionary could be the inclusion of the plural forms of nouns and the inflected forms of verbs. This tool provides insight into the variations in the tense or number of an entry word. This use of the dictionary provides the irregular spelling of words and is helpful in the correct spelling of rarely used words.

Dictionaries often provide the etymology of the word. Etymologies are a valuable aid for extending vocabulary. Knowing a word's origin can help in remembering the word and also provide insight into the meanings of related words with a common origin. Using a dictionary to check the etymology of a word can open up a larger range of words with the same foundation.

Of all of the uses of the dictionary, besides finding the meaning of a word, it is the etymology of the word that can be the most useful. Identifying the age of a word by recognizing that it might have originated in during the Middle Ages often allows the writer to recognize how long particular ideas or actions have been in use. The word "jury," for example, comes from the Latin word meaning "to swear an oath," and in serving on a jury one swears to be nonbiased. The same etymology is evident in the words juror, jurisdiction, and jurisprudence. All of these words entail the use of an oath or the swearing in of something related to expressing an oath.

Dictionaries do provide definitions and are not intended as an encyclopedia, but knowing the different parts and uses of the dictionary can extend its usefulness beyond that of a simple definition provider. The dictionary is intended to provide clear and accurate information about words but also does a good job of providing information that assists individuals in both reading and writing. As such, a dictionary supplies multiple, easy-to-use research tools in a single resource.

Features of the Writing Sample Scoring 4

Appropriateness—The paper's topic and the writer's viewpoint are both well laid out in the first paragraph. The four uses of the dictionary are listed in the topic paragraph and are explored in deeper detail throughout the essay. The language and style fit the writer's audience. The style is formal, but possesses a personalized voice.

Focus and Organization—The writer follows the cues of the writing assignment closely, structuring his or her essay around the specific prompts found therein. The essay follows the course presented in the last sentence of the topic paragraph, and each of the uses of the dictionary is given a complete explanation in the paragraphs that follow, and in the order in which they were initially listed. Different uses for each of the components are examined, but the general focus remains on the use of the dictionary as a research tool.

Support—Each paragraph gives a full explanation of the listed component and the concluding paragraph uses a common sense argument to draw all the parts together. The sixth paragraph clearly offers the writer's choice of the most important use and the examples used support the choice.

Grammar, Sentence Structure, and Usage—The sentences are standardized and vary in form, and the consistent use of the active voice ("Dictionaries provide…," and "The word comes from. . .") make the essay easy to read. There is some stiltedness found in the repetition of "the use of" and "provides" but for the most part the essay is constructed of a variety of sentence forms.

Conventions—Spelling, punctuation, and capitalization are mostly standard throughout the essay.

Writing Sample with a Score of 2 or 1

Besides using the dictionary for looking up definitions of words, it can be used to figure out how to spell words. This is probably how most people got their first taste of the dictionary. Whenever kids ask how to spell something, they are usually told to look it up in the dictionary. Which usually doesn't help much if you don't know how to spell it in the first place.

I am not sure that the inventors of the dictionary meant for it to be used for correct spelling, but that is how it is used these days. Most of us were taught to look up spelling words in the dictionary and then were told to look up a word whenever we didn't know how to spell something. So, we are pretty good at using the dictionary this way.

You can usually get pretty close to the spelling of a word by just saying it out loud and then using those sounds to locate the first part of the word using the guide words at the top of the pages in the dictionary. Sometimes it can be tricky if it is one of those words that have a strange sound and you don't know what the letter is, exactly. It can be a guessing game that takes a long time when you don't know what you are looking for.

Luckily now there are dictionaries built right in the computer software programs that find the misspelled words for you. Sometimes the computer does it for you and automatically changes the spelling of words you use alot. Sometimes you can just right click on it and it will give a whole bunch of words that are close to your word and you pick the one that looks write.

There are other uses of the dictionary, but using it to help you spell is the next most important one after finding out definitions. It was how you first started using the dictionary, and can still be used for that same purpose. The spell checker feature on the computer is an automatic dictionary that is the same purpose as looking words up yourself.

Features of the Writing Sample Scoring 2 or 1

Appropriateness—The writer misconstrues the prompt and writes about only a single use of the dictionary. The prompt does not call for how to use the dictionary for a single purpose; it calls for different uses for the dictionary besides finding word meanings. This essay investigates a single use for the dictionary and while it does offer some support for this point of view, the writer doesn't offer a distinct rationale for using the dictionary to check the spelling of the word, but instead provides instruction in how to use the dictionary for this purpose. The prompt initially points out that using the dictionary to check the spelling of words constitutes a minor use of the possible range of uses, but the writer uses this single usage as the topic of this essay. The writer uses informal language with colloquialisms and idiomatic expressions.

Focus and Organization—While the focus seems to be on the singular use of the dictionary as a way to check spelling, the writer becomes tangential with the introduction of the spellcheck option found on most computers. The writer makes some historical references that are probably common experiences for most readers (asking how to spell a word, only to be told to look it up in the dictionary, trying to determine particular sounds of words), but these experiences don't lend any credence to this selection as the most useful utilization of the dictionary. There is mention of "other uses of the dictionary," but none is explored.

Support—The support seems to be that using the dictionary to check spelling is the most common exercise with which readers are familiar, but there isn't any support to indicate that this is the most appropriate use of the dictionary as a reference material. There is no connection to the usefulness of checking word spelling to writing or researching.

Grammar, Sentence Structure, and Usage—Most sentences follow standard sentence structure, but the opening sentence of the essay has an unclear insubordinate clause and the use of "it" is confusing. Switching from second person to third person throughout the essay makes it very difficult to follow and the use of second person adds to the informality of the essay. There is a sentence fragment in the last line of the first paragraph. There is the use of the word "pretty" as an adverb ("pretty good" and "pretty close") and incorrect noun/verb agreement in the third paragraph ("…it is one of those words that have a strange sound," should be "has").

Conventions—There is an incorrect homonym use ("write" should be "right" in the fourth paragraph) and the word "alot" is two words (a lot)—and probably should not be used at all in formal writing. There is nonstandard comma use before the word "exactly" in the third paragraph.

Index

Pages for Constructed-Response Answers

Pages for Constructed-Response Answers

Pages for Constructed-Response Answers

Pages for Constructed-Response Answers

REA's Test Preps
The Best in Test Preparation

- REA "Test Preps" are **far more** comprehensive than any other test preparation series
- Each book contains up to **eight** full-length practice tests based on the most recent exams
- **Every** type of question likely to be given on the exams is included
- Answers are accompanied by **full** and **detailed** explanations

REA publishes over 70 Test Preparation volumes in several series. They include:

Advanced Placement Exams (APs)
Art History
Biology
Calculus AB & BC
Chemistry
Economics
English Language & Composition
English Literature & Composition
European History
French Language
Government & Politics
Latin
Physics B & C
Psychology
Spanish Language
Statistics
United States History
United States History Crash Course
World History

College-Level Examination Program (CLEP)
Analyzing and Interpreting Literature
College Algebra
Freshman College Composition
General Examinations
General Examinations Review
History of the United States I
History of the United States II
Introduction to Educational
    Psychology
Human Growth and Development
Introductory Psychology
Introductory Sociology
Precalculus
Principles of Management
Principles of Marketing
Spanish
Western Civilization I
Western Civilization II

SAT Subject Tests
Biology E/M
Chemistry
French
German
Literature
Mathematics Level 1, 2
Physics
Spanish
United States History

Graduate Record Exams (GREs)
Biology
Chemistry
Computer Science
General
Literature in English
Mathematics
Psychology

ACT - ACT Assessment

ASVAB - Armed Services Vocational
    Aptitude Battery

CBEST - California Basic Educational
    Skills Test

CDL - Commercial Driver License Exam

CLAST - College Level Academic
    Skills Test

COOP & HSPT - Catholic High School
    Admission Tests

ELM - California State University
    Entry Level Mathematics Exam

FE (EIT) - Fundamentals of Engineering
    AM Exam

FTCE - Florida Teacher Certification
    Examinations

GED - (U.S. Edition)

GMAT - Graduate Management
    Admission Test

LSAT - Law School Admission Test

MAT - Miller Analogies Test

MCAT - Medical College Admission
    Test

MTEL - Massachusetts Tests for
    Educator Licensure

NJ HSPA - New Jersey High School
    Proficiency Assessment

NYSTCE - New York State Teacher
    Certification Examinations

PRAXIS PLT - Principles of Learning
    & Teaching Tests

PRAXIS PPST - Pre-Professional
    Skills Tests

PSAT/NMSQT

SAT

TExES - Texas Examinations of
    Educator Standards

THEA - Texas Higher Education
    Assessment

TOEFL - Test of English as a Foreign
    Language

USMLE Steps 1,2,3 - U.S. Medical
    Licensing Exams

If you would like more information about any of these books,
complete the coupon below and return it to us or visit your local bookstore.

Research & Education Association
61 Ethel Road W., Piscataway, NJ 08854
Phone: (732) 819-8880   **website: www.rea.com**

Please send me more information about your Test Prep books.

Name _____

Address _____

City _____ State _____ Zip _____